D1097965

On Being a Woman

On Being a Woman

THE MODERN WOMAN'S GUIDE TO GYNECOLOGY

Revised Edition

W. *Gifford-Jones*, M.D

THE MACMILLAN COMPANY

NEW YORK, NEW YORK

The Macmillan Company
866 Third Avenue, New York, N.Y. 10022

Library of Congress Catalog Card Number: 76-151163

First Printing

Printed in the United States of America

In the night, imagining some fear,
How easy is a bush supposed a bear.
Shakespeare

Contents

Preface

The Purpose of This Book

THIS BOOK HAS BEEN written for a number of reasons, but probably the primary motive is an attempt to remove fear of the unknown. In my experience as a doctor I have found that women spend much unnecessary time worrying about what goes on in their bodies. A comprehensive handbook that not only explains the function of the female anatomy but also discusses the ills that the female flesh is heir to, may do much to dispel anxiety and to provide a more objective view of what being a woman is all about. For example, the majority of patients who develop pelvic pain, abnormal bleeding, or discharge nearly always jump to the false conclusion that it must be due to cancer. Yet, in nearly all cases, such symptoms are the result of a minor problem. In no way do I wish to underestimate the importance of cancer, but most doctors, including gynecologists, see only a few cases of cancer each year. It is therefore a good idea to put the fear of cancer in its proper perspective by looking at the forest, not just the trees.

Old wives' tales also pose a special problem in gynecology for both patients and doctors. A woman who has a common fungus infection at the vagina may, after talking with a friend, mistakenly worry that it is due to venereal disease. Others may fret that a fibroid growth is malignant. Still others are tormented by the visions of what will happen to them after a hysterectomy.

Today's women are living in rapidly changing times. Millions are taking birth control pills. And before too long, even more of them will be on pills to prevent the ravages of the menopause, which most doctors now consider a deficiency disease that ages women much before their time. Equally important, this book points out that once the menopause starts women can stop taking birth control pills and switch to the long-term natural estrogens. The reasoning is simple: Birth control pills, on very rare occasions, cause trouble, whereas the natural estrogens are virtually trouble-free.

I wish to emphasize that this book is not written for women who indulge in the dangerous game of self-diagnosis. Rather, it is hoped that it will emphasize the need for consulting a doctor at the first sign of trouble as well as the urgent necessity of yearly checkup examinations. Being a little too late in seeking advice can sometimes turn out to be much too late. Although this book is not written to encourage self-diagnosis, it is designed to make women aware that many bothersome problems such as the atrophic or aging vagina, which some patients have tolerated for years, can be easily and quickly cured.

I do not, in this book, discuss normal obstetrics. This is not an oversight, as there are many excellent books already available to the reader, and it would be impossible to adequately condense such a vast subject in a few pages. Furthermore, this book was basically written on the subject of gynecology as there was a great void in this area.

Lastly, I hope it will prove helpful to many busy doctors who find themselves increasingly pressed for time. Napoleon, during one of his numerous campaigns, told an officer that he could ask for anything except his time. Physicians today find themselves much in the same predicament, but they try to spend as long as possible explaining given problems to their patients as well as advising the necessary corrective steps. But on many days the clock moves too quickly, and it is impossible to go into as much detail as either they or the patient would like. Furthermore, a good many patients will have forgotten what the doctor said by the time they get home. It is hoped that this book will help to refresh their minds. In other words, it has been written for intelligent, inquiring women as a supplement to their doctor's advice.

You will also notice that there is a certain amount of repetition in the subsequent chapters. This could not be avoided, since both symptoms and diseases continually overlap and I have also quite deliberately repeated certain essential points because I want to make sure of their impact. Chapter references have been used whenever they seem necessary and helpful, and I hope that the specific categorizing of subjects under their various headings will prove useful to the reader. Michaelangelo while working late into the night on the fine details of his statues used to say "trifles make perfection and perfection is no trifle." The author similarly hopes that he, too, has looked after enough of the trifles to make this not only a useful book, but also one that is interesting to read.

Some Women Talk Too Much

It has often been said that most of man's troubles are man-made, but, as a gynecologist, I am forced to disagree. Every day I see examples of homemade troubles caused by women who simply talk too much. One would think that old wives' tales and medical fiction should be a thing of the past in this enlightened age. But they are not. The lives of many women today are complicated by untold hours of anxiety and worry over some medical fairy tale. And there are days when I spend as much time trying to talk women out of these absurd prejudices as I do in the actual practice of medicine.

What amazes me is that many of the patients who are trapped by these tales are extremely intelligent women who, in normal circumstances, would laugh at such idiotic nonsense. But in times of stress they seem to lose all sense of balance and begin to clutch at straws. They believe the implausible, and even the impossible, especially when a close friend or relative is the vendor of such foolish folklore. They no doubt reason that their intimates would hardly tell them an untruth. Unfortunately, they seldom ask themselves how their confidant has managed to suddenly become such an expert on medical matters. Instead they take the amateur diagnosis at face value, and it sometimes starts a catastrophic chain reaction of problems. Not just problems for the patient, but also problems for the doctor.

An attractive fifteen-year-old tells me she has not had a period for a few months, and is frightened because "bad blood" is collecting in her body and will poison her. A bride-to-be has worried herself sick because of the distasteful picture her own mother has given her of the sexual side of marriage. A young mother worries that birth control pills will cause her to develop a beard. A woman of fifty is depressed because she has been told that at her time of life she will become obese and lose her sexual powers. Another woman of the same age who has been advised to take hormones is concerned that they will cause cancer. Still another woman, who is about to have a hysterectomy, is afraid that she may become insane.

Sometimes I am successful in talking my women patients out of these old wives' tales. At other times I have the feeling that they are just listening to my opinions to be polite. No doubt they think I am trying to trick them or to avoid the real issue for some obscure reason.

The stories most readily accepted as fact are primarily those associated with the emotional stages of a woman's life, and with the organs of reproduction. It is rare that anyone questions whether or not an inflamed appendix should be removed. The doctor's diagnosis is accepted, his advice followed. And if a woman develops pneumonia she wants immediate treatment. Furthermore, she and her friends take it for granted she will recover without any aftereffects. But when something goes wrong with the pelvic organs, reason is thrown to the winds. Women promptly start imagining that the treatment will have all sorts of far-reaching aftereffects, no matter what their doctor says to reassure them.

However, what some people refuse to accept orally they will tend to agree to much more readily when they see it in black and white. I hope that will be the case in this instance. And finally, I would like to remind you that keeping a cool head does much to help in coping with any problems that do arise. A tightrope walker needs perfect balance, otherwise he won't enjoy the fruits of his labors for very long! And by the same token, all of us need good balance and calm judgment in our daily lives.

I hope that all of my readers will approach this book with an open mind and that its contents will help them achieve a truly balanced approach toward an understanding of "women's diseases." And as I have already said, I also hope to clear up much of the dangerous confusion that is constantly being created by irresponsible old wives' tales. There is a well-known legal maxim: "If you take a shot at the king, make sure you kill him." Shooting down ignorant misconceptions, like shooting kings, is not always successful. Sometimes you win, sometimes you lose. But if this book succeeds in getting rid of at least some of the overheated scaremonger talk, distorted ideas, and prejudices—then surely the king has died.

On Being a Woman

CHAPTER I

The ABC's of
the Female Anatomy

The Female Organs

IN ORDER TO BUY the weekly groceries and stay within
the family budget it is necessary for women to have some understanding of simple arithmetic—to know that two plus two equals
four. In the same way it is essential that patients have some
knowledge of elementary anatomy if they are to comprehend
adequately the pelvic problems discussed in this book. For
medical students, who spend the best part of a year studying
anatomy in great detail, this is often a boring and tedious subject,
mainly because they are anxious to get it over with and hurry
on to the real meat of medicine. Fortunately, the knowledge of
pelvic anatomy that is required for the lay reader is simple and
can be quickly explained. Consequently it is time well spent,
for most women know very little about their own organs (as
is only too well demonstrated by the questions they frequently
ask in their doctor's office or following an operation).

I recall one middle-aged woman who was worried because her
teen-age daughter was starting to use tampons during her period.
She was convinced that they might become lost and manage
to end up somewhere inside the abdomen. It was a foolish fear,
since the end of the vagina is practically a blind alley and the

opening into the uterus is no wider than a piece of spaghetti. Once reassured, my patient agreed to go along with her daughter's new-fangled idea, although she still had some doubts. Three months later, during a check-up examination, she confided to me that she was now using tampons herself, and wondered why she had been so long in catching up with the times.

The Vagina and Vulva—Let us consider the structure of the female organs, beginning at the outside of the vagina and gradually working toward the internal organs. The area around the opening of the vagina is the vulva. Before a girl has experienced intercourse this vaginal opening is partially closed by a membrane called the hymen. Just as there are tall and short women, there are also all sorts of hymens, which at times makes it difficult to judge virginity. For example, when a patient has a wide, rigid hymen that nearly closes off the vagina, this is certain proof of virginity, since it would be impossible to have intercourse through such a small opening. On the other hand, in many women the hymen is a poorly developed, narrow, thin, pliable band that only closes off a small part of the vaginal opening. This is the reason why many virgin girls are able to use tampons without any trouble. And since the hymen is also fairly fragile is explains why the first intercourse often tears it slightly, causing minimal, short-term bleeding. But it can cause a good deal of unnecessary alarm if young girls are not aware this bleeding can happen. It can cause equal, if not more, trouble if they get the wrong information. Late one night I was called to the .emergency department of our hospital because a frightened, newly married girl insisted she was bleeding to death. She had been told by her girl friend that if bleeding occurs after the first intercourse an operation should be done to stop it immediately. Actually she just had some minor spotting that was of absolutely no importance and required no treatment other than some calm reassurance. Once again it was the "good friend" who set the stage for this anxiety. It would of course be unusual not to want friends although no one has very many of them. Benjamin Franklin was quite cynical about it when he said "one only has three friends, a faithful dog, an old wife and money in the bank." I'm sure the situation is not that grim. But at least in medical matters much could be said for recommending that women assume they have no friends.

The Labia—On either side of the vaginal opening are small fleshy folds, or lips, called the smaller labia. Next to them are larger pads of fatty tissue, the larger labia. The outside of the vagina and the larger labia are covered with pubic hair.

The Clitoris and Urethra—Between the larger labia are two important structures: the clitoris and the urethra. The clitoris is a firm, small, muscular structure which, like the nipples of the breasts, responds to stimulation, becoming erect and firmer. Its sensitivity produces a pleasurable sensation for women prior to or during intercourse. The urethra is the tube leading from the bladder to the outside of the body.

The Vaginal Canal—is a few inches long and leads from the entrance to the cervix. The cervix is the lower part of the uterus, a small channel running through its center that opens into the uterine cavity, connecting it with the vagina. It is muscular, about the size of a quarter, and during labor it has to undergo tremendous stretching and dilation to allow for the passage of the baby. Since many of the diseases of the cervix are separate in type from those of the uterus, doctors tend to speak about diseases of the cervix and diseases of the uterus, but the cervix is not a separate organ, it is the opening, or neck, of the uterus.

The Uterus—is about the size and shape of a pear. It lies between the bladder in front and the rectum at the back. The wall of the uterus is quite elastic, so that as pregnancy develops it can easily enlarge. As it enlarges, it of course becomes thinner. The thin lining inside the uterus is called the "endometrium," a word which will be used quite frequently throughout this book. The endometrium is a very specialized structure that changes each day in response to the ovarian hormones that circulate in the blood stream. Immediately after the period the endometrium is quite thin, as it loses a good part of its thickness during the menstrual flow. Immediately following the end of the period it again begins to grow, as a result of the stimulation of the ovarian hormones. In a month's time it has regained all this lost tissue, only to lose it again with the

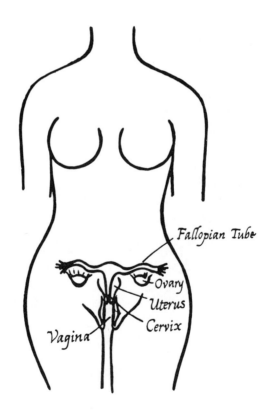

Fallopian Tube
Ovary
Uterus
Cervix
Vagina

next menstrual flow. However, if a pregnancy occurs there is no period, and the fertilized egg burrows its way into this thickly prepared lining and starts to grow. So far as doctors now know, the uterus serves no other purpose than to act as a growing place for the egg. Consequently, removing the uterus by a hysterectomy has no ill-effects on women, in spite of what scaremongers say. It only means that women can no longer have periods or produce children.

The Fallopian Tubes—Hanging like a clothesline from either end of the uterus are the Fallopian tubes, with the ovaries loosely attached to them. A canal runs the entire length of the tubes connecting the uterus to the general abdominal, or pelvic, cavity. Since this canal is exceedingly small, it can easily be closed by infection, and this is a common cause of sterility. The ovaries are hard, whitish structures, about the size of a walnut, and have a very complicated function. First, they secrete the female hormones that are responsible for the normal development of a young girl and initiate her regular monthly periods. Second, they produce the egg that, if fertilized by the male sperm, results in a pregnancy.

How the Organs Function

We mentioned in the previous section that most women are not sure of their normal anatomy. They are equally vague about how their organs work, and most of them only have a very sketchy idea of what happens during the menstrual cycle. Consequently, this section is designed to explain what the period is for, what causes it, and why it eventually stops. Equally important is why it sometimes fails to appear, even though the patient is not pregnant·

Before we proceed any further, let's clear up a couple of misconceptions. Most women think that the period represents just the loss of blood. This is only one side of the story, since in addition to blood loss, part of the endometrial lining of the uterus is also disposed of. Some women believe the bleeding carries away poisonous products, but this is not the case. The menstrual cycle has only one purpose: to prepare the uterus for a possible pregnancy. If a pregnancy does not happen, then the period washes out the old endometrial lining, since it cannot be used a second time. But only the *top half* of the lining is sloughed off, so that the bottom half can immediately start preparing a fresh one.

The hormonal control of the period is reasonably complicated, but let's take a quick look at it. The period occurs because the pituitary gland in the brain stimulates the ovaries to manufacture the female hormones, estrogen and progesterone. Estrogen is produced during the first two weeks of the cycle, causing the endometrium of the uterus to gradually thicken in preparation for the arrival of the fertilized egg. But as you know, most months the egg is not fertilized, and it quickly dies. But since the menstrual cycle has been set in motion for a possible pregnancy, it has to continue on for another two weeks. During that time the ovary produces the hormone, progesterone, which causes further changes in the endometrium. Progesterone has been called "the hormone of the mother," because the finishing touches that it puts on the lining of the uterus are very important for the well-being of the egg, should it become fertilized and a pregnancy begun. Looking at it another way, just as estrogen prepares a soft bed for a possible pregnancy, progesterone goes a step farther by turning down the covers and slipping a hot water bottle between the blankets.

The burning question in the minds of most women is whether a failure to menstruate always means they are pregnant. If the periods have always been regular, a missed period more than likely does mean a pregnancy, particularly if the patient has not used birth control. But, this is not a 100 percent rule. The natural rhythm of the menstrual cycle may be easily broken or temporarily halted by such things as hormone imbalance, illness, emotional disturbance, fatigue, a change of work, excitement of wedding festivities, an ocean crossing, a change of climate, or going away to school.

Late one afternoon a young married girl suddenly burst into tears in the middle of telling me that her period was several weeks overdue. A few months earlier she had decided against the use of birth control pills after reading some controversial magazine article on the hazards of the pill. Now, with her husband still in college, an early pregnancy loomed as a major financial disaster. She also told me that in an effort to make more money she had changed jobs and was working for a high-powered advertising agency. The pressures and tensions of this new environment were turning her into a nervous wreck. So many people were breathing down her back that she was constantly looking around to see who would be the next person to bring her up on the carpet. Satchel Paige once advised "you should never look around, someone may be gaining on you." This advice wouldn't suit some competitive business people who are constantly watching the pack to insure they don't get the worst of the deal. But for this insecure girl who was way over her depth it was certainly sound advice. It soon became obvious, much to her relief, that she was not pregnant. And going back to a job that she could handle restored her periods to normal. She was also advised not to believe everything she read in magazines.

When a period is delayed and the patient does not prove to be pregnant, it is usually because ovulation has failed to occur. At this point the reader might logically ask, what has ovulation got to do with whether or not a period takes place? Ovulation is possibly the most important single event of the entire menstrual cycle. At this time an egg is produced and the ovary starts to manufacture progesterone. This hormone is the one that primarily controls the end point of the menstrual cycle. When something upsets ovulation and it fails to occur, only estrogen is produced by the ovaries; and this hormone sometimes isn't quite strong enough on its own to trigger the period at the proper time. Admittedly estrogen is now and then able to maintain the normal regularity of the cycle in spite of failure of ovulation. But at other times it merely continues to increase the thickness of the lining of the uterus long past the point when bleeding normally occurs. Finally the lining reaches a stage where it no longer can get any thicker, bleeding eventually ensues, and the lining is sloughed off. But, until this happens, women may spend many days of unnecessary worry about the possibility of being pregnant.

What constitutes the normal so far as a period is concerned? This point is discussed in various parts of this book. But since it is such an important question I'll mention it here for two reasons. First, women may worry unnecessarily about small differences that are of no significance. Second, there are instances when changes from the normal pattern represent a danger signal that should be reported to your doctor. Women must realize that what is normal for one may not be normal for another, since no two women are exactly alike. For example, it is not unusual to see a patient who is worrying because her period occurs every thirty-five days rather than the average of twenty-eight days. On the other hand, some patients become alarmed if their periods occur every twenty-one days. Such variations are of no significance so long as the periods have always followed this pattern. If, however, a woman who has always had twenty-eight-day cycles suddenly begins twenty-one-day cycles, this may be the result of disease, and should be checked. It is the change that is of importance. In a similar fashion, it is of no importance whether one woman bleeds for two days and another for seven, so long as this has been an established pattern over the years, and there has not been any change in the amount of blood loss. But should a patient notice the length of her periods increasing or the flow becoming heavier, then the condition should be checked at once by her physician. All this adds up to is that the wise woman looks for change in her own bleeding pattern, rather than comparing it to her friend's or next-door neighbor's.

How many years the period will last depends on how long the ovaries last. Some ovaries continue to produce sufficient amounts of hormones so that the periods continue up to fifty-five years of age or over. But with the majority of patients, the ovaries start to falter earlier; and because of the decreased production of hormones the periods gradually stop, and menopausal symptoms, such as hot flushes, may start. At this point most doctors will advise estrogen replacement therapy (ERT) since the menopause is now considered another disease of aging. This is discussed in detail in Chapter III.

CHAPTER II

New Ideas on Aging

WHY WRITE A CHAPTER on aging when most women are trying to forget about it? I suppose because many old-fashioned women accept the philosophy of "what will be, will be," when in actual fact a good deal can be done to ease many of the problems of later life. Consequently the patient who has stayed away from the doctor's office for twenty or thirty years is simply missing the boat, because medicine has come a long way since the horse-and-buggy doctor; and the specialized field of gynecology is no exception. Chronic annoyances that formerly had to be endured for the remainder of a patient's life can now be cured within a few days. So it is now my intention to present a bird's-eye view of the problem, and to optimistically show that although advancing years may leave a lot to be desired a good deal can now be done to make them more pleasant. But first let's take a look at what scientists are currently doing about solving the problem of why we get older with each passing day. And why it is that aging is today taking on a new significance, and occupying more of scientists' attention than ever before.

Man has many dreams, but perhaps his fondest is to live longer than the three-score years and ten allotted to him; to find the secret of longevity, and delay the approach of death.

Ponce de Leon set sail for the New World in search of the Fountain of Youth. And in Gounod's opera, Faust, embittered by age, made a pact with the Devil to regain his youth. But today the story is entirely different. First of all, scientists have just about eliminated such infectious diseases as smallpox, pneumonia, and diphtheria, to name a few that once caused a terrifying number of deaths. In June 1836 it was a different matter. It was on this date that the Rothschilds, one of the world's most powerful and wealthy families, assembled in Frankfurt, Germany, to attend the wedding of Lionel Rothschild. Nathan Rothschild, his father, developed a sore on his skin that soon enlarged into a carbuncle. On the day of the wedding the inflammation grew worse and immediately following the ceremony Nathan was stricken with chills and a high fever. As the poison swept through his body, frantic couriers sped to England for his personal physician, the famous Benjamin Travers. But when Travers arrived there was nothing he could do, for Nathan Rothschild was gradually but surely dying of blood poisoning. It would not have made any difference if all the great physicians of Europe had been at his bedside, for they all would have lacked one essential weapon—a few dollars' worth of penicillin. Today many different kinds of antibiotics are available which easily cure these infectious diseases. Scientists are therefore looking for new fields to conquer, and some are turning their attention to the degenerative disease of aging. It appears highly likely that before too long our life span will exceed our present average expectancy of seventy-two years. There are of course some skeptics who believe the conquest of age is beyond our reach and is one of the impossibles of life. But there is every reason to suspect that time will prove them to be wrong.

What is aging? During a recent trip to Russia to attend a conference on this subject with a group of Canadian and American doctors, I spent many fascinating hours listening to some answers to this question. And one thing is certain, a sense of extreme excitement is created when scientists talk about this ultimate problem. For drama and intensity, that conference matched the Red Square at midnight—which generates an atmosphere unrivaled by any other piece of real estate I have visited in the world. Furthermore, it appears that there is no reason why the puzzle won't gradually fall into shape, piece by piece. It is just a matter of time. One Soviet scientist hit it right on the head when he told us that if man would spend as much money on this problem as on space flights and atomic research, the secret of extending human life another thirty to forty years could be discovered in one decade. After all, in the past thirty years alone life expectancy in North America has increased from an average of fifty-nine to seventy-two years. This dramatic increase has been the result of advances in medical science; the control of infectious diseases; the discovery of new drugs; a new concept of hormones, as is described in the following chapter; as well as in better housing and eating habits and better working conditions. This is quite an achievement, considering that most cavemen lived to be only eighteen, Roman life expectancy was about twenty-two years, and Englishmen in the Middle Ages couldn't count on more than thirty-three years of existence.

Until recently, most people have thought of old age as a natural process, as inevitable as the fading of the rose petal, the dry brown leaves of fall, the approach of winter. But this is not necessarily so. Medical scientists the world over are becoming more and more aware that aging is just another disease, and that eventually it will be possible to prolong life to three hundred years and even longer. Even more important, this does not mean that we will live longer and look older and older with each passing year. People will not age. Nobody will wander around with wrinkled skin, weak eyes, and rheumatics for the last few hundred years of their lives. Rather, we will stay in the prime of life until death finally comes—most likely by accident. Like Jack Benny we'll all be thirty-nine years of age forever.

Over the years there have been two schools of thought on

aging. One group says it is the result of many external factors: repeated disease during our lifetime, the trauma of childbirth, lack of sleep, too much tobacco or alcohol, climatic conditions, radiation in the atmosphere, to name just a few. After all, they argue, man has lived longer since he learned to control some of these conditions. But the other school of thought believes that this is only half the problem, and that there are clear indications that our present life expectancy has been squeezed to the limit. Now, they argue, we must learn to control internal as well as external factors. And they are now mainly concerned with what happens inside the individual cell, that small unit of life of which the body is composed. It is to this that they are turning their main attention. Most scientists today agree that the process of human aging begins at about the age of thirty, when the cells start to get into trouble. The experts don't think there is any single cause. Rather, it is the result of a lot of complicated chemical and physical changes which take place.

At the moment, there are as many theories as there are scientists working on them. Some believe the cells get clogged with refuse like an old storm sewer, some think the cells forget how to renew their own protoplasm, while others figure that the cells take aboard an excess cargo of proteins. Still others think the cell gets into trouble because of a disturbance of a cellular substance called DNA (Desoxyribonucleic Acid). It is thought that DNA has an important controlling effect on the proper functioning of the cell. Should DNA become damaged, it may result in the gradual death of the cell. At other times, without the controlling effect of DNA, the cells may go on the rampage, dividing in a haphazard fashion that results in a cancer. But regardless of the specific cause, all scientists believe the answer lies in the individual cells of the human body, and that it is only a matter of time before the right answer is found.

If and when that time comes, there are bound to be more and more social as well as economic problems surrounding old age. Many such problems already exist and unless the young-old of the future can find fresh interests and activities, they will either die of sheer boredom, or juvenile delinquency will be replaced by senile delinquency. But for all the trouble it may generate, the extension of man's life span can bestow rewards beyond our wildest expectations. Imagine the benefits to our world if Galileo, Beethoven, Einstein, and Pasteur had each lived another one hundred years.

Unfortunately most of us were born too soon to have the assurance of living to a wrinkle-proof two hundred years. But at least doctors have asked some of the right questions and, step by step, are finding some of the correct answers. This is what makes the practice of gynecology vastly different today than it was thirty years ago. Many diseases that would have formerly killed patients can now be cured. And just as important, many nonfatal but annoying problems, which sap the pleasure from what would be an otherwise pleasant life, can now be quickly eradicated. For instance, in former years women who were lucky enough to survive beyond the menopause were often troubled by vaginal burning, irritation, and discharge which frequently made intercourse either painful or impossible. Now the long-term use of hormones following the menopause will stop this problem. And those who have already developed these chronic irritations can be quickly cured. In the course of this book I will discuss the physiology of the aging process of the pelvic organs and how this may be avoided or corrected.

Doctors are frequently asked by patients whether they are too old to undergo an operation. In recent years the great strides in surgical technique, anesthesia, the availability of blood and antibiotics have enabled surgeons to operate on elderly patients who formerly would have been told to live with their problem rather than accept the risk of surgery. Now it is becoming commonplace to repair injured hearts and, the reader knows, replace entire organs. This means that there has been a fundamental change in the doctors' approach to surgery, because now they primarily treat the disease, not the patient's age. It is no longer merely a matter of using surgery to save a patient's life, since a high percentage of operations are done either to relieve annoyances or to correct problems that if left alone would cause more serious difficulties later on.

In deciding whether or not to do surgery on an elderly patient a number of factors must be taken into consideration. Age, like most things, is a very relative affair. Some women at forty look as if they had been run over by a ten-ton truck while others at seventy still manage to retain the spark and gaiety of life. All doctors have seen seventy-year-olds who have less pain, and more get-up-and-go, following surgery than women thirty years their junior. Yet it is particularly important to take extra care in evaluating the heart, lungs, and kidneys of these older women. Also, any conditions such as diabetes, anemia, obesity, or high blood pressure should be controlled as much as possible before proceeding with what doctors refer to as an "elective" operation.

There is little doubt that aging is going to continue to present people with problems for some time to come. But combined with the better life that medicine continually makes available to us, along with the mature understanding and tolerance that advancing age brings, the latter years can have many compensating factors that youth cannot enjoy for, as Aristotle so aptly said, "there are no boy philosophers."

CHAPTER III

The New Estrogen Treatment and the Menopause

The Truth about Hormones

IT HAS OFTEN BEEN SAID that there is nothing new under the sun. In general, this statement may be true. But the fact remains that there is now a completely fresh and dramatic approach to the whole concept of hormones in their application to specifically female problems and their solutions. And most particularly with regard to the menopause.

Today there is so much talk about hormones that a great many women are confused about the different types. Very simply, hormones are chemical substances produced by various glands which when released into the bloodstream help to control a variety of body functions. For instance, thyroid hormones govern whether the body works in high or low gear much like the accelerator determines the speed of a car. Another hormone, insulin, controls the level of blood sugar. And we will see in this chapter and others that the female hormones estrogen and progesterone also have vital functions. Most women do not know that birth control pills are a combination of synthetic estrogen and progesterone. But when doctors advise long-term estrogens for the menopause they are prescribing straight estrogen, usually from natural sources rather than synthetic.

Doctors prescribe hormones for a variety of difficulties, ranging from their temporary use as birth control pills to their indefinite use in controlling the long-term effects of the menopause. They are also sometimes prescribed on a short-term basis to regulate the menstrual period, control any pain that accompanies it, or to treat a specific disease. Yet it is an unusual woman who accepts her doctor's hormone prescription without some degree of hesitation and doubt. Why should this be the case?

A great deal of the trouble dates back to the time when hormones were in their infancy, and did produce some side-effects for the patient and troubles for the doctor. The early development of hormones such as estrogen presented doctors with some rather interesting and trying problems. I spent an interesting time one evening hearing some of the early tales from a doctor who had been associated with the early development of estrogen.

In 1930 doctors started to collect the urine from pregnant women during the first three months of their pregnancy when the hormone content was high. Since this was during the Depression husbands were often unemployed and women were quite happy to receive one dollar for each gallon of urine. Gradually as more suppliers were obtained the price dropped to twenty-five cents a gallon but this still helped to pay for the doctor's delivery which at that time was about ten dollars. On one occasion some women in the district lodged a complaint with the police department that the doctor was selling alcohol. He was picked up one day and taken to the police station where the captain in charge refused to believe his story. It was only when two other scientists who were working on the project arrived several hours later at the station the doctor was released. On another occasion the scientists were completely unable to unravel why there was so little hormone in one particular sample. It was only after extensive checking that it was discovered that one lady was also emptying the teapot contents into the bottle. A lot of money had gone down the drain to find out that there were no estrogens in cold tea. Possibly the best story of them all involves the research chemist from New York who arrived in Canada to pick up five gallons of pregnant mare's urine. Doctors at that time had shifted from the study of human urine to that of horses and this particular doctor wished to carry out some investigational work on it. Having picked up the urine he started for home, and his troubles began. He was asked at the United States border whether he had anything to declare and promptly replied that he had five gallons of pregnant mare's urine. The custom officials found this rather difficult to believe and since this was wartime, they were suspicious that some very valuable chemicals might be dissolved in it. Furthermore, there was nothing in the customs book of regulations to tell them what to do about pregnant mare's urine. The end result was that the doctor was told he had to leave it at the border and would be advised later on. The scientist pointed out that if he didn't have it within seventy-two hours it would be useless because the product would have deteriorated by that time. About two months later he received a letter advising him that he could pick up his parcel. He was of course by this time furious and threw the letter into the wastepaper basket. Two weeks later he received another such letter and again he threw it away. Finally the third letter arrived telling him in no uncertain terms that unless he picked his parcel up it would be sold within two weeks at a public auction. If the United States customs officials were able to accomplish this sale they certainly deserve a place in history as being the world's best salesmen.

Today, after years of additional research, there is about as much similarity between the old hormones and the present-day variety as there is between a third-rate charwoman and Mrs. Onassis. Nevertheless women continue to worry that hormones will cause them to grow a beard, gain excess weight, or develop cancer. None of these things ever happen with either the hormone creams or pills. But it may be a long time before some women accept this simple fact. Schiller took a rather pessimistic view of mankind when he wrote in *Die Jungfrau von Orleans* "The gods themselves struggle in vain against stupidity." Some of the old-school physicians (and even a few of the younger doctors) tend to share this same attitude and believe it's not only impossible to educate patients, but also it's really better to keep them in the dark about medical matters. Yet it is because of this old-fashioned approach that we often hear women complain that they simply can't get any of the answers from their doctor who continually seems to be skirting around the truth. Fortunately most present-day doctors have become much more optimistic about women and think that if they are told the right facts the majority will accept them and stop this needless worry. And as I've said before that's really what this book is all about. So first let's take a realistic look at what hormones don't do and then what they can accomplish.

The "Beard" Concept. This arose because in the experimental stages of hormone usage, women were sometimes given male hormones for either too long or in too large a dose, and this occasionally resulted in their growing excess facial hair. But not only have today's hormones been refined to a tremendous extent, but also 99 percent of those now used by doctors are female hormones, and therefore could not possibly cause any masculine characteristics.

Gaining Weight. There may be an ounce of truth in the idea that hormones will cause a gain in weight, but it is highly exaggerated, and would certainly never be a valid reason for deciding against the use of hormone pills. Normally, most women gain a pound or two in the week before the menstrual period begins because of the extra fluid which the body accumulates at that time. Birth control pills can also produce the same effect, but it is never enough to cause any excessive weight gain, and once her period is over a woman's weight will return to normal.

Do Hormones Cause Cancer? The answer is no. In fact this whole concept is founded upon a false premise; both male and female hormones are sometimes used to treat certain forms of cancer, which led to hormones and cancer becoming linked in people's minds. Instead of realizing that the hormones were being used to *treat* cancer, they began to believe that hormones *caused* cancer. However, this confusion of ideas is gradually being eradicated. First, because more and more women are taking hormones in one form or another. Second, because the hormone has now been around long enough for it to become clear that there is no higher incidence of cancer among the women who are using it. In fact, some evidence suggests that the number of cases of cancer that occur in this group are lower than the average.

But it is the menopause that pushes the alarm button on hormones more than anything else. This is not surprising, for most people have an inherent fear of this stage of their lives, and consequently are more vulnerable to all kinds of rumors. Adding hormones to the picture just serves to complicate it further, particularly when there is so much lively debate at bridge as to their relative merits.

However, to sum up, hormones can be extremely beneficial to a number of conditions, particularly the menopause. When they are recommended by your doctor there should be no hesitation in taking them. Failure to do so means that women are forfeiting the benefits of present-day medicine. To say no to hormones is the same as turning down penicillin, insulin, or any of the other advances in medical treatment.

Estrogen Pills and the Menopause

For centuries the menopause, like old age, was regarded as a natural process, something that women just had to endure. But doctors are now successfully challenging this out-of-date concept. They look upon the menopause as a deficiency disease, as obsolete as a Model-T Ford. It is no longer considered a normal physiological process, but a disease of aging that can be safely prevented. Of course there are some doctors who resist this change, a minority who believe that the menopause should not be tampered with, that it only lasts for a short time and is best treated with reassurance and mild sedatives. Others will go a step further, and only use hormones for women with noticeably bad symptoms, but eventually discontinue them. However, the majority of doctors are moving in step with the times, and are advising their patients to take female hormones indefinitely with the onset of the menopausal period. At a recent meeting of the American College of Obstetricians and Gynecologists, doctors were told "estrogens are not the fountain of youth, but may well be the springs that feed the fountains."

Even a century ago the menopause was not something which gave doctors much concern—simply because women did not live long enough to develop either menopausal symptoms or their long-term effects. The majority died coincidentally with the ending of their ability to produce children. For example, most of the women born in 1900 did not have an average life-expectancy beyond forty-eight years. What a difference today, when the average female life-expectancy has increased to seventy-three years! This means that for about thirty years most women will have to face a deficiency in the female hormone, estrogen, which has been aptly described as "what makes a girl, a girl."

Until recently, doctors were still looking upon the menopause as a temporary disturbance which would eventually correct itself. And the fact that some women sailed through it with only minimal trouble, or even none at all, made many doctors feel that the complaints of their other patients had a purely imaginary basis. Now, however, the medical profession sees the problem very differently.

They realize that although some symptoms may result from emotional tension and the wear and tear of advancing age, the real villain of the piece is the sharp fall in the female hormone, estrogen. It is a deficiency in estrogen which causes hot flushes, cold spells, headaches, insomnia, anxiety and depression with which many women are plagued during this stage of their lives.

It is particularly important that modern women understand the real causes of the menopause, because this is a time when even the most intelligent women may become prey to quite ludicrous fears. They are convinced that the menopause signifies a change for the worst. How could it mean a change for the better when they hear about all the terrible things it can cause? Someone has told them about a friend who became insane during her change of life. Another says that women automatically become obese with its onset. Still others talk about the loss of sexual desire—to most women the most terrible threat of all.

For example, I was once consulted by a distraught woman who was sure that her healthy and well-adjusted response to sex would end with the onset of the menopause. What could be done to avoid it, she asked. Were there any drugs she could take? What about hormones? Millions of women ask these same questions and have the same fears every year, usually because of some foolish, illogical remark by an ignorant friend.

Admittedly, the menopause does represent a minor change in a woman's life, but there is nothing abnormal or damaging about it. No tricks will be played on her. The menopause simply means the end of the female's reproductive stage, when her periods, and the possibility of childbirth end. And nowadays most doctors are advising the indefinite use of estrogen for two reasons. First, taking this hormone immediately stops any annoying symptoms that may be present. Second, a great deal of scientific evidence has been accumulated that shows that the long-term use of this hormone helps to slow down the aging process in certain parts of the body. The estrogen pill is therefore one of the early steps in medicine's attempt to produce a wife who doesn't wear out. Furthermore it will give women a tremendous psychological boost knowing they finally have something other than the artificial support of make-up to help them keep up with their husbands.

To repeat, the menopause is merely part of the overall aging process, no more, no less. Even before the female hormones became available the worst that could ever happen to a woman was that she had to put up with the few annoying symptoms. And, as the reader will see, certain areas of the body did tend to age more quickly. But women have never gone insane, grown fat, or lost their husbands because of the menopause. If such things do happen, it is because they would have occurred anyway. Women need psychiatric help at times other than during the menopause. People get fat at all ages. And husbands can be lost for many reasons. It is the acceptance of this illogical reasoning that can cause the damage. The women who spread alarmist rumors (without any real medical knowledge) do not bother to recall the millions of females who went through the menopause in the past without any trouble. It is always the isolated case that attracts attention, and gives the scaremonger the ammunition she needs to frighten her friends.

Yet not all the stories come from friends, some women create their own tall tales, either unknowingly, or for devious reasons. For instance, some women who have been chronically unhappy about sexual relations all their married lives frequently fasten upon the menopause as a good excuse for ending sexual relations. They blame the menopause for the diminishing of a sexual desire which they never possessed in the first place. It is regrettable that such women will spread stories amongst their friends as a means of assuaging their own feelings of guilt. And it is never difficult for them to find a listening ear.

One last point. Women who have been frightened by old wives' tales should realize that the menopause has its good points. Many women are, for the first time, totally relieved of the constant fear of an unwanted pregnancy. No longer is there the anxious wait for the next period. To some women this even puts a new emphasis on sex. Now they can relax and enjoy marital relations fully.

Most women become aware that the menopause has started when there is a change in the bleeding pattern, starting somewhere between thirty-five and fifty-five years of age, and taking many different forms. For instance, only a small group will suddenly miss a period and never have another one. Rather, the majority will notice a gradual lessening of bleeding, with either fewer periods, decreased bleeding during the periods, or a combination of both. On the other hand, some women will gradually notice a pattern in which there is neither rhyme nor reason. Bleeding may become very irregular, frequent, heavy or prolonged. This increased bleeding is usually not associated with any disease. But more bleeding than usual should *always* be checked by a doctor. Unfortunately, most women immediately jump to the false conclusion that any abnormal bleeding is due to cancer. This is rarely so, but to make sure doctors do a dilatation and scraping of the inside of the uterus, or what is commonly referred to as a "D and C." This removes the inside lining of the uterus, which can then be subjected to a microscopic examination that will detect the presence of any malignancy. At the menopause this precautionary D and C is important, because cancer is more common at this age, and should be detected early, while it is 100 percent curable. Consequently, women who experience increased bleeding in one form or another should not wait to see if it is going to continue, as this means loss of valuable time if any trouble is present. How much better to consult the doctor early and obtain the reassurance and peace of mind that can be given to nearly all patients.

But women should also consult their doctor to obtain relief from the annoying symptoms of the menopause. Foremost of these are the hot flushes and cold spells. One woman described it as like being in a cold room with steam rising from her. Another said it felt like blood rushing to the head and then feeling wet all over. Still another said it would be wonderful if you could undo the cork at the top and let the steam out. Other women may notice night sweats, headaches, pins-and-needle sensations in the fingers, or general nervous tension that are both unpleasant and unnecessary to endure.

Scientists now believe that lack of estrogen not only causes these bothersome symptoms, but is also responsible for harmful metabolic effects on numerous systems of the body. Let me briefly mention some of the more important problems.

Atherosclerosis. A disease in which the arteries become narrowed by fatty deposits on their walls, believed to be related in part to an estrogen lack. It is a proven fact that during the reproductive years women rarely have heart attacks, but in their sixties, when they have been deprived of adequate estrogen for many years, they start to suffer from as many heart attacks as men. Some scientists believe that lack of estrogen is in part responsible for the increased levels of cholesterol and other fats in the blood which may be related to heart disease. Others are convinced that the degenerative changes in the blood vessels affect not only the heart, but also other areas in the body. For instance, high blood pressure has been found to decrease on long-term estrogen treatment. Furthermore, questions are now being raised as to whether premature senility may be in part related to lack of estrogen. Admittedly the theories surrounding these problems are still controversial, but piece by piece the evidence seems to be fitting into the proper place, linking lack of estrogen with premature aging of the arteries.

Osteoporosis. A disease in which the bones of elderly women become brittle, thin, and break easily. It has been said that the only constant thing in life is change, and bone is no exception to this rule. Prior to the menopause there is a good balance between the production of new bone and the production of old bone. But in elderly women the formation of new bone slows down, while the absorption of old bone, unfortunately, remains the same. The net result is that the bones lose some of their bulk and become less dense and more porous. This problem effects about one out of every four postmenopausal women and many doctors believe it is in part due to the result of chronic estrogen deprivation. There are many reasons for this assumption. Most old people who break their hips are women, and they also happen to be the ones who have not been taking estrogens. Furthermore, women have a tendency to shrink in height as they age, sometime a few inches, because of the thinning and bending of the bones comprising the spinal column. Conversely, women who take estrogen usually do not break their bones or shrink in size. Furthermore, some doctors are impressed by the fact that women with osteoporosis and low back pain can frequently be helped by taking estrogens.

For many years it has been a well-established fact that women age more quickly than men. Now doctors feel that this too is related to lack of estrogen, causing the breasts to sag, the skin to become dry, wrinkled, and devoid of its former elasticity. Admittedly, estrogen will not completely stop the aging process. But it can certainly go a long way in helping to slow it down.

Senile Vaginitis. Following the menopause, many women's vaginal lining starts to age more rapidly than other areas. It becomes irritated, sore, inflamed, and bleeds easily. Some women will notice increasing vaginal discharge. Others will experience bleeding during intercourse, or find that intercourse gradually becomes painful, and the vaginal opening constantly irritated. There is little doubt that this condition has not only caused a great deal of discomfort over the years, but also has been a prime factor in many unhappy marriages. Unfortunately, even today this is still too often the case, because senile vaginitis continues to be one of the most neglected problems in medicine. And the irony is that it is one of the easiest conditions to diagnose and treat, or better still, to prevent. Its existence can be quickly confirmed by an examination of the vagina. And no long and costly treatment is required to change a severely irritated vagina to one that looks thirty years younger. The simple nightly insertion of an estrogen cream will, after one week, result in a dramatic relief of symptoms. Then, to guarantee that the vagina will continue in a healthy state, a daily dose of estrogen will be advised. However, for a full discussion of this very common problem and its treatment, the reader is referred to the section on senile vaginitis in Chapter XVII.

The When and How of Taking Hormones

As I mentioned at the start of this chapter, an increasing number of doctors now believe that the advantages of long-term estrogen treatment far outweigh any of the disadvantages. They argue that the menopause is no different from any other disease of aging, and if we have the means to treat it, why not do so? After all, when our eyes begin to fail, very few of us refuse glasses, and only a fool would refuse insulin, if the alternative was to die of diabetes. More and more doctors therefore conclude that with the onset of the menopause all women should take a daily estrogen pill *whether or not they have symptoms*, because the latter can be a most unreliable index of an estrogen lack. For example, a woman can be without any apparent symptoms and still be suffering from an extremely irritated vagina.

Hormones can be given by either pills or injections, and your doctor may favor one approach over the other for a variety of reasons. For instance, women who habitually forget to take the pill for long periods may be better off receiving a hormone injection every now and then. However, this method has certain disadvantages, as it is impossible to predict how long the injection will remain effective. Some women are relieved of their flushes and other symptoms for a few weeks, others for a month or more. It therefore becomes a hit-and-miss affair when the injections are given. And as mentioned previously, even when symptoms are absent, many doctors believe hormones are still needed to protect women from heart disease, brittle bones, and senile vaginitis.

Consequently, it is generally felt that the majority of sensible women are more conveniently and effectively treated by estrogen pills. This method does away with the need to return frequently to the doctor's office and the inconvenience of needles. The cost is lower and a predictable daily level of hormone is ensured.

Estrogen pills can either be from natural sources, or synthetic (man-made). The major advantage of the natural estrogens is that they are virtually free from side effects, such as nausea and vomiting. Synthetic estrogens, on the other hand, produce nausea in a high percentage of women. In addition to this, women taking natural estrogens often feel better than those on synthetics. There is also abundant evidence in the medical literature that natural estrogens do have an effect in preventing or delaying the onset of osteoporosis, senile vaginitis, and other conditions mentioned earlier in this chapter, but less is known about the action of synthetic estrogens in these conditions. Some synthetic hormones are a little less costly than natural hormones but the difference is not great and, in either case, estrogen therapy is relatively inexpensive.

Your doctor will advise on when and how to take the pills. Some gynecologists believe estrogen should be started before the periods end, particularly when hot flushes or other menopausal symptoms are bothersome. Other gynecologists wait until the periods have stopped for a few months before they recommend them. Similarly, there is slight variation in how the pills are taken. Some doctors will tell patients to take a pill each day for three weeks out of every four or, more simply, for the first three weeks of every month. Other doctors think it is better for women to use a tablet every day of every month. Women who have had a hysterectomy, with removal of both ovaries, are usually advised to take them this way. But regardless of what routine is recommended, most doctors agree that estrogen should be continued as long as a woman lives.

No one has ever shown that long-term taking of natural estrogens causes trouble. But since women will sometimes be using them for as long as thirty years, they may tend to wrongly blame the estrogen pill for anything that occurs during that time. If a patient develops pneumonia or an ingrown toenail while taking it, most people would never think of blaming estrogen. But if bleeding problems start, some might point their finger at it. Very often they would be in error, for a pelvic examination will reveal a polyp, fibroid, or an early malignancy that would have occurred whether or not the patient was taking estrogen. Less frequently, they might be proved right, for on rare occasions estrogen stimulates the endometrium (inside lining of the uterus) to the point where a slight spotting or bleeding occurs. This bleeding, when it's due to estrogen, is of no importance and does not require any treatment other than adjusting the dosage of hormone. The trouble is that doctors cannot be sure the bleeding is due to estrogen, as it might also result from an early cancer. To rule out this chance, they usually advise a D and C.

There is one further point which should be discussed. What about the increasing number of women in their forties who are on the birth control pill? At what age should they start taking estrogens? These women obviously do not wish to become pregnant, but they also do not want to take birth control pills any longer than is absolutely necessary. We mentioned earlier that women usually develop menopausal symptoms at some point during their forties, as an indication that their change of life is at hand. But this red light doesn't always flash on for women taking the pill, because birth control pills contain some estrogen along with the other female hormone, progesterone. Since there may be enough estrogen in these pills to stop any symptoms from appearing, it becomes a guessing game as to whether or not the menopause has started.

Many women sensibly ask whether it makes any difference if they continue on the birth control pill, particularly when they feel fine. Fortunately there is a simple answer. In my chapter on birth control, I mention that there has been too much scaremonger talk about the dangers of this pill. Nevertheless, it must be admitted that some fairly good evidence has been presented by doctors which suggests that birth control pills can occasionally cause serious problems, such as bloodclots in the brain and lungs. And even if this is an extremely small risk why push your luck if you don't have to? Natural estrogen, on the other hand, is trouble-free. In addition, estrogen is normally produced throughout the entire menstrual cycle, whereas progesterone is limited to the last two weeks of the cycle. Most doctors therefore feel that it is more natural to give continuous estrogen than continuous progesterone. Also, there is no evidence progesterone is needed for the menopause and, being excess baggage, the sooner it is stopped the better.

To carry out this change-over is quite easy. Some doctors will simply switch from the birth control pill to natural estrogens. And as an added precaution they may suggest the use of a contraceptive cream for a short time, until it is apparent the periods are over and there is no further chance of pregnancy. Others will test to see if the menopause has started by advising their patients to stop the birth control pills for a few months to see what happens. If the patient develops hot flushes and the period fails to appear the menopause is present. Estrogens are then started by the doctor.

I trust the reader now understands the merits of taking a daily pill of natural estrogen at the start of the menopause. And I would again caution patients not to listen to the scaremongers who denounce hormones. Remember these predictors of woe usually possess one important trait that helps them propagate this nonsense. It's the simple fact that they give the outward appearance of being so totally sure of their opinions. Both these soothsayers of doom and their friends would be well-advised to remember the practical wisdom of the old Negro who counselled: "It's not the things you don't know what gets you into trouble, it's the things you know for sure that ain't so!"

CHAPTER IV

Common Menstrual Problems

Premenstrual Tension

MANY WOMEN SUFFER from various aches and pains before the start of the menstrual period. Some complain of difficulty just a few days before their period. Others may notice a change for as long as fourteen days before its onset. Certainly the majority of women are well able to live with this problem, but some find it extremely annoying. In fact it is sometimes the husband who has insisted that an appointment be made with the doctor to see what is wrong with his usually easy-to-live-with wife.

What causes premenstrual tension is a debatable point, but one fact can be agreed on: For some reason the body holds on to more fluid at this time of the month than at any other time. It is this increased collection of water in the tissues of the body that is generally believed to be responsible for the symptoms. But there is less agreement as to the cause of the water retention. A number of doctors think it is due to a temporary change in the hormones. Some blame one hormone, some another. Other doctors believe that a toxin is liberated by the lining of the uterus when it starts to break down, just prior to the onset of the menstrual period.

The symptoms of premenstrual tension are numerous, and vary in number and severity from woman to woman. Many women develop minor degrees of depression and are difficult to live with at this time. Others become emotionally upset, often for no good reason. Still others complain of headaches, nausea and vomiting, and tight feelings in the legs. A common complaint is bloating of the stomach or a feeling of being bloated all over. This symptom, when it is confined to the lower part of the abdomen, is believed to be due to the increased blood flow to the pelvic region which occurs during this time and which causes congestion of the female organs. For the same reason women often complain of a tingling feeling in the breasts or an enlargement and tenderness of the breasts. Fortunately, with the onset of the period these symptoms quickly subside.

What can be done to relieve premenstrual tension? Those women who believe that their monthly discomfort is the result of disease often just require the assurance that it is not, after which they are quite willing to put up with it; and many decline any other treatment. Premenstrual tension is such a commonly recognized phenomenon that most women who feel out of sorts for a few days before their period realize it is a normal process and never bother to see their doctor. Consequently treatment is usually reserved mainly for those women with severe symptoms that start a week or more before their period. Since it is the increased collection of water in the body that appears to be the cause of the trouble, the logical form of attack is to get rid of it. This is just what doctors do, and it can be accomplished in two ways. First, they advise women who suffer from distressing symptoms to limit the amount of liquids that they drink before the onset of their period. Second, the excess water can be eliminated by the use of drugs called "diuretics," which stimulate the kidneys. These drugs are usually started a number of days before the expected onset of the period. Usually one pill is swallowed every morning, which causes increased urination during the day and results in a marked improvement of the symptoms.

Painful Periods in the Adolescent Girl

It is not an unfamiliar sight to see a rather agitated mother enter the doctor's office with her young daughter. Usually both mother and daughter are of a tense type, in other words "like mother like daughter." Some of these girls experience pain with the very first period. Others notice it after two or three years of normal periods. The pain may start a few hours, or one or two days before the bleeding, or just at the onset of flow. Some complain of low stomach pain. Others of back pain. Still others of both. Sometimes the pain is present in the thighs. There is also a great variation in how long the pain lasts. With some it may be for a few hours, but others may have it for one or two days. Certainly some girls look on it merely as an annoyance which a few aspirins will take care of. A few are severely incapacitated, with pain, nausea, vomiting and, sometimes, fainting spells. Usually the skin of this type of girl will become quit' clammy, and she will perspire freely. In such cases, the doctor will be called regularly to the girl's home to give an injection which will relieve the pain. What is the cause of these extreme symptoms? Most doctors believe it is because the contractions of the uterus at this time are more pronounced in some girls than in others. Others believe that the contractions don't vary much from one girl to another, but the individual's reaction does. The tense, emotional girl will have more pain than the cool, calm, and collected type. Still other doctors try to explain it on more specific psychological grounds, such as an unhappy home life or problems at school or work. Some believe it may, in part, be the result of either little or no preparation for the onset of menstruation and what it signifies. Certainly mothers or friends who refer to the period as the "curse" do little to help a susceptible girl. In similar fashion, the mother who has always suffered from menstrual pain, and who makes a point of telling her daughter that it will be the same for her, is usually condemning the girl to a lifetime of similar experience.

As a Latin proverb so apty points out "if you always live with those who are lame, you yourself learn to limp."

Not too long ago a distraught woman led her daughter into my office. The mother proceeded to explain in great detail how she had suffered for years from painful periods because of cystic ovaries. A few months ago her daughter had started to have pain, and the mother was totally convinced that it was due to cysts forming on her ovaries. No doubt she had been drilling this theme into her daughter's head, because the girl was obviously upset by all this alarmist chatter. As it turned out there was nothing wrong with her. She was having normal, mild menstrual cramps, which had been greatly exaggerated by her mother's concern. Reassured that her pelvic organs, including her ovaries, were perfectly healthy, she left the office quite happy.

Then there are the mothers who insist that whenever their daughters are having their period their lives should come almost to a standstill insofar as sports, work, and other activities are concerned. This automatically makes the girl think that something must be seriously wrong with her. As you can see, there are many possible causes for menstrual cramps, and although they are a reasonably common complaint, most of the girls a doctor sees do not have anything seriously wrong with them either psychologically or physically.

However, the doctor's first responsibility is to conduct an examination and make certain there is no disease present. As the reader would suspect, adolescent girls can develop some of the diseases that cause painful periods in older women. But this is unusual. No doubt some of you are wondering how a pelvic examination can be done on a girl of this age, when the hymen is still intact. When this *is* the case, a pelvic examination, in the true sense of the word, cannot be accomplished. Fortunately, however, by inserting a finger into the rectum the doctor can feel the female organs just as well as by doing a vaginal examination. On the other hand, some girls have a poorly developed hymen, so a pelvic examination does become possible.

But the point I want to stress is that nearly all girls will be told their female organs are perfectly normal. Sometimes this alone will remove the girl's worry, and no further treatment is needed. Reassured, she is able to put up with a little bit of pain. But some girls are still so inconvenienced for a day or two each month that further treatment is required. Again this may mean little more than a few aspirins or codeine. But what about those who, month after month, need injections for pain? A number of things can be done. Most of these young girls can expect complete relief by taking one hormone pill daily for the first three weeks of their cycle. This stops the process of ovulation, and for reasons which are not altogether clear, the next period is painless. This method may only give temporary relief. But it does have one very important psychological result. The girl discovers, much to her surprise, that something *can* be done to completely rid her of pain.

There are other procedures that are sometimes advised. Doctors know that a fair number of these girls are relieved of their pain after a normal pregnancy. It is generally thought that this relief is the result of stretching the opening of the uterus during the process of delivery. It is believed this injures the nerves in the lower part of the uterus, so that they are less able to send pain impulses to the brain. If this is so, why not stretch the cervix (opening of the uterus) in a girl who is not contemplating a pregnancy for a few years? Doctors who have gone along with this reasoning have had fairly good success. It requires hospitalization for a day or two, as well as an anesthetic. Then, while the patient is asleep, the cervical opening is gradually stretched. Some girls are helped permanently, others for a few months, still others not at all. Should the pain continue to recur in the same degree, what else can be done? In these cases, doctors occasionally do what is called a "presacral and uterosacral neurectomy." In this operation, the surgeon cuts the nerves that carry painful sensations away from the uterus. By interrupting this nervous pathway to the brain, nearly all girls with this type of pain are permanently cured. But doctors do not advise an abdominal operation until all other methods have failed.

Painful Periods in the Older Woman

Painful periods in the older woman are not necessarily a cause for worry, as they can result from spasm of the uterus, similar to the type experienced by the adolescent girl. Many patients will say they have had cramps with their periods all their lives, and that the pains have not changed. The majority of these women have no disease and have learned to live with their monthly discomfort. Nevertheless pain is more likely to indicate real trouble in this group than with the adolescent girl. There are two situations in which this is particularly true: first the woman who has experienced menstrual cramps all her life and then finds that they gradually or suddenly become much worse; second the patient who has never suffered from menstrual pain but who suddenly develops it later on in life. It is well to remember that a change of this sort does not always mean trouble, for the pain may result from only a minor disturbance. Yet the doctor should be informed of it at once, for he is the person best able to judge whether a problem exists.

Since pain is such a universal symptom it can be caused by many diseases and these are discussed in detail in other chapters of this book. I only now intend to briefly summarize the more common reason for pain in the older woman. I should also point out that the pain is usually accompanied by some type of abnormal bleeding which many be in the form of heavy, long, frequent periods or bleeding between periods.

Fibroid Tumors, which are so common in middle-aged women, may in some cases cause menstrual pain. Yet these benign (1 oncancerous) growths may remain small in size for years and never require any treatment. And they never turn into cancer, so there is no need for worry along that line. Many small fibroids go completely unnoticed, and only those few that en-large in size sometimes cause discomfort. Fibroids are discussed in detail in Chapter XIV.

Pelvic Infections are another frequent reason for menstrual pain. Here again the majority of infections are so mild that they pass unnoticed in many cases. When, however, extensive scarring of the uterus, tubes, and ovaries has occurred, pain with the periods is sometimes a prominent symptom, and surgery may be required. A section dealing with this type of infection will be found in Chapter XIV.

Pelvic Endometriosis (internal bleeding) may also occur at this age. Chapter XIV again includes a full description of this condition, and the possible forms of treatment. However, like mild cases of pelvic infection, it requires no treatment in most cases, and fortunately goes away at the menopause, when the periods stop. On the other hand, if the pain becomes severe, surgery may be required to correct it. In the case of a young girl the surgery removes the endometriosis but preserves the female organs. Women nearing the menopause, however, are usually treated by a hysterectomy with removal of the tubes and ovaries. During the last few years important studies have been made regarding the treatment of this problem. At present many young girls are being satisfactorily treated with hormones, so that in the future surgery may be needed less frequently.

The Tipped Uterus. There are other, less common, problems that cause menstrual pain. Sometimes undue tension and worry will make minor cramps seem much worse. At other times, a tipped uterus may be partly responsible for the pain when it is associated with one of the above conditions, such as infection or endometriosis. However, unassociated with disease, a tipped uterus is of no significance in 99 percent of cases. A full discussion of this condition will be found in Chapter XII.

To sum up, menstrual pain in the older woman is sometimes

of importance, and at other times of little or no significance. But there is only one way to make sure: a pelvic examination by your doctor. Anything short of this is just guesswork, and may cause a delay in treatment. It is therefore important to consult your doctor at the first sign of trouble, so that it can be diagnosed and treated in its early stages. As the reader would suspect, the earlier a disease is treated the better the results.

Premature Onset of the Period

Most girls start their periods around thirteen, but they may occur under normal conditions as early as ten or as late as eighteen. It is unusual, however, for the periods to start before ten, although the development of the breasts and the pubic hair can normally occur as early as eight.

Although it is unusual for girls to start bleeding before ten, the majority who do so are perfectly healthy, and there is no reason for parents to become unduly alarmed. In the great majority of cases the bleeding occurs merely because the delicate hormonal mechanism that starts the periods has shifted into gear at an earlier age. Just why this happens is a complicated subject; but in all probability the pituitary gland, often referred to as the master gland of the body since it controls the actions of so many of the other glands, is responsible. By producing hormones, it in turn stimulates the ovaries that manufacture the female hormones. These female hormones then circulate in the blood, and cause the lining of the uterus to grow, and finally bleeding occurs.

When bleeding starts at an early age it is usually a shock for the parents and the child, and obviously it is important that both parties be reassured as quickly as possible. It is important that the girl should be immediately examined by a doctor, and tests done to rule out the very few rare problems that can occasionally cause both early bleeding and premature sexual maturity. But as mentioned earlier, the majority of cases are merely caused by earlier glandular activity, and can be classified within the normal limits of a girl's natural growth.

In some cases, doctors will advise the use of hormones to insure normal development, but in other instances some education of the parents and child is all that is needed. The girl should be told the facts of life in terms she can easily understand, so that she will not be frightened by the appearance of bleeding. All this amounts to just good sense, rather than making a federal case out of the problem.

Bleeding between Periods

This type of bleeding can result from a number of problems, the majority of which are of little importance and easily corrected; but again it is vitally important that an early visit be made to the doctor. Should bleeding occur between periods, it is important to discover at what part of the menstrual cycle the bleeding was noted. For example, slight spotting or bleeding sometimes occurs about halfway between periods, and may last anywhere from a few hours to two or three days. Usually this bleeding is due to ovulation when the egg escapes from the ovary, and there is a temporary drop in the hormonal level of estrogen. This transient drop in the hormonal level temporarily leaves the lining of the uterus without enough hormone to stop it from bleeding, so that bleeding may occur for a few hours or a few days, until the hormonal level is once again normal. This midcycle bleeding may occur only once, or in some women it may be almost a constant feature. In fact it is worth mentioning that on rare occasions midcycle ovulation bleeding can also be associated with either mild or extremely severe pain. This is because at the time that the egg pops out of its small sac in the ovary a small amount of fluid is also released, which may irritate the peritoneal lining of the inside of the abdomen. At other times, as the egg breaks its way through the outer surface of the ovary, it may rupture one of the small blood vessels on the ovarian surface and, depending on the amount of bleeding, varying degrees of peritonitis occur. This internal bleeding, which of course the patient cannot see, is usually of small amount, quickly stops, and produces mild pain for only a few hours. When, however, the pain is more severe, or lasts longer and happens to be on the right side, it is difficult at times to differentiate the pain from that caused by appendicitis. Careful observation of the patient and blood studies are then required. Not infrequently, the patients report that the pain is on one side one month, and the other side the next month, and this helps the doctor considerably in arriving at the proper diagnosis.

Some women also notice slight staining or bleeding a few days before a period is due. This is usually the result of what doctors refer to as "teetering hormonal levels." Let me explain it this way. The period normally starts because of a rather abrupt drop in the level of female hormones circulating in the blood. If, however, the ovary falters gradually, rather than quickly, in its production of hormones, the bleeding may come on slowly for a few days before the regular bleeding occurs. This is of no importance and requires no treatment, but should be reported to the doctor.

It is also important to realize that bleeding that occurs either halfway between periods or at other times can be the result of other problems. A full discussion of abnormal bleeding and its causes will be found in Chapters XIII and XIV.

Frequent, Heavy, Prolonged, and Irregular Bleeding

The reason I have grouped these four problems together is that they are so frequently associated. Patients can, of course, notice only one of these symptoms, but in many instances two or more are present.

Possibly the worst error women make is to compare their

bleeding with a friend's or next-door neighbor's. We all realize that no two individuals are the same in temperament, size, or the amount of work they can do, so why should their bleeding pattern be the exception? As I have already said, it is the *established pattern* over a period of years that is the significant factor in menstruation. Variations in this pattern between one woman and another have no meaning and are of no more importance than the difference between a woman who weighs 100 pounds and another who weighs 125 pounds. Similarly, some women use ten pads for a period, whereas others may require twice as many. Consequently rather than comparing themselves to each other, women should look for a change in their own established bleeding pattern, particularly when it is a change to more bleeding rather than less. If, and when, this happens a prompt visit to the doctor is in order.

There are times in a woman's life when doctors expect to see temporary variations in the menstrual cycle. They are not surprised, for instance, to see either frequent or infrequent periods in teenage girls when menstruation is just starting. Some girls will immediately begin regular periods with normal bleeding. But others frequently need anywhere from a few months to a year or more before the delicate hormonal system that controls the periods gets into balance and regular monthly bleeding starts. This never worries doctors, nor should it concern patients, because sooner or later the right wheels suddenly click into place. If on the other hand, the bleeding does become troublesome in this age group, controlling the periods with hormones for a few months is usually all that is required. Should the bleeding persist in spite of this, a D and C may be advised by the doctor, but in general doctors try to stay away from doing a D and C with younger girls.

Just around the menopause the periods may also start to change, characterized by either increased bleeding or delayed or missed periods. These temporary upsets at the beginning and end of a woman's menstrual life may, of course, occur at other times and are usually unrelated to any major problem. Sometimes it is the result of some tragic event in the family or a change in occupation or a move to another city or merely a temporary variation in the production of hormones by the ovaries. A detailed discussion of other possible causes will be found in Chapters XIII and XIV.

What about bleeding after the menopause? The main rule to follow is that any bleeding should be reported to the doctor when it starts at about six months after the periods have, to all intents and purposes, stopped. This bleeding may similarly be due to any of several problems and may occur with or without pain, depending on its cause; and it may be the primary reason why the patient seeks medical attention. Even when the abnormal bleeding is accompanied by pain, in the majority of cases examination will reveal some benign problem that can be easily corrected. But again, it is most important that an immediate examination be carried out by your doctor.

Dysfunctional Bleeding. This is a term frequently used by doctors, because many of the women who consult their physician regarding a bleeding problem are eventually given this diagnosis. Dysfunctional bleeding may have considerable variation, such as spotting immediately before the period, between periods, frequent, heavy, prolonged or irregular bleeding; in fact, the bleeding may assume any form, but in this case it is usually present without any pain. In order to diagnose it, your doctor will do a thorough pelvic examination, blood studies and, finally, a D and C. But the long and short of it is that, in most cases after all the tests are done no disease of any kind is found. This of course is the happiest diagnosis, particularly since the D and C frequently corrects the bleeding. In most instances doctors believe the spotting between periods or the change in the menstrual flow results from a temporary hormonal upset, which is frequently caused by the ovaries failing to ovulate each month. At other times doctors are unable to offer any explanation for it.

Dysfunctional bleeding, therefore, is unimportant 95 percent of the time, yet there are occasions, particularly in women approaching the menopause, when it becomes troublesome. In these cases, frequent, prolonged, or nearly constant bleeding continues, in spite of one or more D and C's, which gradually cause anemia and general fatigue. Once the D and C has been done and the doctor is certain no serious disease is present, hormones may be used for a few months to temporarily regulate the bleeding in the hope that once they are discontinued the bleeding pattern will return to normal. If this fails to happen and the situation continues to look pretty grim, doctors may still decide to do nothing further on the off-chance that the bleeding will simmer down.

It is possible that they feel much like Lefty Gomez, the great New York Yankee pitcher who, with the bases loaded and with three balls and no strikes, kept refusing to throw the next pitch to one of the all-time outstanding hitters. Finally, the catcher walked out to Gomez and said, "Look, I've signaled you to throw every pitch I know and you keep shaking your head. What do you want to throw him?" Gomez replied, "I don't want to throw him anything."

As a final recourse, a hysterectomy (see Chapter XII) may be advised since, in most such cases, the patient does not want any more children, and she and her husband are tired of the inconvenience and worry caused by her condition, and want something done to end it.

As I have already said, you will find further information on the different types of bleeding in Chapters XIII and XIV; but in all cases my main purpose is to show that most changes in the bleeding pattern are due to minor problems not cancer, and a quick trip to your doctor is all that is needed to put your mind at rest.

However, two conflicting forces are presently at work in determining whether or not women seek early advice from their doctor. On the good side is the fact that twentieth-century women have largely discarded the remnants of Victorian modesty, and for the most part have no hesitation in submitting to pelvic examinations. Furthermore, the vast communications network of television, radio, newspapers, and magazines has disseminated information on medical matters to an unparalleled extent and has particularly advocated the wisdom of early diagnosis and treatment. Confronted by all this advice, many women do the wise thing and consult their physician at the first sign of trouble.

On the bad side, one must include the highly dramatized television shows and some written articles, which tend to cause undue fear about cancer and other serious diseases. It may be that the drive to educate the public regarding the need for early diagnosis has also tended to convey the impression that early pain, bleeding changes, discharges, and lumps, are very frequently due to cancer, when this is actually far from the case. The simple fact is that every gynecologist sees hundreds of patients each year with this type of problem, and most of these doctors could count on both hands the number of cases that are due to malignancy. Unfortunately some women fail to realize this. They procrastinate about seeing their doctors because they are afraid of an inescapably bad verdict. Yet, 99 percent of the time they will discover that their trouble is the result of something quite other than cancer.

Failure to Menstruate

In the section of my preface entitled, "Some Women Talk Too Much," we discussed a common misconception about the monthly period, and I think it would be advisable to repeat it here. Contrary to what a great number of women think, the menstrual period does not rid the body of any poisons. Consequently, if for one reason or another, a woman fails to menstruate, no harmful products collect in her body to cause any further trouble. The only purpose of menstrual bleeding is to prepare the inside, endometrial lining of the uterus for a possible pregnancy—no more, no less. Now let's have a quick review of the physiology of the menstrual cycle before we proceed further.

Very briefly, in order for menstruation to appear, the pituitary gland situated in the brain must produce hormones, which circulate in the blood and stimulate the ovary, not only to ovulate, but also to produce hormones of its own called estrogen and progesterone. These ovarian hormones then proceed to circulate in the bloodstream, in turn causing the endometrial lining of the uterus to grow to such a point that on the twenty-eighth day of the month, bleeding starts. Consequently, should there be any disease of the pituitary gland, the ovaries, or the uterus, the periods may be absent.

The most common reason for a missed period during the childbearing years is, of course, pregnancy. It is unfortunate that because of this so many women live from month to month in a state of chronic fear. Many arrive at their doctor's office a few days after a missed period to ask whether they are pregnant. This, for many reasons, is an impossible question for the doctor to answer. First, even though most women believe they are quite regular, if they keep an accurate record they will find that they actually do vary a few days each month. Therefore going into a state of panic when the period is supposedly two or three days late is quite unnecessary. Second, the uterus does not change significantly in size for the first few weeks of pregnancy, so that doctors are unable to detect any enlargement in the early stages. Third, pregnancy symptoms, such as early morning nausea, breast tenderness, enlargement of the breasts and frequency of urination, may not be present at this time. A good many women want to know whether a pregnancy test will give them a reliable answer. Sometimes it will; but again, this test is more accurate when it is done two to three weeks after the missed period, rather than immediately after it. Furthermore even pregnancy tests can be wrong. This means that there is no sure-fire way of giving a 100 percent correct answer immediately after a missed period, even though both the patient and the doctor may suspect that there is a good possibility of a pregnancy being present.

Young girls who have either failed to menstruate by sixteen

or have stopped following a few months of bleeding, may or may not have something wrong. In general, if a girl has not menstruated by the age of sixteen, it is advisable to seek medical advice, because, in very rare cases, a girl may be born without a vagina, uterus, or ovaries. And obviously, if the uterus is absent, there is no way a period can occur. If, on the other hand, the ovaries are absent, but the uterus and vagina are present, the doctor can prescribe hormones to produce the monthly bleeding. Doctors prescribe this treatment not because it is important for the patient to menstruate, but because it is essential that such adolescent girls receive adequate amounts of the female hormone, estrogen, to insure normal development of the breasts and other female characteristics. Doctors obviously cannot create ovaries or a uterus if a girl is born without them. But fortunately surgeons can actually build an artificial vagina, in the event that one is lacking.

The problems we have just discussed are extremely rare, but there is one that occurs more frequently. It is referred to by doctors as the "imperforate hymen." It simply means that the hymen, which normally closes off a part of the vaginal opening in virgin girls has, in such cases, closed it off completely. Normally this condition goes unnoticed until the girl begins to menstruate, and even then it may be undetected for a period of time. But since, when this condition is present, the vaginal opening is completely blocked by the hymen, none of the menstrual flow can escape, and the blocked blood remains in the vagina behind the obstruction. Although this condition can be tolerated for a few months, it sooner or later becomes apparent as the trapped blood gradually causes increasing distension of the vagina, resulting in abdominal pain each time the bleeding occurs. Once the diagnosis is made it is a simple matter to deal with. All that is necessary is simply to cut a small hole in the hymen, which allows the blood to escape.

In determining why a sixteen-year-old-girl has not menstruated, the doctor initially makes sure the pelvic organs are present and that the so-called secondary sex characteristics, such as the breasts, have also developed along normal lines. He may also give hormones to determine whether the pituitary gland and ovaries are working well and also to see if the uterus is capable of bleeding. Once these tests have taken place, the patient and her parents can usually be reassured that in all probability the periods will start within a year or two, and that there is nothing to worry about.

What about girls who start to menstruate at thirteen, have fairly regular periods for a couple of years, and then stop menstruating? Again this is usually not serious, because it is extremely common for young girls to skip not one, but sometimes many months, during the first few years of their menstrual life. This is because the ovaries fail to ovulate, which most likely is due to the fact that the hormones produced by the pituitary gland and ovaries have not reached their right balance. But sooner or later the natural adjustment is achieved, and once again the periods become regular. Should this fail to happen, it is imperative that detailed studies be done to ascertain the state of the pituitary gland and the ovaries. If such an examination reveals a major problem, the trouble will usually be involved with the ovaries. Just as some people are born with a weak heart or weak kidneys, some girls are born with inadequate ovaries. Sometimes, for the first few years of life, these ovaries are capable of producing enough of the female hormone to produce a monthly bleeding, but then their strength gives out and, although they still continue to produce hormones, the concentrations are not great enough to cause bleeding. At the present time there is, unfortunately, nothing that can be done to make weak ovaries stronger. Doctors, therefore, have to be content with supplying additional estrogens to insure adequate development of the female characteristics.

Although the pituitary gland, and another gland called the hypothalmus, are, with the uterus, sometimes responsible for failure to menstruate, it is, nevertheless, the ovaries that are the crux of the problem in most cases. We have seen that girls who are born with extremely weak ovaries may never start to menstruate or, if they do, it may be only for a year or two. Furthermore, women in their late twenties or early thirties can also suddenly stop menstruating because of what doctors refer to as "relative ovarian failure." In such cases, what happens is that the ovaries no longer produce sufficient quantities of the female hormones, so that the uterus cannot be sufficiently stimulated to bleed. Actually this is exactly what happens at the time of the menopause when, in normal conditions, the aging ovary finally gives out. But other things can happen to the ovary apart from its inability to produce adequate amounts of hormones. For example, not too long ago it was discovered that ovaries sometimes develop an extremely thick outer covering, which prevents the egg from escaping from the ovary at the time of ovulation. And since regular monthly ovulation is necessary to insure regular periods women with this condition will sometimes go many months without bleeding. It also means that these women are unable to become pregnant since, if the egg cannot escape from the ovary, it cannot be fertilized by the male sperm. This difficulty, which doctors call the "Stein-Leventhal Syndrome," can often be cured by performing an operation on the ovaries, in which a wedge-shaped piece of ovarian tissue is removed from one surface, after which the ovaries are stitched back together again. This procedure has generally been successful, in that pregnancies have afterward occurred. More recently, drugs have been used to stimulate ovulation. (For further discussion on the subject of sterility, see Chapter IX.)

Does obesity have any effect on menstruation? Four hundred years before Christ the Greek physician Hippocrates stated that "fat men are more likely to die suddenly than slender." This comment is still true, and we now also know that obese people are more likely to develop flat feet, diabetes, hypertension, arthritis, and many other troubles. In the case of women, they are also more likely to develop irregular, infrequent periods and, on occasion, may go many months without menstruating. It would seem that the German proverb that "fat hens lay few eggs" can also be applied to women. Just why obesity should give rise to lack of ovulation, which in turn produces either infrequent or absent periods, is not definitely known. But the fact is that a significant gain in weight is often the culprit in such cases.

At other times worry can be the responsible factor affecting menstruation, because chronic anxiety usually attacks our weakest link. In some people it causes stomach ulcers. Other individuals develop high blood pressure or become subject to heart attacks. And sometimes the menstrual period is affected, either on a temporary basis, or for long stretches of time. It is common knowledge that when young girls have school problems, move away from home, or change jobs, their menstrual period may fail to occur. This applies equally to middle-aged women. I recall one single woman of thirty-five who had lived with her widowed mother for years. They were terribly dependent on one another, and when her mother died the woman's periods stopped. Ten years later she still had not menstruated. A case such as this is somewhat unusual, because the periods generally return once the patient's problems have been resolved or she has made some mental adjustment. But no two people react the same way to worry, and whereas one woman can tolerate any number of crises without any effect on her periods, another may miss a period because of some seemingly trivial difficulty.

There is one other situation that might be worth mentioning at this point. It is astounding how many women undergo pelvic surgery and remain totally ignorant of what was actually done to them. I recall a forty-year-old lady who had been operated on in another country ten years previously. Immediately after the operation her periods ceased. It was only by finally writing to the hospital where the surgery was carried out that she discovered both her ovaries had been removed. This woman had worried for years that something was seriously wrong with her, because she had been only thirty years of age when her periods ceased. A simple explanation of the surgery that she had undergone would have taken only a few minutes and could have saved her many years of unnecessary anxiety. And believe me, she is not an exception. Any number of women ask whether they will continue to menstruate following a hysterectomy. They simply do not understand their own bodies well enough to realize that once the uterus has been removed it is impossible to have a menstrual period.

I trust the reader now understands that failure to menstruate can result from many problems, some of which are quite normal, others abnormal. Sometimes, the trouble is easy to stop during an initial visit to the doctor's office, but now and then various tests have to be done to pinpoint it. Fortunately, however, as has been indicated in this chapter, in the great majority of cases failure to menstruate is due to a minor problem, and not to serious disease.

In ending this chapter remember that some of your friends may consider themselves menstrual experts. But keep in mind that just because they are women who experience the monthly period, it still does not make them doctors; and they should not pass judgment on matters in which they have not been trained. Apelles, the great Greek painter, gave some sound advice about people who meddle in other people's business. A cobbler, on looking at one of the artist's paintings found an error with the drawing of a shoe buckle. Like Napoleon, the cobbler should have stopped while he was winning. But foolishly he then went on to criticize the drawing of the legs, about which he knew nothing. Apelles made the remark that has lasted to this day, when he said, "The cobbler should stick to his last."

CHAPTER V

A Commonsense Approach to Sex

Sex and the Premarital Checkup

IF A GIRL IS ABLE to get by the onset of her periods without trouble, there are other traps she may fall into. In these days, false modesty has largely become a thing of the past, and most girls are better prepared for the sexual side of marriage than their predecessors. Yet, unfortunately, doctors still have to deal with serious problems which could have been avoided if there had been less talk and more thinking. Not infrequently, I see a young girl who finds the sexual side of her marriage a chronic nightmare. Usually such a girl comes from an extremely strict home where sex has either never been discussed or has been continuously downgraded. It is probable that her mother has repeatedly referred to sex as dirty, something to be avoided, and merely accepted with distaste as a duty to one's husband. Sometimes such remarks are made by a woman disenchanted by her own marriage. But frequently the statement that sex is sinful comes from sincere parents, who are making a genuine attempt to raise a wholesome daughter. It is the wrong approach. What they are trying to say is that their daughter should wait until the right man comes along, with whom she will be able to enjoy married life to the fullest extent. Yet this is not the impression they convey; and, unless their daughter has a mind of her own, years of this type of indoctrination cannot be erased by a short marriage ceremony which is supposed to make sex legal, acceptable, and morally right. Susceptible girls may therefore find the adjustment difficult, and a great deal of marital trouble ensues. Some, after a few months of marriage and proper advice from their doctor, will develop a more healthy attitude toward sex. Others are never able to rid themselves of their past, and live out their lives merely putting up with the sexual side of their marriages.

Downgrading sex is one mistake. Making it too complicated is another. Certainly the nonsense that has been written on this subject does little to clarify the situation. I am thinking of articles that deal with such topics as "How to Live With Your Husband," or "What Women Should Know About Sex," and which tend to overemphasize and exaggerate the sexual side of marriage. One wonders whether sex is as complicated as these experts would have us believe. No doubt, their advice does help some people, but I am also convinced that they often merely confuse others by too much talk. Is sex such a complicated matter that it requires a two-hundred-page book to explain it? Furthermore, many books go into so much detail that they make people believe sex needs a scientific approach rather than a spontaneous one. They fail to realize that there are people everywhere who are sexually happy without ever having read a book on the subject and who are merely enjoying what comes naturally and instinctively.

This means that most sensible couples do not need a lawyer to figure out their sex lives for them. Admittedly, however, there are couples whose marriages *can* be salvaged by some practical advice. And there are also others that a dozen marriage counselors or social workers cannot help. But it is worth a try; for sex, although only a part of married life, is nevertheless sufficiently important that it can either make or break a relationship. As one wise physician once stated, "if the bedroom is not right, then every room in the house is wrong." Another sensible philosopher said "sex is only twenty percent of the marriage—but it is the first twenty percent."

Unlike the Victorian days, when any frank discussion of sex was effectively taboo, more women now visit their doctors for premarital examinations. Nevertheless, a large number still do not bother with a premarital checkup. This is really quite amazing when one considers it. Here we have a situation in which each person is picking a life partner, for better or for worse, and yet so few individuals bother to make sure of each other's health. Rather, they are willing to let their emotions run wild and hope that all is well. Fortunately, the majority of couples are physically sound, so little is lost. But there are the unfortunate few who do have something seriously wrong with them, which they find out only after they are married. And, on occasion, this happens after the thrill of romance is over. Of course, I do not advocate a mating bureau, or an IBM machine, to determine which couples are best suited to each other physically and emotionally. But I do suggest some common sense in picking a lifetime mate. Isn't it logical that a person with severe heart disease, diabetes, or any other problem should be aware of her condition and inform her chosen partner *before* marriage? The possibility of problems developing after marriage is a chance we all take, but the record at the start should be as clear as is humanly possible—no more, no less. Think of the care we take in purchasing a car, even though we shall only drive it for a few years!

In some parts of the country, an examination is compulsory in order to obtain a marriage license. In such cases, the primary reason is to make certain both individuals are free of venereal disease. But there are many other reasons for a premarital examination, apart from a general checkup. The majority of women are eager to learn about the various methods of contraception. Others are interested in discussing the sexual side of marriage, particularly because many young girls are not as well informed on this subject as they would like to have others believe.

I do not wish to give the impression that I am an expert on sexual matters. But after listening to the complaints of hundreds of married women over the years, certain points seem to recur time and time again. Let us talk about some of these problems, and how they can be avoided.

One of the common difficulties encountered immediately after marriage is the inability of the couple to have intercourse due to a tight unruptured hymen at the vaginal entrance. In most girls this is quite thin and easily stretched, but a few have an extremely thick hymen which has to be dilated and cut to allow entry to the vagina. An examination done a few weeks before marriage will reveal this condition and stop a very painful introduction to the physical side of married life that may have a lasting effect on the young woman's attitude. In the majority of cases girls can be shown how to dilate the hymen gradually, using a well-lubricated finger. Only a small number have to go to a hospital. The first case that I encountered was shortly after graduation from medical shool, when I was employed for few weeks in a large Canadian resort hotel in Quebec. Since there was no hospital nearby, I performed the surgery in the office, using a local anesthetic. A few days later a much happier couple left the hotel.

Another important aspect of the premarital examination is to dispel any old wives' tales the young girl may have heard. If she has been taught that sex is unpleasant and one of the liabilities of married life rather than a benefit, now is the time for the doctor to discover her attitude. A frank, open discussion is needed, and it may take more than one visit to unravel all the fears that have been built up over the years. Nevertheless, it is time well spent. The alternative is too often a distraught, tormented girl who walks into her doctor's office many months later sobbing that her marriage is falling apart.

Fortunately, the sexual act is a perfectly natural phenomenon, and therefore the majority of normal people do not require a Solomon to figure it out for them. But, there are some useful hints that may help to allay any fears that may be present during the first act of intercourse. It is always the unknown, the unexpected, that worries us. For example—the knowledge that a small amount of bleeding may occur during the first act of intercourse, because the hymen at the entrance of the vagina may tear slightly, may save many girls from needless worries. And, since one's first attempt at anything is always associated with some degree of tension, particularly something so personal as sexual intercourse, there are other precautions which can be taken. A warm bath, a drink, and a small amount of lubrication around the vaginal entrance, will all help to make this initial act more pleasant and relaxed.

We cannot leave the subject of sex before we discuss the female orgasm, or what is usually referred to as the "climax." Many girls, having heard about the climax, enter marriage believing their first night will be a bonanza of heavenly bliss. Such total satisfaction may occur with some women, but it is by no means universal. The opposite is true of men, for they are more easily satisfied. And, unless there are problems of impotence, a male orgasm occurs at the end of intercourse, with the discharge of fluid mixed with sperm. Conversely, what happens in women has always been a less easily explained phenomenon. In fact, it is even difficult for a woman who usually experiences an orgasm to explain it to a friend who has never had one. It would be about the same as trying to convey the warm glow that a bottle of wine can bring to your dinner to the president of a temperance society!

Furthermore, women often react to an orgasm in different ways. Some women cry. Others become violent and scratch or bite. Still others state they feel good all over, and have a sensation of vast release. Then there are those who say they see flashes of light or have chills going down their spine. Often the orgasm begins as a tickling sensation in the region of the clitoris, gradually increasing in intensity, and finally spreading to the outside and inside of the vagina. But regardless of how the orgasm affects different women, most who experience it are well aware that it has happened.

The first scientific study on sex was carried out a few years ago by Dr. William Masters and Virginia Johnson in St. Louis, Missouri. When they published their book, *Human Sexual Response* in April 1966, they immediately became the center of the most explosive controversy since the Kinsey Report. But unlike Kinsey, who merely asked questions regarding the sexual habits of Americans, Masters and Johnson took the next big step by taking sex right into the laboratory. A total of 382 women, between 18 and 78 years of age, and 312 men from 21 to 78 years of age masturbated and copulated in the laboratory, during which time their heart rate, respirations, blood pressure, and other physiological reactions, were monitored. In addition, certain significant visual responses were recorded on film. To some people, this was a shocking experiment, but to others it was labeled as the most progressive move yet attempted to finally determine what happens to the human body during the sex act. Some of the findings, such as the increase in the heart rate to between one hundred and forty to one hundred and eighty beats per minute in orgasm, compared to the normal of around seventy, were more or less predictable. And their experiments on alcohol merely confirmed what Shakespeare had said four hundred years ago about its effect on sexual response: that a little stimulates, and a lot depresses. But the laboratory findings also shot down some sacred cows. It was discovered that the size of the penis has little bearing on whether a male can satisfy his partner. In addition the experiments showed that many postmenopausal women continue to have strong sexual drives and that a male in his late seventies can be sexually effective, providing he is in fairly good health, and has a responsive wife. Possibly the most important discovery was their documentation of the intensity of the female climax, which showed that there was no physiological difference between a clitoral and a vaginal orgasm. Furthermore, they found that the marriage manuals were wrong in preaching that the ultimate goal in the sex act should be the ability of both partners to achieve a simultaneous orgasm. Couples who think that nothing has been achieved when this does not occur were proved entirely wrong. So, although the study raised some eyebrows, it did succeed answering some long-sought questions about satisfactory intercourse.

At this point the reader might ask why it is so easy for men to enjoy sex when it is sometimes such an elusive thing for women? Again, this is not an easy answer. But there are, nevertheless, certain points which do seem to apply to the women who experience this trouble. As I mentioned earlier in this chapter, the prudish and restricted background of some women plays a definite role. It may take months or even years before the idea that sex is dirty and something to be avoided can be completely erased from their minds. But not all women who have difficulty achieving a satisfactory culmination of the sexual act come from this sort of background. What, then, are the other causes? A frequent problem is a husband who is either too rough or too quick for his wife. Most men are easily aroused and frequently have an orgasm long before the woman is satisfied. This can often be corrected by explaining to the husband the need for more prolonged love-play prior to the act of intercourse. Most women are stimulated by touching the neck, thighs, lips, breasts, and clitoris. During this so-called excitement phase, the nipples become erect and congested and, even more important, there is an increase in the amount of vaginal lubrication. Although there are no major glands in the vaginal lining, Masters noticed a "sweating phenomenon," in which droplets somewhat resembling ordinary perspiration appeared in the vagina. This sweating provides the main lubrication during intercourse. It was also observed that just prior to intercourse the vagina tends to increase in length and width, the breast increase in size, as does the clitoris. These changes arouse the woman to the point where she is more ready and anxious to participate in intercourse and finally to achieve a satisfactory orgasm. Very passionate women will achieve the climax within a minute or two, but for most it takes a longer period of time. In addition whereas the majority of women will have one orgasm, some women appear to have multiple orgasms during a single act of intercourse.

The important point that young women about to marry must realize is this: The sexual side of their marriage may take time to develop to the fullest extent, and they should not be discouraged and disappointed if their first night is not what they had imagined. There are few good things in life that come easy, and for some women sex may be in that category. Given time, mutual understanding, and a candid discussion of marital problems, the adjustment can be accomplished. This is why the premarital checkup is so important. (It is also at this time that the various methods of birth control should be frankly discussed with your doctor, particularly if you wish a planned family program. Birth control is discussed in detail in Chapter VI.)

Sex and Marriage

The majority of couples who are sexually unhappy are usually incompatible in many other ways. They do not share the same interests and goals in life and so, over the years, they draw apart both sexually and socially. Once the romance of marriage is over there is nothing left and slowly but surely they drift apart. But sharing and planning things together is not the entire answer. The personalities of some couples are just mutually out of tune, and how they ever originally got together is sometimes hard to figure out. Look around at your own friends to see just a few of the misfits of marriage. A dozen marriage counselors with time to spare could not rectify the personality conflicts that exist between such people, for it is a hopeless situation. There would be more sense in trying to get an English bulldog and a cat to shake hands.

Certainly there are times when one has to conclude that the computer could have done a better job in bringing the right people together. And with computers affecting nearly every segment of our society, it is highly unlikely that marriage will escape their attentions. Particularly since too many marriages are still settled by the light of the moon. This works fine for Hollywood and in story books, but by the cold light of dawn it too often proves a poor long-term investment. In some future society individuals may conclude that marriage is too important to be decided by a game of Russian roulette and will turn to the computers for help. Considering our high divorce rate, with its disastrous consequences for children, it is unlikely that the computer could do any worse. Yet, as I have already mentioned, there are couples who are mutually compatible on every other basis except sex. What has gone wrong in such cases?

Some married couples immediately start off on the wrong foot by trying to live with their in-laws. Not only does this cause endless practical problems, but it rarely results in a happy sexual life. As one of my patients once remarked "it is rather difficult for my husband and me; you can hear through the walls at night." Better to live in a single room, or to postpone marriage, than to try to rely on the financial support of in-laws. One wise man once observed that "when poverty comes in the door love flies out the window." Time and time again one finds this to be true, for if too much worry and effort are spent on financial problems, little energy is left for sex and companionship. It is only when financial peace of mind returns that the sexual drive is restored. Certainly living within our means is one of the strong points of a happy and prosperous marriage. They would be well advised to follow the philosophy of Henry David Thoreau when he wrote "I would rather sit on a pumpkin all by myself, than be crowded on a velvet cushion."

I mentioned in the previous section of this chapter that some women have been conditioned to think of sex as being dirty, which frequently leads to sexual trouble. But there are some women who have no such faulty, preconceived notions about sex, and who initially have an excellent sexual relationship with their husbands. Then the relationship starts to break down, and they complain that their husbands are neglecting them. Frequently, the reason is obvious. One glance shows that, as wives, they leave a lot to be desired. At some stage in their lives they seem to have thrown in the towel and just let their appearance go to the dogs. Certainly a wife who constantly looks as though she has been dragged through the wringer is not going to receive the same attention as a woman who makes a real effort to be attractive. It is not surprising that some husbands begin to show a lack of interest when they are faced with wives who seem to be permanently in curlers and unattractive slacks. To be sure, all wives can't look like Sophia Loren, particularly when they have to spend untold hours washing diapers, ironing clothes, and performing a multitude of other necessary trivia. Yet they should do their best to make themselves as attractive as possible throughout their marriage. Furthermore, if handled properly, a sexual relationship should grow and deepen with practice. Also, any marriage is enormously helped if, besides love, there is a genuine liking, a companionship stemming from many ingredients other than passion. This is the solid rock on which a lasting marriage and a truly satisfactory sexual relationship is based.

Women are frequently embarrassed to admit that they do not enjoy sex and come to consult their doctor about some other problem. A great number use the excuse that intercourse has become painful and therefore is no longer enjoyable. With some of these women, examination will establish a genuine reason for the pain. But if the checkup shows everything to be normal, any pain is usually due to an emotional problem. Usually after repeated visits to the doctor such women will finally admit that all is not well with their marriage. Many have proof their husbands have been unfaithful. Others merely suspect it. Yet the end result is the same. In their endeavor to rid themselves of their husband's attentions they either consciously or subconsciously complain that sexual relations are painful. If they can be told that there is no foundation to their suspicions of infidelity, marital relations again become normal. But should their fears be proven correct, then often little, if anything, can be done.

One pretty young girl once consulted me because she dreaded intercourse and did everything in her power to avoid it. Finally she admitted that during their first year of marriage, when she was three months pregnant, her husband was unfaithful. Until that time she had enjoyed sex, but since then it had become a chronic nightmare. In such a situation, it is extremely difficult to reestablish the marriage. As that particular woman stated "we live together just because of the children."

Another major handicap to a happy sexual life is the constant fear of pregnancy, which has a drastic effect on many women. Certainly most women who have four of five children have little desire for additional pregnancies. In these days of rising costs, families have neither the time nor money to adequately care for the larger families of earlier years. No two mules can do the same amount of work, and so it is with women. Some can look after six children with relative ease. But there are many whose capacity is one, two, or three children; more than that is just too much. Their physical and mental constitution is unable to cope with it and trouble begins. Chronic fatigue is the common symptom. But this leads to further developments, such as a desire to avoid sex. Some are just too tired for it. Others develop an increasing fear of intercourse, because the possibility of another child is too much to bear. Sooner or later, this causes further trouble, for a husband who is continually pushed away may begin to wander. What a demoralizing situation for a democratic society! It is odd that we can live where we wish, marry the man or girl of our choice, do the type of work we enjoy the most, and yet have no right to determine the size of our family. The situation becomes even more ridiculous when one considers how much is being said about the problem of world overpopulation. It is my own hope that the day will soon come when legalized sterilization will be the right of every citizen living in this or any other society. Relieved of the day-to-day fear of pregnancy, a great number of marriages that now end up in divorce courts might be saved. And what could be worse than to begin life as an unwanted child? Today a great number of people are shouting for their inherent God-given rights. Youth decries the hypocrisy of its elders, the scarring of our environment, the inequalities of our society, and demands a greater voice in the nation's affairs. Unions claim a greater percentage of the country's wealth. And women's liberation groups insist on equal rights with men. Many indeed have solid justifiable complaints, for it is obvious there is a moral, economic, and social sickness eating the heart out of our nation. But surely those of us in middle age can't be all that bad and youth all that good. Having just given a talk to a group of clean medical students who had the misfortune to be thrown into a new but filthy hippie-dominated dormitory, one must conclude that some youths would be better advised to spend more time bathing and less time shouting. It would indeed be interesting to see how a cabinet composed of middle-aged, unshaven, unbathed hippies would run our country. But in all the clamor for fairness, surely the unborn child has the greatest claim of all in asking that he be given the inherent right to be wanted, loved, and cared for. To deny this is the worst crime of all.

In view of the sexual revolution that seems to be sweeping the world, it is difficult to know what the future holds for marriage. Certainly sex is now more of an open book, and there is a more liberal approach to sexual standards than in the past. A few college students have already taken the step of living together, free of the entanglements of marriage, and it may be that this form of trial marriage will spread to other segments of our society. Yet it is highly unlikely that the family unit will end. Rather, there will be greater emphasis, in the years ahead, on the question of combining the right people. However, regardless of how the initial marital choice is achieved, couples will still have to work at marriage in order to do a good job. Good marriages, like good generals, are rare. As one wise Frenchman once remarked, "It requires far more genius to make love than to command armies."

CHAPTER VI

Birth Control

In a world that is increasing at the rate of over two hundred thousand people daily, the last half of the twentieth century may well be remembered by future generations as the time when something constructive was finally done to stem this massive buildup of population. It has often been said that "necessity is the mother of invention," and the tremendous amount of research currently concerned with the problem of overpopulation is indeed evidence of the truth of this statement. I believe that it should be the right of every couple in a democratic society to decide what size they want their family to be. And if religion is not an issue, then all that is necessary is to decide upon the safest and most logical method of birth control. For example, a young married couple that is still attending college usually requires a 100 percent effective contraceptive, in contrast to other couples that may prefer to wait a year or two to start their family, but would not be too upset if a pregnancy ensued.

The older contraceptives, such as the diaphragm, jellies, and condom, are still popular, and are extremely effective if used correctly. Yet some people find them embarrassing and awkward and unfortunately many fail to use them consistently. Consequently when a pregnancy results, they blame the method.

when actually the fault lies with themselves. A moonlit night, a few drinks at a party, and sometimes all the best planning goes out the window and a new arrival comes in by the door. Now, however, millions of women are taking all the chance out of pregnancy by a method commonly referred to as "the pill." Others are using a new revolutionary device that has become known as an IUD, or the intrauterine device. I will discuss these two methods first, since most women who are presently seeking birth control information are primarily interested in them.

The Pill

We are frequently told that there are only two things certain in life: death and taxes. Now, however, one can easily add another: the proven reliability of the birth control pills, for they are practically 100 percent effective when used correctly. In fact, even when a woman forgets to take the occasional pill, it still remains by far the most foolproof contraceptive available. Like all drugs, the pill has caused some problems, but I think the reader will see that its assets far outweigh the liabilities.

The main question women want answered is whether or not the pill is safe. In order to adequately answer this question it is first necessary to ask why there should be such doubt in their mind in the first place? One reason is quite obvious. During the past few years a number of medical reports have been issued linking the pill with abnormal clotting of the blood. Statistically it has been shown that women on the pill do have a greater chance of developing thrombophlebitis (an inflammation of the veins usually in the legs) and pulmonary embolism (a blood clot in the lungs). For example, of those in the twenty- to thirty-four-year age group who are not taking the pill, doctors normally expect two women in every one million to die from a blood clot. It appears, however, that for those taking the pill about fifteen in every million will die from this disorder. Yet in view of the tremendous furor surrounding the pill one has to look for other reasons to account for such mass hysteria. After all this is not the first new drug that has had an occasional bad effect. In fact let's make one point crystal clear—there are no drugs, old or new, that always give 100 percent beneficial results. Even the so-called miracle drug penicillin now and then causes a severe allergic reaction that may result in the death of a patient. But it is most unusual for a woman at a bridge club meeting to question the use of this drug or other drugs or to be fearful of them. Why? A good deal of it is because the pill affects the female reproductive organs. This small part of a woman's anatomy is the sensitive heart of her emotions and anything that affects it, such as the pill, is open to suspect. But apart from this, it doesn't take too much to get some people worried. Some individuals in our society can even find something sinister about a Coca-Cola ad. Unreasonable patients' fears are always difficult to handle—even in the best of circumstances—but there has been added complication with the pill.

We live in an age of mass communication. At no other time in the history of medicine has the communications media subjected women to such a detailed blow-by-blow dissertation on the merits, but in particular the dangers, of the pill (the smoking scare hasn't been much different). It's a very basic human rule that it's much easier to worry people than reassure them, and the press were quick to capitalize on this point. It has resulted in numerous articles with melodramatic titles that mean nothing but get the reader's attention. And all too often the writers of these scare stories are no more knowledgable about hormones than most doctors are about Picasso paintings. Consequently to get their material for the story, they interview a number of physicians who, being quite human, often disagree with one another—not so much on general basic points, but on less important ones. Unfortunately these differing opinions are greatly exaggerated; and equally important, after presenting varying points of view, the writer rarely reaches an opinion. The reader is therefore left holding a loose bag of theories and is more fearful than she was before she read the article. In this particular instance I think one can justifiably criticize the press. For although their "alarm approach" has been good business, it has left too many worried readers. But one must also accept the good with the bad, because at times the press has been more alert for good news than some members of the medical profession. For example, I can recall magazine articles written by lay writers praising the Pap cancer smear long before some of my medical colleagues were willing to use it. So in this instance one has to doff one's hat to the media for quickly helping to bring this to the attention of women.

But other factors have also been at work to create an atmosphere of suspicion and concern. The FDA (Food and Drug Administration) has ruled than an insert must be included with every pill prescription that warns the patient of possible side effects and states that anyone taking the pill should be under the care of a physician. It also informs the patient that a pamphlet prepared by the AMA (American Medical Association) warning of the possible side effects of oral contraceptives can be obtained from the patient's doctor. Now no one can be criticized for trying to keep patients well informed on medical matters. After all that is what this book is for. And that is why the cancer society and a host of other organizations try to educate the public. If that is the wrong approach then we had all better fold our tents and steal silently away in the night. But there is a marked difference between informing patients and worrying them.

The point of contention is why does the FDA focus so much on the pill? Admittedly this isn't the first drug that has come under its attack. Currently the FDA is trying to restrict the use of amphetamines (speed drugs) in order to curb their abuse by teenagers. It does an important job and no one would deny it is its right to be on the lookout for legitimate trouble. But is the pill problem a bona fide one? One could argue that it is not considering the vast amount of research to date on the pill. It would be just as logical to place an insert with each prescription of cortisone, penicillin, or a variety of other drugs. But this is not done because these other drugs do not have the religious and moral wrappings associated with them.

It is noteworthy that the AMA has made its position quite clear on package inserts of any kind directed to patients. It flatly told the various legislative and administrative branches of government that it was against inserts because it believed it was the doctor who should inform the patient about the prescription drug and any possible hazards. But unfortunately the inserts became a political football, and because of these pressures and sensational publicity the FDA had little choice. The only concession to the AMA was to allow it to prepare and distribute the pamphlet. For it was the AMA's feeling that medical information of this kind should come from the doctor, not from government or industry. Behind these political overtones lies the unfortunate fact that the poor patient now gets a double-barreled salvo on the risks—one from the insert, the other from the pamphlet. Confronted by such a series of warnings why shouldn't women wonder if something is amiss, particularly when they can get other drugs without such detailed messages?

What about doctors? Have they helped trigger any of these fears? In one sense they have, because doctors are not machines and therefore are not immune to either their own ideologies or to public opinion. Any discussion on the pill, therefore, has some of the earmarks of a round-table debate on legalized abortion in which medical opinion is always flavored with a touch of individual philosophy. It follows that some doctors who have a personal prejudice about birth control have strongly opposed the pill for other than medical reasons. Yet whatever the motives, these remarks by a physician do tend to put the stamp of authority on any discussion that is out to veto the pill. In the minds of many women, the wheels must grind out the message: If some doctors are worried, maybe something is wrong.

Furthermore, doctors by the very nature of the game they play, develop an inborn caution about the diagnosis and treatment of disease. In spite of this, now and then they get their fingers badly burned, particularly when using new drugs. Just take thalidomide as one tragic example. So when prestigious bodies such as the AMA and the FDA zero in on the pill to such a degree, doctors tend to become even more ultracautious. This happens even when they're not too sure why they should be wary in view of the proven safety ratio of the pill. And it is hard for them to completely ignore the almost-weekly barrage of articles in journals and medical newspapers overplaying the possible risks of the pill, even though they all cover much of the same ground. So some of this does rub off a little on doctors, and they become defensive.

Yet it is unfortunate that when doctors catch what really amounts to the "politicial pill disease" they use too many unwarranted "ifs" and "maybes" when discussing the pill with patients. Obviously this wariness must rub off on patients to a certain extent—to their detriment.

But is all the worry justified? Since the root of it stems from the statistics on death from blood clots, let's analyze that first. The British report, as mentioned earlier, showed that in the twenty- to thirty-four-year age group, fifteen women in one million users of the pill died from blood clots. In the same age group only two women not using the pill died from blood clots. It therefore appears that there is a seven times greater risk of dying from blood clots for women on the pill. Furthermore, it has been shown that hospital admissions for nonfatal blood clots was about nine times greater for women using the pill than in those not taking it. On the surface these statistics look rather damaging, but it is always wise to consider the other side of the coin and use some common sense—which is unfortunately uncommon. For instance, if the same number of women become pregnant, statistics indicate that approximately 225 die from the various problems of childbirth (admittedly, not all one million women would become pregnant if taken off the pill). But nevertheless, the hazards of the pill are much, much less than the risks of additional pregnancies. Why, therefore, should the government, press, and some doctors repeatedly emphasize the dangers of the lesser risk? Furthermore, proving something by statistics has always been a very risky game, for it's a well-known fact that you can prove almost anything you want by this method. In fact its been said there are three kinds of lies: lies, damned lies and statistics! Yet even assuming the figures are correct, it is also well to remember that all of our daily activities involve some risk. Look at the slaughter on our highways and the drownings in our lakes. These are major risks that are more common than the number of women who die while on the pill. On occasion the author has spent some very pleasant moments swimming in the Caribbean, and I imagine there is a very small chance that I might get my leg bitten off by a shark. The point is, these chances do not stop people from driving cars or winging their way to a favorite Caribbean beach. It's the old philosophy of "you pay your money and you take your chance." I of course do not mean to be either facetious or to leave the reader with the impression that we should not do all we can to reduce any risk either big or small. But we do not live in a utopian world, and possibly never will; but we can say that if all the risks in life were as small as those for the pill it would be a much safer world for all of us.

Time and time again it's also been said that there is no drug that has ever been so thoroughly tested as the birth control pill. Equally important these studies have shown that the "safety ratio" of the pill is probably as high or higher than of any other drug. It is therefore worthwhile to speculate how other drugs that are commonly used would stand up to such careful scrutiny? What differences would one find between one million women between the ages of twenty and thirty-four who take a laxative every day and a similiar group that does not? And what about others who are more prone to reach for headache pills or swallow unnecessary vitamin pills than those who do not? It's quite conceivable that such a detailed statistical analysis might show some startling findings. But I wonder if it did would it receive the notoriety surrounding the birth control pill? I would hazard a guess that it wouldn't because there isn't the same interest in headache pills or high-caloric foods. After all obesity causes countless more numbers of deaths than the birth control pill, yet this doesn't make the headlines. One could argue that if the FDA wanted to do a thorough job, it should request that fancy desserts be labeled as hazardous to health. To sum up, dangers of the pill are extremely small, and there is no need for panic.

In discussing the pros and cons of the pill it is also necessary to consider the consequences if you don't take it.

Many women are inconsistent in their thinking about the pill —they want an easy method of contraception that is 100 percent effective and never has any side effects. At the moment, unfortunately, there is no such animal, and if patients won't accept the exceeding small risk of the pill they will have to accept the risk of becoming pregnant. This is a most important point, because the risk of bearing another child far exceeds the risks of the pill. And equally significant this risk is a double-edged sword. On one side there is a chance of dying at some stage of the pregnancy. But it is the other side that is rarely mentioned in discussions about the pill. In short, what effect an additional pregnancy will have on the woman's total well-being? For example, what will another pregnancy do to existing varicose veins, the patient's weight or blood pressure? What effect will the pregnancy have on an already strained back? And often of even greater importance, what will it do to the patient's vagina? Will the passage of another child through it further weaken the tissues so that the bladder falls down and results in the annoying loss of urine when coughing or sneezing? Or will an additional pregnancy cause so much more stress in the family that a stomach ulcer is the final outcome? Carrying this line of reasoning along a little further one can quite logically theorize that a certain number of these women will have to have an operation to repair the fallen bladder, cut out the stomach ulcer, or remove the varicose veins. And how many women will die from this surgery? In the case of the woman who develops high blood pressure as a result of increased tension, by how many years will her life be shortened? And I want to emphasize that the statistics that state that seven times more women who are on the pill are likely to die from blood clots, just don't take these variables into consideration. The cold, unemotional statistical analysis not only tells you nothing about these other effects on the woman but also nothing about what happens to the marriage.

It's food for thought as to how frequently extra children strain the pocketbook or nerves so much that the marriage ends up in the divorce court, which in turn has far-reaching consequences for both the children and society. In a world that is increasingly plagued by crime, pollution, alcoholism, and drug addiction it is important to assess the role played by illegitimate and unwanted or neglected children. In the United States alone there are 300,000 illegitimate children born annually, and again in the United States it's been calculated that there are 750,000 unwanted children who are born each year who will be unloved, neglected, and often abandoned. Furthermore, it has been shown that one in six brides is pregnant at marriage, and 50 percent of them are in their teens. Surely it's hardly necessary to carry out a statistical survey to determine what effect these children will have on our society. Good sense alone dictates illegitimate and unwanted children cause more trouble than those who live in a home where there is love and laughter.

The statistical findings that correlate the pill with death from blood clots must be critically analyzed. The figures tell you nothing about the increased number of women not taking the pill that will die in childbirth, and straight numbers do not register the full impact of the general deterioration of the patient's health following repeated pregnancies. Furthermore, there are some gynecologists who believe that the deaths in the British study will be shown to be associated with a disease that was present in the women before they went on the pill. I've also spoken to a number of statisticians who say they could not come to any statistical conclusion from the

British study. They all mention that there are so many variables to consider, such as the state of the patient's health before she went on the pill, her diet, the effect of climatic conditions, and what effect worry might have on the overall picture. It may well be that the fear of taking the pill is actually doing more harm than the pill, for worry does cause changes in the blood-clotting mechanism.

These statisticians also point out that the British study, which showed that fourteen patients in a million died from blood clots while on the pill relative to two in a million who died and were not on the pill, was an exceedingly small number from which to draw any good conclusion. Nearly all summarized the findings by stating the figures might be statistically valid (true) but they were certainly not statistically significant (important). The figures also point out something that is food for thought. They show that if you are on the pill there is a slightly greater chance of dying from a blood clot than if you are not taking the pill. So let us assume the patient pours the pills down the drain and subsequently becomes pregnant. The figures then show that pregnancy increases the chance of developing a blood clot; in fact being either pregnant or on the pill has approximately the same risk of death from a blood clot. Looking at it another way, it means that the patient not only has the same risk of dying from a blood clot if she becomes pregnant, but also she exposes herself to the many other dangers of pregnancy. So I trust that when the readers come across another article on the perils of the pill they will have a better understanding of the total picture.

In addition to the worries about blood clots, women have also been exposed to another penetrating fear. Since the pill came on the market a few doctors have questioned whether the pill would cause the development of cancer over a period of years. They could have speculated it might cause one of a dozen other diseases as easily and few would have given it a second thought. But the word cancer sets up a nervous chain reaction. Unfortunately cancer and the pill have been mentioned in the same sentence, so let's see if there is any element of justifiable fear.

One thing the fear-mongers have on their side is that cancer does not develop overnight. As mentioned in the chapter on cancer this disease is not white one day and black the next, but may takes ten years or more to become an outright malignancy. This is because agents producing cancer may take up to ten years to cause even the preliminary changes that doctors call carcinoma-in-situ. This is an early change strictly limited to the surface of the tissue, and it may or may not go a step further. But it is well documented that even if it does continue on it may take many more years before it becomes a true cancer invading normal tissue and spreading to other areas. And the longest study on the pill has only been going on for approximately ten years. But after ten years no increase has been noted in the number of women who develop either cancer of the uterus or breast. Time, therefore, is more and more on the side of the great majority of doctors who feel that the pill has nothing to do with the development of any cancer.

The link-up between cancer of the uterus and the pill is related to two facts. First animals have developed cancer when given large doses of estrogen over a prolonged period of time. Second estrogen may cause hyperplasia (thickening of the lining of the uterus—see Chapter XIII), and a few of these patients later develop endometrial cancer. Since the birth control pills contain estrogen, the question is: can the pill cause the same effects? There are several reasons for thinking otherwise. The animals that were given estrogen received very large amounts and for a long period of time. And there are absolutely no convincing studies to show that it can produce the same thing in humans. The hyperplasia theory also holds very little water primarily because so many women have hyperplasia and relatively few develop cancer. The author has given long-term natural estrogens to patients for years and very few develop hyperplasia, let alone cancer. And since hyperplasia is such a common disease (it's caused by failure of ovulation), it follows that now and then a patient with this problem will also develop cancer. In other words she will in all probability have developed a cancer even if the hyperplasia had not been present. After all patients with bronchitis sometimes develop lung cancer, but no one believes the cancer develops from the bronchitis. Another bit of evidence against the hyperplasia theory is that endometrial cancer usually occurs after the menopause—the very time the ovaries are producing the least estrogen. Furthermore, cancer of the uterus has been around for years, long before doctors had estrogen tablets or the pill to give to patients. It is also a good idea not to forget that the birth control pills contain not only estrogen, but also synthetic progestin. And the progestin part of the pill has exactly the opposite effect, which is to keep the endometrial lining thin. And hyperplasia cannot develop in a thin lining. So even if we assumed that on rare occasions hyperplasia might change to cancer, one would have to conclude that the birth control pills help to prevent cancer rather than cause it because in effect they stop hyperplasia from developing. It's equally significant that some of the synthetic progestins can be helpful in cases of advanced endometrial cancer. Patients who have been in dire circumstances have had considerable improvement when given large doses of this drug. It hardly seems likely, therefore, that the birth control pill could cause cancer, when one part of the pill—namely progestin—has these beneficial effects.

What about the pill and breast cancer? The finding that estrogen could produce breast cancer in mice triggered this fear. But the part of the story that should have been emphasized was the fact that enormous doses had to be given over a long period of time. But once again people worried because the pill contained estrogen. But again one has to remember that the pill also contains synthetic progestin, so it's impossible to compare the pill to straight estrogen. Furthermore, in humans there is absolutely no evidence that estrogens can cause cancer of the breasts. It is well known that women who have taken estrogens for as long as thirty years do not have a higher incidence of this disease than women who have not taken this hormone. But there is an important distinction to be made when talking about the effect of estrogen on breast cancer. It's well known that estrogen can accelerate the growth of an existing breast cancer in women who are either still in the child-bearing years or at least pre-menopausal. But there is a great difference between accelerating a cancer and actually causing it. We also know that prior to the menopause women who have widespread breast cancer may be temporarily helped by removal of the ovaries, which takes away the major source of estrogen. Yet how do you explain that following the menopause giving estrogen often causes a shrinking of the tumor mass and a dramatic fading away of the metastatic cancer in the bones, lung, and skin? Most important cancer of the breast has been around for centuries, long before the advent of the pill or estrogen. Certainly any disease that affects about one in every sixteen women—whether or not they are on the pill—must be caused by something else. Add it all up and once again common sense dictates that the pill, although it does not cause cancer, has resulted in a lot of unnecessary worry.

However, in 1956, when the pill was first introduced, it was only natural that women should ask a lot of questions about it. Most people resist change, particularly something as revolutionary as the pill. And the fact that it was a hormone added to the problem, because hormones have always been a favorite target of the scaremongers. I have seen many intelligent women become incredibly apprehensive the moment any suggestion is made of their taking the pill. No doubt they have the idea, and sometimes justifiably so, that just because something is new it doesn't necessarily mean it's good. However, what most women failed to realize when the pill first became available was that it was not a new drug in the strictest sense. The birth control pill contains chemical hormones closely related to other female hormones (estrogen and progesterone). These have been used for many years to treat other pelvic problems without causing any serious side effects. The pill represents an improvement over these other hormones, because it is more potent and can also be produced economically for mass use. And as the reader would suspect, the pill itself has gone through a number of major transitions from the first rather heavy dose pill to the smaller mini pill of today. Today the pill is manufactured by a number of different pharmaceutical companies that use slightly different formulas and various trade names. In general, there is as little difference among their products as between a Ford or Chevrolet. And although some women were initially hesitant to take advantage of them, there is now little question that their use will expand phenomenally in the next decade. One interesting change has already taken place. Not too long ago it was the doctor who suggested the pill. Today, it is usually the patient who requests it.

The pills work by preventing the production of eggs by the ovaries. Normally, following menstruation, the pituitary gland stimulate the ovary to produce another egg and on about the fourteenth day of the cycle this egg escapes from the ovary, and pregnancy may or may not result. The birth control pill temporarily stops this process. No egg is released; and without an egg to be fertilized, pregnancy cannot occur.

It is also believed that the progestin part of the pill has two other effects in addition to helping estrogen suppress ovulation. First, it makes the endometrial lining quite thin, so that if by a one-in-a-million chance ovulation does occur the egg cannot settle into a nice soft bed and start to grow. In Chapter II I mentioned that estrogen normally prepares a soft bed for a possible pregnancy and progesterone goes a step further by turning down the covers and slipping a hot water bottle between the blankets. But when you take away natural progesterone and substitute synthetic progestin, it is as if someone came along and literally threw the mattress off the bed. Second, progestin changes the cervical mucous, making it more difficult for the sperm to get inside the uterus.

How are the pills taken? Currently there are two types available, either the 21-days pills or the 28-day ones. For the first cycle, each type is started on the fifth day of the menstrual period, counting the first day of the menstrual flow as day one. The 21-day pills are taken daily for 21 days and then stopped for one week. Usually the period begins within three days after discontinuing the pills. In other words, if a woman completes one cycle of taking the pills on Monday, she automatically starts them again the following Monday—whether or not the bleeding has stopped. This simple routine of three weeks on the pills and one week off is continued as long as the pills are prescribed by her doctor. One further important point. On rare occasions, no bleeding occurs when the pills are finished. Should this happen, it is still essential to start the pills again in one week. Failure to do so could result in a pregnancy. The 28-day routine is even simpler because the first 21 pills contain hormones, while the last pills are just sugar. While the patient is taking these last seven sugar pills the period will most likely start and also end. But regardless of whether the period has started or ended, once the last of the pills is taken another package is immediately started by the patient. The big advantage is that women never stop taking the pill once they start it and do not have to remember what day they stopped the pill and what day the have to start taking them again. Looking at it another way, once a patient starts a pill on the fifth day, she forgets about the fifth day of subsequent cycles and simply continues to take a pill a day for as long as she is on the pill. Women frequently worry about what would happen if they forget to take a pill for one day. While a pregnancy rarely results from this mishap, it is important to take the missed pill as soon as possible. For instance, if a woman normally takes her pill with breakfast and then later in the day remembers that she has forgotten to do so, she should take it immediately. If, on the other hand, she remembers one morning that she did not take a pill on the preceding morning, she should immediately take two pills. But missed pills are to be avoided. So women should get into the habit of taking one at a particular time, such as when brushing their teeth, with breakfast, or the evening meal.

To make things even easier, most of the companies making the pills number them and have the days of the week printed on the package, so that forgetful women can check whether or not they have taken a pill on a particular day. As the reader might guess it is much more serious to forget to take the pills in the early part of the cycle when the idea is to stop ovulation. Forgetting to take the pill a few days prior to the onset of the period will merely mean that the bleeding may start a little earlier. But most women are so interested in preventing an unwanted pregnancy, that they leave very little to chance. But now and then a pregnancy does occur in spite of the pill. This is usually because the woman has either failed to take a pill or two or when the period fails to occur she waits longer than a week before going back on them. Women should therefore be certain to check with their doctor if there is any doubt in their minds as to how they should take the pills. Winston Churchill following the fall of Singapore made the poignant remark that one should take absolutely nothing for granted when dealing with vital issues. He severely criticized himself because he had not asked about the defenses of this city. He said: "I ought to have asked. The reason I had not asked was that the possibility of Singapore having no landward defenses no more entered into my mind than that of a battleship being launched without a bottom."

Now let's talk about the occasional side effects that a few women suffer from while taking the pill. However, it should be remembered that there has been a good deal of talk about this aspect of the pill, which may, in part, be responsible for some of the symptoms. If people expect something to happen, it's amazing how easily the mind can play tricks on them. For instance, if patients are given sugar pills and told they will be questioned later about their symptoms, a significant number actually do develop nausea, headaches, and other problems. Nevertheless, the majority of adverse reactions are the result of the pill, and I'll briefly mention the most common ones.

Nausea and, occasionally, vomiting may be troublesome for

the first month, but fortunately this is usually a temporary problem. Women should be patient for a few weeks. Fortunately the lower dosage pills are now much less likely to cause this trouble. Other women complain of headaches, tenderness and fullness of the breasts, and a weight gain of a few pounds. The headache problem is a paradoxical one since the pills at times cause headaches and in other instances may relieve them. The temporary weight gain is caused by the estrogen, which decreases the excretion of salt by the kidneys; this excess salt holds onto the water and results in an increased collection of fluid in the body. So it's better to look on this as water weight and not true fat weight. Furthermore, obesity is such a complex and universal problem with so many variables that one would literally have to put women in glass cages and observe them from morning to dusk to fully realize what's going on. For example, it may be that the pill stops them from worrying about becoming pregnant and therefore they are more relaxed and eat more. Or it may be that they eat the same but because they worry less they burn up less nervous energy. Suffice to say weight gain is of no importance, and if it is more than a few pounds one should look for something else that's causing it rather than the pill. A few women also complain of skin pigmentation, particularly on the face. These areas of pigmentation are similar to the type that occur during a pregnancy, and doctors refer to this as "the mask of pregnancy." Just what causes these large areas of pigmentation is not known, but luckily other than their cosmetic effect, they are of no importance. Various creams and ointments are available that can ease the problem. Luckily the pigmentation rarely becomes so pronounced as to require stopping the pill.

Again some women become so depressed that they must discontinue the pill. Depression like obesity is difficult to evaluate because depression is similarly such a widespread disorder. Who isn't depressed now and then? And often these periods may last for considerable lengths of time. So in trying to evaluate whether or not the pill or something else is the culprit, doctors often feel much like the store merchant who was convinced that half his advertising was of no value; but the trouble was he didn't know which half. Yet unlike the merchant who could lose his business by stopping the wrong half, doctors can very easily discontinue the pill for a few months to see what happens. If the depression continues, it's obviously due to some other problem. If the depression is relieved, it is usually better to back off and use some other means of contraception. I have known of a few instances where this has not been done, and the end result has been a very severe depression that could have been prevented. Certainly doctors, like generals, should know when to retreat.

There is another group of patients that fails to resume menstruation for a few months after going off the pill. Normally it lasts just a few months, but it may continue for a year or longer. Why this happens is debatable, but the reader will recall that the pill works by acting on the pituitary gland, which in turn stops the production of eggs by the ovaries. In one sense it's the same as if you placed your arm in a sling for a few years and then finally removed the sling. It would be unusual if the arm wasn't a little stiff for a short time. Certainly 99 percent of the time the pituitary and ovaries start working again either immediately or in a few months. But if they do not, doctors have other drugs to help bring on the period. One of these, Clomiphene —a new drug that helps to stimulate the ovaries—is discussed in the chapter on sterility.

One further point that should be mentioned is that some patients will have very slight spotting between periods, particularly while taking the last few pills. Again, this is usually temporary, and corrects itself with subsequent menstrual cycles. Doctors refer to this as breakthrough bleeding, which simply means the pill is not strong enough to stop the lining of the uterus from bleeding. Just as the steel structure in a building must be of sufficient strength to hold up the building, so the pill must contain ample hormones to stop the uterus from bleeding—particularly during the latter part of the cycle when it is more than likely to occur. Should it become troublesome, the pill may be temporarily increased to one pill in the morning and another in the evening until the bleeding stops. At other times the doctor will merely shift to a slightly stronger pill. But on rare occasions this fails to work and the spotting develops into outright bleeding that may be very irregular and last many days. This "on and off" bleeding can be confusing because the patient has no idea whether it is or is not a period. Usually since the doctor is in exactly the same boat he will advise stopping the pills and most likely suggest a D and C. This is because the bleeding may result from a polyp, fibroid, or another problem totally unrelated to the birth control pills. If the D and C discovers a polyp or something else to explain the cause of the bleeding the pill can be used again. But even if the D and C reveals nothing, which would indicate the pill is the culprit, the doctor may still try the pill a second time. Yet should the problem recur, the doctor will then advise another type of contraceptive.

Just to round out the picture I would also like to point out some rare symptoms which the reader should be aware of. For instance, now and then pain will develop in either the legs or chest or the patient will notice an unexplained cough or blurred vision. These symptoms, particularly the blurred vision, are extremely rare; but since they may be associated with a blood clot, they should be reported to the doctor immediately. In the future there is an extremely good chance that these symptoms will become even rarer with the lower dosage pills. The FDA has recommended that doctors try to use the pills containing the lowest amounts of estrogen. This is because a recent study has shown that the pills containing over fifty micrograms of estrogen were more likely to produce blood clots. The pills that are currently in use contain anywhere from fifty to one hundred micrograms of estrogen, and consequently many doctors are now switching to those pills that contain the smallest amount of estrogen. The big drawback, however, with the low-dosage pills is that breakthrough bleeding is more likely to occur.

The only way to find out is to try them, and if it doesn't occur then the patient may as well use low-dosage pills.

Yet looking at the other side of the picture, these drawbacks are minimal and more than balanced by the beneficial effects. I've already mentioned the one big plus at great lengths namely the commonsense limitations of one's family. Yet there are other side benefits that are of equal help for some patients. For instance, women who used to have painful periods can often be relieved of this problem. Other women who have had a long history of irregular heavy periods, find that not only are their periods regular, but also the bleeding is much less. Usually most women bleed much less and also for a shorter time while taking the pill. Women who are either entertainers or athletes can also postpone their period to a more convenient time by taking the pills for a few extra days. The length of the time the pills can be taken is still being determined by doctors, but a five-year period is generally accepted by most physicians without any question. And more evidence is accumulating to show that in all probability there is no need for any time limit. What has caused more debate over the last few years is who should be allowed to take the pills. I refer in particular to whether or not high school and university students should be given a prescription for the pill while they are still single. It's my personal feeling they should; and most doctors now take this stance, assuming that it's better to write a prescription for the pill than be faced with the multitude of problems that an unwanted pregnancy presents. In short anyone who is exposed to sex should also be exposed to the pill. And it goes without saying that a little bit of exposure is sometimes all that is needed. I recall one time during a radio interview, a woman called the station and asked if she should give up the pill since she was now leading a relatively quiet life. She was strongly advised to continue with it until she was leading a totally quiet life! I gave this advice for very good reason, because so frequently I see young girls crying about their unwanted child and naively saying "I didn't do it very often." It doesn't do any good at this point to tell the girl she's a little stupid because the error has already been made. Too often you see young girls who have gone on the foolish assumption that it won't happen to me and that a miss is as good as a mile. What they fail to remember is that when they get hit, it's a 100 percent hit. Mark Twain purportedly said that "We're all a little stupid, only in different ways." But at least all of us should try to take the risk out of those things where there doesn't have to be any. It is also disheartening that a time when such foolproof contraception is available to women, doctors are seeing more single girls who are pregnant than at any other time. This is sometimes the result of the doctor's refusal to give them the pill, at other times of a somewhat lackadaisical attitude on their part to obtain it.

In the event that a patient wishes to start these pills following a pregnancy, most doctors advise waiting until the baby has been weaned. If, on the other hand, the baby is being bottle-fed, the majority of women will have a period within four to six weeks following the delivery. And the pills can be started at that time. However, it should be kept in mind that it is quite possible to become pregnant before the first menstrual period occurs. If patients are going to have intercourse before that time, other contraceptive means should be used such as the condom or the contraceptive jellies, with or without a diaphragm. But for the type of patient who is not smart enough to come in out of the rain, the best approach is to put them on the pill just as they are leaving the hospital.

For women around 45 who have been on the pill, sooner or later the question arises as to whether they should stop taking it because their change of life may have begun. Since birth control pills contain some estrogen the usual menopausal symptoms, such as hot flushes, may not be present. Also because the pill results in continuing regular periods, it is impossible to be certain whether or not the menopause has started. One approach is to stop the pills and see what happens. If no bleeding occurs and hot flushes start, then the menopause has begun. But if regular periods continue and there are no menopausal symptoms, it indicates that the change of life is still a little way off. During this test interval it is advisable for women to use a vaginal contraceptive cream to avoid pregnancy. At this age the possibility is extremely small, and the use of contraceptive cream provides virtually 100 percent protection.

Many women ask if they can continue taking birth control pills to stop the menopausal symptoms. Some doctors use this method, but the majority do not for two main reasons. First, there is no point in taking birth control pills if the patient can no longer become pregnant. Second, why take the two hormones —estrogen and progesterone—which are present in all of the pills, when one hormone—estrogen—will do? As we know, sometimes two heads are better than one, but in this case one pill is better than two. In short, progesterone is not needed for the menopause. It's merely excess baggage. Consequently most doctors advise women to change to natural estrogen tablets. (See Chapter III.)

An increasing number of patients will use the pill in the years ahead because it is a foolproof method of contraception. And the majority of women prefer to have their babies by choice, not chance. Removing the constant fear of another pregnancy is the main reason why the pill has been so widely accepted by women. Many patients are very happy because they have been able to discard the mechanical devices. Furthermore, although the pill has no specific effect on the sex drive itself, it has improved the sexual lives of many couples who no longer fear pregnancy.

Since we are living in a youth-oriented culture, one thing deserves very special mention. The birth control pill offers all ages complete freedom from worry of pregnancy. But too many young people fail to realize it offers absolutely no protection from the hazards of venereal disease. And in a society that increasingly accepts almost unlimited sexual freedom, all indicators seem to point toward an increase in both syphilis and gonorrhea. I wish to stress here, as I've stressed elsewhere, that the condom is still the best means available to guard against venereal disease.

What of the future? Robert Browning once said "a man's reach should exceed his grasp, or what's a heaven for?" He implied that it's only by reaching for the stars that we have been able to land on the moon. I suppose the same is true for the never-ending search to find the perfect contraceptive. At present a number of attempts are being made to achieve this goal. For instance, a pill is being developed that can be taken once a pregnancy has started that will result in an abortion. Another approach is to give women injections twice a year. It may even become possible to immunize women against their husband's sperm so as to be protected from pregnancy for several years. And as the search for the perfect contraceptive goes on, more and more scientists are turning their attention to the male. At the moment it's possible to immunize an animal against its own sperm, thus causing infertility for several months. It's also theoretically possible to use drugs that will act on the cells of the testes and prevent formation of sperm cells.

What prods doctors is the hair-raising fact that it took somewhere between a quarter of a million and a million years to bring the world's population to about three thousand million, but this feat will be repeated in the next thirty-five years. At the time of Christ the world's population was about two hundred and fifty million. During Queen Elizabeth's reign it had jumped to five hundred million, but by 1965 it had reached three thousand million. In the United States alone it is estimated that the population will reach three hundred and seventy-five million in another fifty years' time. Looked at another way, a world "population clock" shows that there were 3.9 babies born every second in 1969 and 1.7 people died every second. This means that there was a net gain of 2.2 persons per second, 132 per minute, 190,000 per day, and more than 1,330,000 every week. Therefore during 1969 seventy-two million people were added to an already over-populated world. It takes little imagination to envision that sooner or later something has to give. Just consider the fact that an average American pollutes 3,000,000 gallons of water, uses 21,000 gallons of gasoline, drinks 28,000 gallons of milk, eats 10,000 pounds of meat during his lifetime, and add 500 pounds of pollution to the atmosphere each year. This is why we are already seeing the first symptoms of disaster in our overcrowded highways, the pollution of air and water, and the crime and delinquency on our streets. Laboratory experimentation with rats has shown that when they are given ample room they all live together in a peaceful way. But, when they are crowded into smaller areas they become irritable and frequent fights occur among them. The same thing is already happening in certain segments of our society, and this progressive erosion of many human values will continue unless there is a stabilization of our population. Failure to control this monster will have effects as devastating as a nuclear explosion.

But will man be smart enough to do something about it before it's too late? The problem is that while our scientific thinking sends rockets to the moon, our emotional thinking is back in the Dark Ages. One writer recently pointed out that pilgrims used to travel to Mecca by camel over miles of desert, which gave them plenty of time to think and meditate. Now they arrive at the shrine by plane, much in advance of their minds. This inability of the mind to keep up with technological change and accept practical solutions to present-day realities continues to hinder progress in many parts of the world. For example, a recent report from Bombay, India stated that the family-planning movement had come under attack by religious groups in many Asian countries. Led by orthodox monks, these groups are pressuring the government into throwing out the birth control programs. They argue that birth control is planned murder. But their real motive is evident when the Buddhists in Ceylon say that the country's Buddhist majority will become a minority with the next twenty years if the use of contraceptives continues. They point out that the Roman Catholics, Moslems, and Ceylonese Hindus refuse to participate in family-planning clinics, and Buddhists are the only ones using contraceptives. Similarly, in India, the right-wing Hindu party is also severely critical of family planning. It too worries about becoming a minority—in spite of the fact that the Hindus number 450,000,000 and there are only 70,000,000 Moslems. This type of medieval thinking will make a minority of all of us.

But how can we be critical of the developing nations when the United States has also made a political football out of the pill? And the pill has not only already brought great benefits to mankind, but must also be looked on as one of the most important priorities of our time. For example, if we never find a cure for cancer, the world is not going to come to an end. But it's apparent that the failure to curb the population explosion will eventually bring utter havoc to this planet. Since the pill represents one of the major weapons to combat this catastrophe, surely the medical profession and others should stop their senseless bickering over the infinitesimal risks of the pill. Instead they should turn their energies to attempting to solve the many urgent social problems of our nation. Nero played the fiddle while Rome was burning. Hopefully the nations of the world will not stand by idly and debate on the fine points of birth control while our civilization also burns. Unfortunately history has a habit of repeating itself. For as Santayana points out, those who do not learn from history are condemned to relive it.

The Intrauterine Device

Madame Bertin, the milliner to Marie Antoinette, is supposed to have said "there is nothing new save that which has been forgotten." She could have been talking about the intrauterine device, because the basic principle of the IUD has been known for centuries. About a thousand years ago the Arab discovered he could prevent his camel from becoming pregnant by inserting a small stone in the uterus. Now there has been renewed interest in this dramatic approach to birth control, which is usually referred to as the loop or, simply, the IUD. This small plastic device bears no similarity to the diaphragm, which is merely placed in the vagina, and can be inserted and removed by a woman without any problem. The IUD must be inserted by a physician, since it is placed *inside* the uterus and is left there permanently, or a least until there is no longer a chance of pregnancy. Before the invention of the IUD other materials, such as platinum and gold, usually in the form of a small ring, were used by doctors of many countries. The IUD, therefore, merely represents an improvement over these earlier devices and, for reasons doctors are still not certain of, it is nearly 100 percent effective in preventing pregnancy.

Some doctors prescribe the IUD at any time during a woman's reproductive life. Others are hesitant to advise its use until after a patient has had one or two children. They reason that there is a very slight possibility that insertion of the IUD could introduce infection into the uterus. And, if this was severe, it could result in sterility. Women who decide on this method of contraception should also realize that now and then a pregnancy does occur, and they must be willing to accept this very small risk. But the good thing about the IUD is that it does away with having to think about pills, diaphragms, and contraceptive creams.

The insertion of the IUD is quite simple and painless and takes only a few minutes in the doctor's office. It is done by gently dilating the cervix (opening into the uterus), following which the narrow plastic device can easily be pushed into the uterine cavity. Usually it is carried out immediately following a menstrual period, as it causes less bleeding at this time. Furthermore, doing it then insures that it is not being placed inside a pregnant uterus. What should patients expect after the insertion of the IUD? Some will have no pain. But most women will experience mild abdominal cramps for a few hours. This discomfort is easily controlled by a couple of aspirins or codeine, and it is extremely rare that the IUD ever has to be removed because of pain. On the other hand, bleeding, or a bloody discharge, may occasionally cause problems. Women should realize that it is normal to expect bleeding after its insertion, which can vary considerably in both amount and duration. Sometimes this bleeding persists for only a few days. At other times, there is nearly constant bleeding or a bloody discharge that requires one or two pads a day for a month or longer. Such prolonged bleeding usually simmers down; but now and then it does not, and the IUD has to be taken out. All this means is that women should accept the fact that intermittent bleeding during the first two months is quite normal, and unless it becomes very profuse they should not worry about it. Also, since the bleeding does not follow any definite pattern, it may be quite difficult to establish what bleeding represents a period and what does not. In many cases the period comes a little early, but it can also be late, or occur at the usual time.

Occasionally the IUD falls out of the uterus. If this happens, it is usually during the first two months. Consequently, to be certain it has not occurred, patients are advised to see their doctor after a few weeks. However, this is becoming less and less of a problem as improvements are made in its design, and should not be a deterring factor in the use of the IUD.

The Diaphragm

The diaphragm is still widely used and no doubt will continue to be popular for some time, even though many couples who formerly relied on it have now changed to either the pill or the IUD. The diaphragm provides protection in two ways. First, it acts as a physical barrier, which stops the majority of sperm cells from making contact with the cervix. Second, the spermicidal jelly or cream kills any sperm that does happen to get by the diaphragm. Certainly, the method is a very safe one if used correctly. This means that the diaphragm must be fitted by a doctor, and its use and method of insertion must be adequately explained to the patient. Furthermore, it must be used all the time. One occasionally hears of a woman becoming pregnant while using a diaphragm, and, as a result, she will be likely to lose faith in the effectiveness of this method. But nine times out of ten the woman is at fault, not the diaphragm. One of the most common errors is the failure to use it consistently, because some women make the false assumption that it is not needed during their "safe" time of the month. In other instances, the diaphragm is either inserted incorrectly, or not left in long enough. Still other women fail to get refitted after a pregnancy, when a slightly larger size is usually required.

Today there are many different styles of diaphragms that can be purchased. Most of them are placed in the vagina with the help of an inserter after a small amount of contraceptive jelly has been placed on one side of the diaphragm. It is best to place the diaphragm in the vagina just prior to intercourse, and it should not be removed for approximately fifteen hours. On its removal it should be washed, dried, and powdered.

Contraceptive creams are also available that can be used without a diaphragm, and these are also extremely effective. They are particularly suitable for women who do not wish to be bothered by the insertion of the diaphragm or women who cannot be fitted with a diaphragm prior to marriage. Most virgin girls have a reasonably snug vaginal opening, and any attempt to determine the size of the diaphragm would be extremely painful. However, after a few weeks of marriage the hymenal ring becomes stretched, and the diaphragm size can then be determined quite easily.

Today, therefore, women have a variety of choices available to them in this rapidly changing field. In fact, in view of the number of methods available, many women become confused and do not know how to decide which will be the best for them. The truth is that all the methods are good, and all are better than using nothing. However, at different stages of a woman's reproductive life, one form of birth control may be more advisable than another. Most married couples will wish to postpone a family for a year or two, but their reasons may be more important in some cases than in others. As I mentioned earlier, an unexpected pregnancy could end a college student's career. In such case, where there can be no margin for error, the pill is, at the moment, superior to any other method. On the other hand, if it does not matter too much if pregnancy occurs, then other methods, such as the contraceptive jellies, with or without a diaphragm, may be used. But it should be kept in mind that there is an extremely slight element of risk involved with these procedures. Later in life, when a woman has completed her family but does not want to be bothered by pills or the inconvenience of inserting a diaphragm, the intrauterine device is frequently the best solution. And it can be easily removed by her doctor should she change her mind at any time.

The Condom

The condom, commonly referred to as "the rubber" or "the safe," is used by some couples, but it is not too popular with the majority of them. This is because most men do not like wearing something over the penis, since regardless of how thin the condom may be, it nevertheless interferes with some of the sensation. In addition, since it is usually applied just prior to the actual intercourse, it means a temporary delay while it is being placed over the penis, and many couples find this objectionable. Yet, there are some who are quite happy with this method, and if used properly it is still one of the safest means of contraception, particularly if the condom is checked prior to its use to make certain there are no holes in it. The best method is to blow it up slightly and check to see if there are any air leaks. Then it should be placed on the penis, leaving a good half-inch between the end of the condom and the end of the penis. This not only allows for the ejaculation, but also for movement during intercourse, making breakage less likely. In the event that the condom slips off it must be immediately pulled out of the vagina and a spermicidal jelly introduced. If this is done immediately it is very unlikely that a pregnancy will result, but if no jelly is available the next best solution is to take a douche. Which brings up the further points that some couples always use a spermicidal jelly along with the condom, for added protection. The jelly can be placed inside the vagina prior to intercourse, and will kill any sperm that might happen to escape. For women, who are troubled by a dry vagina, it also acts as a lubricant.

Condoms have one further important use, which is to prevent such diseases as gonorrhea and syphilis. It would be foolish to deny the fact of premarital experience, for it not only exists, but it is also more common than it was in former years. Consequently, if single people are going to have intercourse then they should take care not only to prevent pregnancy, but also to decrease their chance of contracting a venereal disease. Without a doubt, the most reliable way to prevent this dual problem is by the use of a condom. Failure to take this precaution may result in venereal disease, and if this is not treated quickly it can result in a host of other unnecessary problems. Franklin, writing in *Poor Richard's Almanac*, points out how failure to take care leads to other things. He says, "For want of a nail the shoe was lost; for want of a shoe the horse was lost; and for want of a horse the rider was lost; being overtaken by the enemy, all for the want of care about a horseshoe nail." In short, being careful pays off.

Sterilization

More and more couples are asking whether one or the other can be sterilized. And more frequently the answer is "yes," simply because like therapeutic abortions a more liberal trend is in the air. This is because doctors and society are throwing off some of the sacred-cow thinking about this procedure and now consider it as merely another means of contraception. After all, if the patient has a right to *temporarily* stop an unwanted pregnancy by using the pill, why shouldn't she also have the right to *permanently* stop pregnancy by sterilization?

Sterilization, however, continues to be surrounded by a good deal of misguided thinking, primarily because it has always been associated with emotional and religious pressures. I pointed out elsewhere in the book that young women often find the sexual adjustment to marriage difficult if they have been drilled for years in the concept that sex is dirty and bad. The church and the laws of many nations have similarly preached the same theme with regard to sterilization, so it's no wonder there is much anxiety about the effects of this operation. It was usually impossible to obtain permission for sterilization unless the patient was suffering from a bad heart, failing kidneys, or some other serious problem. Add the psychological effects of these restrictions to the fact that it also involves an operation on a very sensitive, emotional part of a woman's anatomy and it is no wonder many women (and their husbands) spread misconceptions about this type of surgery.

Let us first discuss what sterilization does not do. Possibly the greatest error is confusing sterilization with castration. Castration involves removal of the sex glands (namely the ovaries of a woman or the testes of a man), and these organs are not touched by sterilization. So since the ovaries are not removed, the female hormones are in no way changed by the operation. Another misconception is that the surgery will stop menstrual periods. But again this is not the case, since the uterus is not removed. One can therefore state in the strongest possible terms that there is absolutely no change in the normal functioning of a woman's body. The ovaries continue to produce the female hormones estrogen and progesterone, which in turn act on the lining of the uterus and each month the period occurs. The next important hurdle is to convince couples that sterilization will have no effect on their sexual life. How could it? In the section on hysterectomy I've shown that even removing the uterus and ovaries has no effect on a patient's sexual feelings. Consequenly, in a sterilization procedure when these organs are not even removed, there is no logical way it could cause any psychological or physical sexual change.

Another myth is that sterilization is a reversible procedure which can be undone at a later time. It's an extremely grave error to assume this because 99.9 percent of the time sterilization is permanent. It is therefore important for the patient to realize that you simply cannot put a zipper on the tubes that can easily be reopened at a later date. Admittedly, doctors do have surgical techniques that are available to repair tubes that have been either damaged by disease or by a former sterilization procedure. Sometimes this involves removing the damaged portion of the tube and joining the ends together again, or it may be necessary to reimplant the tube into another part of the uterus. But when you consider that the hole in the tube is about the size of a needle it's small wonder that these operations usually fail. A few surgeons who have had extensive experience in performing this type of delicate surgery report good results in about 30 percent of the cases. Usually, however, the end result is much worse. The only sensible approach is to consider sterilization an irrevocable decision.

Possibly the final fear and fallacy is that sterilizations often do not work. One cannot deny that on rare occasions a pregnancy does occur, but let me reassure you that the failure rate is very, very small.

How does a sterilization work? In order for a pregnancy to occur, the sperm has to swim into the uterus, emerge through the tubes, and fertilize the female egg. The purpose of the operation is to stop this from happening by tying and cutting the tubes. This is the operation that doctors refer to when talking about sterilization. It requires an abdominal incision of about the same size as that used for an appendectomy. It's an extremely safe procedure and carries even less risk than having the appendix removed. I might point out that not all doctors use the same technique. The great majority of surgeons just cut and tie the tubes. Others go a step further, and as an additional safeguard they bury one end of the tube deep into the wall of the uterus. Since it is a simple operation most patients are able to leave the hospital in a few days. And, of course, the operation is immediately effective. In view of the current interest in sterilization, new techniques are being developed for this procedure. For instance, there are small optical instruments that can be inserted into the abdomen through a very small incision. The surgeon then looks through the eye-piece and after finding the tubes is able to cut them using a cautery.

Some gynecologists feel that the best operation for sterilization is a hysterectomy. This may come as a shock to some of the readers, so let me explain why this is the case. A hysterectomy is 100 percent effective because without the uterus it's impossible for the patient to become pregnant. Also, since the uterus serves no useful purpose other than for pregnancy, why not remove it so that fibroids, cancer, infection, and other diseases can't develop in it later in life. Leaving the uterus in may mean another operation at some future time. So in many ways this is a much more logical approach, particularly for women who wish a sterilization done when they are in their late thirties or early forties. But since it is a departure from the long-established approach to sterilization, most patients and their doctors tend to shy away from going this further step. They would argue that the thinking is a little radical, and why carry out a larger operation when a smaller one will do. Let the future take care of itself. But in the event that a hysterectomy is done, it still does not involve castration because in nearly all instances the ovaries will be left in place.

At this juncture the reader might wonder if women are ever castrated during a sterilization, and 99 percent of the time the answer would be no. Yet there are a couple of exceptions to this general rule. For example, those doctors who feel a hysterectomy is the best way to sterilize a woman also argue that the ovaries should be removed even if they're not diseased, as a few may become cystic and require another operation at a later date. It is a continuation of the same philosophy mentioned above—namely, let's get it all over with at one time. Further, at age forty the ovaries only have a few years left to produce sufficient amounts of estrogen, so they may as well be taken out.

The situation may also arise during surgery that the ovaries are found to be diseased and have to be removed. Remember these last few examples are given just to give the complete picture, but in a great majority of cases the ovaries are left alone. Even if they have to be removed, it is not a major calamity. The patient will merely be given a daily pill of the hormone estrogen which will keep the menopause from occurring.

When should couples consider having a sterilization done? This is an individual decision, for all people have varying ideas as to the size of the ideal family. The main point is that couples should be absolutely certain they want a sterilization done. If there is any doubt, it is much better to forget it and use other means of contraception. There is also a time to be sterilized and a time not to be. For a thirty-five-year-old mother with six children there is little doubt. But for a twenty-five year old woman with two children it requires a good deal of mature thought. One or both children may die. Or the woman may become a widow or divorcee and remarry. Here sterilization could be followed by regrets. Consequently, I usually advise these patients to use contraceptives for a few more years before making such an irrevocable decision.

In recent years there has been an increasing tendency for the husband to be sterilized. This is because it is easier to do in the male, since it does not require an abdominal incision. In fact this simple operation is often done in the doctor's office using a local anesthetic. The surgery merely involves making a small incision in the scrotum and cutting and tying off the vas deferens. This small tube carries the sperm, and by blocking it, no sperm are ejected during the intercourse. Some men are rather reluctant to have it done for fear it means castration and loss of manhood, and will have an adverse effect on their sexual life. This is not the case, since the male glands are not removed: men are just the same after the operation as before. It takes more than merely cutting the vas deferens to change a man's attitude towards sex.

CHAPTER VII

Pregnancy

Diagnosis of Pregnancy

IT IS A RARE WOMAN WHO, on one or more occasions, does not spend a few sleepless nights wondering if she is pregnant. And, unfortunately, there is no absolute way to be sure of the diagnosis during the first weeks after conception has taken place. A young woman who normally has regular periods and then misses one, certainly stands a good chance of being pregnant, particularly if there has been no attempt at birth control. If the missed period is then followed by early morning nausea, vomiting, breast tenderness, and increased frequency of urination, the presence of a pregnancy is almost certain. But as I discussed in the section "Failure to Menstruate," in Chapter IV, there are many factors that can stop periods, so it is wrong to jump to a hasty conclusion. For example, a slight normal delay in the period may cause sufficient worry to produce some of the early symptoms of pregnancy. And sadly enough, some women submit to an abortion who are not pregnant.

How then can you be sure of the diagnosis? If we are talking about 100 percent certainty, it means waiting until somewhere between the fourth and fifth month, when the fetal heart can be heard, the baby's outline felt, and X rays can show the fetal skeleton. But, if patients are willing to accept a 99.9 percent diagnosis, it can obviously be made much earlier than the fourth month.

What makes the diagnosis of pregnancy difficult in some cases? The crux of the whole problem is whether the patient consults her doctor during the first few weeks of her pregnancy or whether she waits for three or four months. I am sure most women believe that it would be easier for a doctor to make a diagnosis of pregnancy after it has been present for three months than during the first few weeks. This reasoning is correct, as long as the patient with the three-month pregnancy consulted the doctor shortly after her missed period. For example, if a woman is examined shortly following the missed period and the uterus is found to be normal in size, and then a month later it has become larger, the patient is in all probability pregnant. But should a woman postpone seeing the doctor until the third or fourth month, examination will show a pelvic mass which may present certain difficulties in diagnosis. If the patient has marked breast changes and other symptoms of pregnancy, the mass is in all probability an enlarged uterus. Yet it could also be a uterus enlarged because of fibroids. Then, in the obese patient, or one who cannot relax, it is sometimes difficult to determine between an enlarged uterus and an ovarian cyst. Not knowing what the pelvic findings were a month or two earlier puts the doctor at a distinct disadvantage, for he has nothing with which to compare his present findings. Consequently, he has to wait a few more weeks to make certain that the fetal heart appears and that the uterus increases in size.

What about the pregnancy test? In the great majority of instances there is no need to use it, because whether the patient is pregnant or not makes little difference, and a little time and patience will decide one way or the other. On the other hand, there are certain occasions when the early diagnosis of pregnancy is extremely important. The young, unmarried girl obviously wants to know as quickly as possible if she is pregnant. Then there is the woman who has missed a period and later begins to bleed, and the problem arises as to whether she was pregnant and is now having a miscarriage. Another problem is presented by the patient who misses a period, and then complains of abdominal pain, with or without bleeding. Doctors then have to ascertain whether the patient is pregnant and if so, is the pregnancy in the uterus or in the tube? (We will talk at some length about tubal or "ectopic" pregnancies later in this section.) The pregnancy test sometimes comes in handy in cases like this although it can also be quite misleading. Most patients have the mistaken idea that it invariably gives the correct answer, but this is not always so. Sometimes, the tests will say the patient is pregnant when she is not. Conversely, it may label her as not pregnant when she is. However, during the last few years, a variety of pregnancy tests have become available and their accuracy has improved. Therefore, in any of the foregoing situations, such tests are an important aid to the doctor; but like other laboratory tests they form only part of the overall picture of the patient's condition.

Before leaving this subject, there is one further method that has been used for a quick diagnosis of pregnancy during the last few years. This involves the use of hormones which may be given by either a single injection or in pill form for a few days. These hormones cause a rapid stimulation of the inside lining of the uterus which, in a few days, results in bleeding if the patient is not pregnant. However, should the patient fail to bleed, a diagnosis of pregnancy is quite probable.

False Pregnancy

One of the most interesting problems in medicine is the so-called imaginary or pseudo-pregnancy. Women who have unsuccessfully attempted to get pregnant for many years and those nearing the end of their reproductive life are more likely to develop this rare syndrome. I can vividly recall being asked to see a patient who had been in labor for a day and had failed to deliver a baby. Examination showed that she was not pregnant. Of course, most women are discovered to have a false pregnancy long before they reach the labor room, but it is not unusual for them to fool themselves and their doctor for a few months.

Doctors are not certain what causes a false pregnancy, but these women all have one thing in common: an extreme yearning to become pregnant. And in some way this intense longing for a baby reaches such proportions that pregnancy symptoms occur. Some women will stop menstruating and develop early morning nausea and vomiting. Others will notice an increase in the size of the breasts, and sometimes even pigmentation will occur around the nipple. Still others will go a step further and notice a progressive increase in the size of their abdomen, and this is often what fools both the patient and the doctor. And as if this were not enough, a few women will think they actually feel fetal movements; and, as mentioned above, in the final stage they actually go in labor.

Most cases will of course, be detected within the first few months, when the doctor finds that although the stomach is gradually increasing in proportions, the uterus has nevertheless remained the same size. On the other hand, if the patient first presents herself at the doctor's office when the abdomen is quite distended, it may be impossible to feel the uterus, and an X ray of the abdomen will be required to show that there is no fetal skeleton present. The most difficult aspect of this whole problem is to get some women to accept the fact that they are not pregnant. Once they are convinced, however, the symptoms quickly subside.

Ectopic or Tubal Pregnancy

William Shakespeare, in *The Rape of Lucrece*, writes that "no perfection is so absolute that some impurity doth not pollute." Shakespeare, who had the uncanny ability of hitting things right on the head, might just as easily have been talking about ectopic pregnancy as anything else. For although Nature starts a pregnancy in the right place over 99 percent of the time, the fact is that now and then it slips up and in about one case in every two hundred the pregnancy starts to grow inside the tube instead of inside the uterus. It is, of course, impossible to put a seven-pound baby inside a small tube, and consequently, the diagnosis must be made as quickly as possible and surgery carried out.

What causes a tubal pregnancy? In Chapter I, where I explain how the female organs work, I mentioned that following ovulation the egg quickly enters one of the tubes on its way to the uterus. If intercourse has occurred at about the time of ovulation, the egg may become fertilized on its journey down the tube; and under normal circumstances it finally reaches the uterus where it becomes attached to its wall and a normal pregnancy starts. The problem with tubal pregnancy is that the fertilized egg never reaches the uterus. In the majority of cases this is because there has been a previous infection which has partially blocked the small channel that runs through the tube, but on rare occasions there is absolutely no apparent reason.

What happens when the pregnancy starts to grow in the tube? In a few lucky cases, the egg attaches near the opening into the tube. After growing for a few weeks it falls out into the pelvic cavity. This happens because the egg is so near the tubal opening that it follows the path of least resistance, literally falling out of the end of the tube, and is gradually absorbed. Doctors are not certain just how often this occurs, but unfortunately most ectopics do not end in this fashion. In most cases the egg usually travels further down in the tube before it reaches an obstructed area, where it starts to grow. This is when the trouble begins, because unlike the uterus, which was specifically designed for a pregnancy, the tube can neither expand, nor does its lining have the capacity to nourish the growing egg for any length of time. Consequently, sooner or later the pregnancy becomes too large for the tube, and it ruptures from the increased pressure.

The diagnosis of ectopic pregnancy can be as easy as falling off a log, but in some cases it is one of the most difficult diagnoses in gynecology. The patient with the acute type of ectopic is usually rushed to the emergency department of the hospital with the diagnosis written all over her. This is because sudden rupture of the tube has produced internal bleeding, and the patient quickly goes into a state of collapse. In talking about this acute type of ectopic, doctors frequently refer to the "bathroom syndrome." This name arises from the fact that just before the tube ruptures there may be a small amount of internal bleeding which causes rectal irritation, and gives the patient the false feeling that she needs to go to the bathroom. Then on attempting a bowel movement, the increased straining causes rupture of the tube resulting in more bleeding, and the patient rapidly loses consciousness. Of course it does not always happen in this way, but most patients complain of sudden pain from the initial rupture, which is soon followed by the usual symptoms of blood loss, such as weakness, perspiration, cold clammy hands, rapid pulse, and final collapse. Usually by the time the patient is seen by the doctor, the abdomen is distended from blood, and it is obvious that blood transfusions and immediate surgery are required.

The chronic type of ectopic pregnancy is another story, for it can masquerade at times under a number of different disguises which makes the diagnosis quite difficult. In most cases there has been some change in the menstrual bleeding but this may vary considerably. Some women may miss a period. Others may have it a week or two late. Still others have the period at the normal time, only to find it is a little less in amount. And just as important as the change in the bleeding pattern is the presence of low abdominal pain, which similarly varies from patient to patient. Some complain of occasional stabbing pains, but most describe it as a dull aching sensation, and it is only when bleeding into the tube occurs, or sudden rupture, that the pain becomes severe. The other symptoms of pregnancy, such as morning nausea and breast tenderness, may also be present. This means that a young girl who misses a period and then experiences abdominal pain and vaginal bleeding may have an ectopic pregnancy, although the same symptoms can also be present with the common miscarriage. Consequently in order to narrow down the diagnosis, doctors do a pelvic examination to see if they can feel an enlarged tube. This can be quite easy with a thin patient, who has no difficulty in relaxing, but with an obese patient, who tightens up during a pelvic examination, trying to find a small enlargement of the tube can be extremely hard. And in such cases a pregnancy test is not of much value since, if the pregnancy has died, the test may show nothing. Furthermore, even if the test points toward a pregnancy, it still does not inform the doctor whether the pregnancy is in the tube or in the uterus. Doctors therefore have to go a step further and, should there be any doubt in the diagnosis, they will hospitalize the patient and examine her when she is asleep. Under an anesthetic the abdominal muscles become relaxed, and the surgeon then has a greater chance of feeling any small mass that may be present in the tube. During this procedure he may also insert a small needle through the end of the vagina to see if there is any blood in the pelvic cavity. Should blood be present it strongly suggests the presence of an ectopic pregnancy. In other cases, a small optical instrument will be inserted through the same area, or through the abdomen, which allows doctors to look directly at the tubes and ovaries. And going a step further, sometimes an incision will be made in the same spot, to get a better look at the tubes and ovaries. If an ectopic is found, immediate surgery is indicated before the rupture occurs. This involves removing either the entire tube or part of it.

CHAPTER VIII

Miscarriage or Abortion

MOST PATIENTS THINK the word "abortion" refers to the criminal interference of a normal pregnancy, no doubt because those who carry on the work are labeled "abortionists." But this is only one aspect of the term, for doctors also use it to describe the loss of an early pregnancy, although the majority of people have become accustomed to using the word "miscarriage." We will see in this chapter that there are basically two kinds of abortions: spontaneous ones which result from an act of nature and induced abortions, which may be either legal (therapeutic) or criminal. Let's first talk about abortions which occur strictly by chance.

Spontaneous Abortion

Why do spontaneous abortions occur? Doctors sometimes find it hard to explain the exact cause, but with those that occur during the first ten to twelve weeks of pregnancy aborting is usually due to a defective egg, which soon dies and must be expelled by nature. But after the twelfth week other things are usually at fault. In these cases, a normal egg may start to grow in the wrong location in the uterus. This may result in either the inability of the placenta (afterbirth) to nourish the growing egg or failure of it to remain adequately attached to the uterine wall. Then there are a few situations when the trouble is not in the uterus but can be pinpointed in some other part of the body. For example, an operation for the removal of an acute appendix may create sufficient irritation inside the abdomen to cause uterine contractions strong enough to result in an abortion. Patients with diabetes or thyroid deficiencies may also have trouble.

However, women have a quite unnecessary fear of certain types of mishaps. Slipping on ice, light blows to the stomach, and car accidents have all become firmly fixed in the public mind as a major cause of miscarriages, but most doctors do not believe that a normal pregnancy can be hurt by minor injuries. Let's look at it this way. When an elderly lady falls and breaks her hip, the cause of the fracture is not so much the fall as the fact that her aging bones have become brittle and weak. By the same token, doctors feel that you simply cannot jar a normal pregnancy loose, but only one that is in some way defective. Doctors also hear patients talk about miscarriage occurring after the sudden death of a loved one, and again this is a debatable point. Most people forget the large number of pregnancies that continue after sorrows of one sort or another, so that in all probability the occurrence of a miscarriage during a crisis is strictly coincidental.

What are the main types of spontaneous abortions? The earliest one is called a "threatened abortion," in which slight spotting or bleeding occurs some time during the early weeks of pregnancy. Fortunately the bleeding usually stops and the pregnancy is not affected. But should the bleeding and cramps continue, part of the pregnancy may be discharged, resulting in what doctors refer to as an "incomplete abortion." (Less frequently, the entire pregnancy is expelled, but this type of complete abortion is the rarity rather than the rule.) The final type of miscarriage is called a "missed abortion," which means the embryo has died but an actual abortion does not occur, in spite of abdominal cramps, slight bleeding or a fairly constant brown-ish discharge. Sometimes it may be several weeks or months before the embryo is discharged. But doctors know it has died because the uterus either fails to increase in size or becomes smaller, the breasts return to normal and tests may fail to show the presence of any life. Sooner or later the uterus will expel the pregnancy, and a D and C may be done. Fortunately this type of abortion is relatively rare. However, when it does occur the most difficult problem is to convince both the patient and her relatives that the proper treatment is to let nature take its course and not to rush in and remove the pregnancy. Most missed abortions are expelled within a few weeks, after which a D and C can be safely done; but if one is attempted earlier it may cause rather heavy bleeding.

Can doctors be certain of the final outcome if bleeding appears in the early stages of a pregnancy? Generally speaking, the answer is no, but there are certain clues that are sometimes helpful. A small amount of bleeding, lasting only a few hours or a day or two, is often due to a condition doctors call "implantation bleeding." During the early weeks of a pregnancy the small egg is literally burrowing its way into the wall of the uterus in order to gain a secure foothold, and this digging action now and then causes minimal bleeding. But should the bleeding continue for many days, suddenly increase in amount, or change to a constant brownish-red discharge, the outlook is less favorable. Such bleeding usually means that part of the placenta (afterbirth) has separated slightly from the wall of the uterus. Sooner or later it will be followed by low abdominal cramps and the patient aborts. How well doctors can prophesy the end result also depends on when they first see a patient. For example, if the patient delays seeing her doctor in spite of moderately heavy bleeding and pain which continues for a number of days, by the time she *does* see him the cervix (the opening into the uterus) may have become quite dilated. If this has occurred, there is no hope of saving the pregnancy. Conversely, if the doctor had seen his patient a day or two earlier, the cervix might still have been closed, and there would have been some hope for the final outcome. The doctor's forecast also depends on whether or not the abortion comes on slowly or suddenly. As we have seen, when the bleeding is minimal, and lasts for a few days only, the resolution of the problem may still be favorable. But when an abortion comes on suddenly, with heavy bleeding and cramps, 99 percent of the time the pregnancy will be lost. And while we're talking about bleeding in the early weeks of pregnancy, it may be worthwhile to mention that some women entertain the unnecessary fear that any kind of bleeding indicates that they are going to have an abnormal baby. There is no scientific foundation for such an apprehension. If the baby has died it will eventually abort. Otherwise, it will probably continue to develop normally.

What doctors do for an abortion depends in part on whether it occurs before or after the twelfth week of pregnancy. Since miscarriages before the twelfth week are usually caused by a defective egg, the embryo has normally been dead for a few weeks by the time bleeding begins and treatment is therefore futile. If, on the other hand, the bleeding occurs because of some minor problem, and the pregnancy is normal, the bleeding will stop regardless of what is done.

Following the twelfth week the situation is not the same. By this time there is normally a healthy fetus, and some other condition is responsible for the bleeding. In such cases, a few days of rest in bed and a prescription of mild sedatives and hormones may be beneficial. Quite often a couple of days of bed-rest will stop the bleeding, but if it does not there is little point in preventing the patient from getting up. Failure of the bleeding to stop usually means that the pregnancy is going to be lost regardless of what is done, and the patient may as well get it over with as soon as possible. A good many women have young children to take care of, and prolonged bed-rest is neither practical nor helpful.

The use of hormones in the treatment of miscarriage has come to the fore in recent years, because in some cases there appears to be a deficiency of the hormone, progesterone. However, it must be admitted that there is still a great deal of controversy as to whether many, if any, pregnancies are preserved by its use. Certainly prior to the twelfth week progesterone can do nothing for an abnormal egg, and in such cases its use will merely delay the inevitable abortion. A good many doctors, therefore, reserve hormones for habitual aborters, that is, women who have had three or more consecutive abortions. In such cases, there is nothing to lose, and possibly something to gain, if hormones are started about ten days after the missed period in the hope that the additional quantities of progesterone will help nourish the growing egg and give it a healthy start.

So far, we have been dealing with situations where the doctor has time to try some form of treatment, but there are occasions when bleeding comes on so quickly that an immediate D and C must be done, to remove what is left of the pregnancy, and to control the hemorrhage.

Surgery has relatively little place in the overall treatment of miscarriage, except for those patients who have a fibroid uterus and who have aborted a number of times. Sometimes removing the fibroids will preserve a pregnancy for its full term. But doctors never make a hasty decision to do this type of surgery because they have all seen women with multiple fibroids in the uterus who sail through their pregnancy without a single problem. Similarly surgery is usually not advised for a tipped uterus, but it may finally be resorted to after a number of miscarriages in the hope that it may prevent future aborting. Another rare problem arises with the woman who has a uterus divided in two by a septum (partition), which has been present since birth. Removal of this wall of tissue will occasionally stop the abortions.

Then there are those women who regularly lose their baby after the fourth month of pregnancy. A pelvic examination, done just before the pregnancy is lost, shows the very interesting fact that in such cases the cervical opening into the uterus is dilated, and the patient's membranes (commonly called the bag of water) are seen protruding through the opening. Shortly after this, the membranes break, the amniotic fluid is lost, and labor begins. Some of these patients may have had the cervical opening injured during a previous pregnancy, but in others there is no definite reason why this condition develops. However, in recent years doctors have been performing an operation which produces excellent results. They place a plastic band around the opening into the uterus, which prevents the cervix from stretching. Since the band does not dissolve, patients who complete their term must either have the band cut or be delivered by caesarean section. (It should be emphasized that this operation is only employed with those women who have repeatedly lost their child during the latter months of pregnancy. It is of no help to those who abort during the first three months.)

Therapeutic Abortion

There are two types of induced abortions: therapeutic ones that are done by ethical physicians, and criminal abortions that are usually carried out by incompetent people who have no medical training. We will first talk about criminal abortion, which has caused such havoc over the years. And since legalized abortion is currently such a controversial subject, I'll discuss how it has evolved in four different parts of the world. We will see that legal abortion in Japan is totally accepted as a way of life. Conversely in Great Britain, although large numbers of abortions are being done, many segments of the population still find it a barbarous act and continue to fight for repeal of the law. And in the United States the situation is even worse—for there is presently no equality or uniformity in the various states on this tremendously sensitive matter. Even in those states such as New York, Hawaii, and Alaska that have passed laws allowing abortion virtually on demand, great injustices are taking place. And surely nothing can bring the law more quickly into disrepute than a failure to apply it equitably.

We will see that much of blame must fall on many members of the medical profession who are failing to push for more efficient facilities to carry out this procedure and who are directing so much criticism at their colleagues who are doing them. So often their attitude seems to be "why is a good doctor like you doing abortions?" I trust this chapter will explain that basic question and also many other aspects of this highly complex matter.

Criminal Abortion

Joseph Stalin once said that "one can walk with the devil until one reaches the end of the bridge." It may well be that many nations, more recently the United States, are in fact nearing the end of the bridge as far as criminal abortions are concerned. Some countries such as Japan and more recently England have pretty well closed the door on criminal abortions simply by legalizing abortion. In these countries women can acquire an abortion from a competent doctor merely by asking for one. Other nations such as the United States are rapidly liberalizing their laws on abortion. Still other countries like Canada have a long way to go. In the long run criminal abortions will be history, partly because of improved methods of contraception such as the pill and partly because legalized abortion will be a fact of life in all countries. It is, however, somewhat incongruous and unjust that for the moment geographical boundaries, particularly in the same country—such as the United States, are in effect dictating what is right and what is wrong. What makes it right for a woman in New York State to have an abortion on demand, whereas it is denied to a woman in Massachusetts. Time will correct these disparities, but too often politicians tend to move at snail-like paces in catching up with the mood of the times. During a recent trip to Lebanon I saw some writing on the wall of the prince's palace. It said "one hour of justice is worth a thousand months of prayer."

Hopefully the legislators will follow this advice and quickly put an end to the useless loss of life from backroom abortionists. Yet since criminal abortions remain one of the major concerns of society let's talk about this problem.

Just how many illegal abortions are done each year in North America is anyone's guess, but the figure most authorities quote is one million. This rough estimate merely points out the magnitude of the problem, for it is believed to be the third biggest racket in the United States, with only gambling and narcotics ranking behind.

Who does abortions and what are the motives? Sophocles, in 450 BC, wrote that "Money lays waste cities, it sets men to roaming from home, it seduces and corrupts honest men and turns virtue to baseness, it teaches villainy and impiety." He may as well have said men will do anything for a piece of silver, including the wanton murder of women in the prime of life. Who does the abortion cuts across all walks of life. A good many women are tricked into believing they have been referred to a responsible physician, and on very rare occasions this is the case. One well-known abortionist admitted to performing over five thousand abortions in his lifetime with only two deaths. But for every doctor of this caliber, there are thousands of non-medical abortionists ranging from retired real estate men, mechanics, and insurance salesmen to cab drivers.

What kind of person submits to such a hazardous procedure and why? Here again the whole gamut of society seems to be susceptible, for rich and poor, educated and illiterate, have beaten paths to the abortionist's door. And contrary to what most people believe, married women with families outnumber single girls making this tragic journey. The blight of some married mothers received public focus a few years ago, when women who had taken thalidomide early in their pregnancy fought unsuccessfully to get abortions in the United States. One of them journeyed in desperation to Sweden, where an abortion disclosed that she would have given birth to a badly deformed child. But except for instances of this sort the majority of women resort to such extreme measures for the simple reason that another child is not wanted.

Some women attempt to produce a miscarriage themselves by taking castor oil, falling down the stairs, or vainly and dangerously attempting to insert a knitting needle or some other object into the uterus. Others insert pills, such as potassium permanganate, into the vagina, which accomplishes nothing except to burn a hole in the vaginal lining, often resulting in severe hemorrhage. After these useless attempts fail, many women decide to have the child, but others eventually make a final desperate contact with an abortionist.

How are abortions done? A majority of abortionists are at least wise enough to know that a D and C is a very tricky operation on a pregnant patient. Even gynecologists, who carry out a legalized abortion during the third month of pregnancy under the best of conditions in a hospital have an extremely healthy respect for this procedure. This means that a nonmedical person operating in an ill-lighted, poorly equipped bedroom, without the aid of anesthesia, blood, or trained personnel is walking a very fine tightrope. It is indeed no exaggeration to say that an experienced gynecologist could lose a patient in such conditions. As a result, abortionists usually try something short of an actual D and C. A favorite method is to insert packing into the cervix (opening into the uterus) in the hope that the irritation will cause the uterus to contract and finally expel the pregnancy. But the danger here is that a small amount of packing has no effect and a large amount will cause a severe hemorrhage.

Another common approach is to inject solutions of soap or other substances into the uterus, using a small catheter (a tubular instrument for inserting into the bladder to remove the urine). This may cause enough irritation to result in contractions. But this method, and any others that are attempted, can have disastrous consequences. Not infrequently, the catheter method causes an air embolism in which air bubbles get into the circulation, resulting in instant death. But it is not only the danger of death that threatens the patient, but also the far-reaching aftereffects; since, in nearly all cases of criminal abortion, some degree of infection occurs. This may result in complete sterility or in chronic pelvic pain which plagues the patient for years and often finally makes a hysterectomy necessary.

What else can go wrong? It depends in part on what is attempted, and how far the abortionist pushes his luck, but certainly hemorrhage leads the list. This is because the wall of a pregnant uterus gradually but surely becomes thinner, softer, and more vascular as the uterus enlarges. At this point the reader might logically ask why it is so tricky to do a D and C on a pregnant uterus when so many patients are advised to have one done following a miscarriage. On the surface this might seem to be a good comparison, but there is a difference of night and day between these two problems. During a spontaneous miscarriage the uterine contractions gradually increase the thickness of the uterine wall; and before the D and C is done, drugs are given to further increase the tone and thickness of this wall. But when the pregnancy is quite normal and the uterus has no intention of giving it up, a vastly different set of rules apply. Here fools often rush in where angels would fear to tread and not only produce uncontrolled bleeding but also perforate the thin uterine wall resulting in further bleeding and the additional complication of peritonitis. And in their clumsy efforts to empty the uterus some further bungle the job by pulling back loops of bowel through the torn uterus.

Women often ask whether there is a pill they can swallow that will cause an abortion. Obviously if one was available doctors and abortionists would use it. It is because of the absence of a simple method of getting rid of a pregnancy that abortionists must resort to these other means of emptying the uterus. To stop this sort of murder countries like Japan, England, and many Communist countries have allowed women a carte blanche approach to abortion. Let's see how it has worked in

Japan since 1948 and in England since 1968. Then let's take a good look at what is currently happening in the United States and Canada.

Legalized Abortion in Japan

In Japan more than one million legal abortions are performed each year. A few years ago, in order to satisfy my curiosity and also to write a story for a national magazine, I visited Japan and traveled more than one thousand miles, discussing the problem with general practitioners, gynecologists, public health officials, hotel managers, and cab drivers. Previous to my criss-crossing of the country I visited the population control center in Tokyo where I asked the crucial question: Why did Japan make abortion legal? The answer was simple. The impending population explosion that is threatening the West became a cruel fact in Japan many years ago. Japan is a nation of limited living space. Ninety-five million people live on islands that are smaller in total area than the state of California. With its 142,688 square miles, Japan is roughly the size of Newfoundland, and only 16 percent of the land is arable. As a result, large families and limited space and resources have bedeviled Japan for centuries. Even a hundred years ago it was common practice to dispose of new and unwanted girl babies by throwing them into the river. But with the aftermath of the Second World War, these age-old population pressures were aggravated beyond measure. In a country impoverished by war, the Japanese government had to find means of dealing with a birthrate that had risen from a prewar rate of 30 per 1,000 to 34 per 1,000 by 1947. Since a cheap, effective contraceptive for the masses was, and is yet to be developed, the only practical solution for the government of that time was to legalize abortion. So in 1948 the Eugenic Protection Law was passed. Although it did not state that any woman could have an abortion upon simple request, it did give the doctor unlimited power to decide who was eligible, without fear of interference.

Why were there no public outcries or impassioned speeches against this law? It is perhaps difficult for the Westerner to comprehend that religious feeling was no real hindrance. Only one-quarter of 1 percent of the population of Japan is Christian. And although the doctors associated with the Christian-supported hospitals were against it, the vast majority of Japanese are either Buddhists or Shintoists, and in these religions the developing baby has no rights until birth. Consequently when abortion was legalized, it was accepted as a practical necessity by the very practical Japanese.

The Eugenic Protection Law is designed to prevent the increase of inferior descendants and to protect the life and health of the mother by either sterilization or abortion. It guides the doctor in determining which of these two operations should be performed in the case of such diseases as schizophrenia, manic-depressive states, mental deficiencies, psychopathic tendencies, degeneration of the nervous systems, muscular degeneration, malformations of the body, epilepsy, blood diseases such as hemophilia and hereditary deafness. Also included, are abnormal sexual desires, repeated criminal offenses, and rape. But it is Section Four of Article Fourteen of the Eugenic Protection Law that gives the doctor practically unlimited freedom, for it states that any pregnancy can be interrupted if the mother's health may be affected seriously by either physical or economic consequences. All the doctor needs is the consent of the patient and her husband. If the husband refuses to say either yes or no or if there is no husband then the woman merely signs the required papers herself. If the woman is either feeble-minded or insane, her husband, guardian, or the mayor of her city may give consent. Applied practically, this clause enables any woman to easily obtain a legalized abortion. For instance, if she already has two or three children it can be argued that another pregnancy will affect her health because of the economic situation. One more mouth to feed would strain the family's budget and food supplies, thereby indirectly affecting the mother's well-being. (It should be remembered that although the Japanese standard of living is the best in the East it is still low by Western standards.) Even though its economy has grown miraculously since the Second World War, the gap between the earned and desired incomes of these able, ambitious people has probably become even wider.

Section Four is open to an even broader interpretation. Newly married working women, for instance, may obtain abortions by arguing that pregnancy will interfere with their work. I also asked the obvious question as to what would happen if a healthy, married woman who was not working and who could well afford to have a family wanted an abortion. I queried a number of doctors on this single point. Most of them stated they usually tried to dissuade such women and delayed referring them to a gynecologist in the hope they would change their minds. Others (and most of them smiled when asked) replied they would most likely arrange an abortion. As one doctor in the Ago Bay district remarked, "Many people in this area suffer from beriberi, which I can always use as my reason." In spite of such comments I had the specific impression that Japanese doctors were as interested in their patient's welfare as doctors elsewhere and that they merely considered that they were protecting their patient from a criminal abortionist by consenting to her wishes.

In rural Japan there is another reason for abortion, and this is the custom of trial marriage. Although this custom is gradually dying out, it is still practiced in many regions. I discussed it with a country doctor in Kashikokima who explained that the man and woman live together on a temporary basis to see whether they are mutually compatible. Usually the man goes to live at his prospective bride's home, sometimes for as long as one or two years. As might be expected, pregnancy often results, and if it occurs before they decide to marry this doctor said he would perform an abortion.

In contrast to North America, where the majority of abortions are illegally performed by unqualified people, all abortions in Japan are done by gynecologists. To obtain his license the gynecologist applies to the medical association, and all other doctors must by law refer patients requiring an abortion to him. One gynecologist in Osaka stated that he regularly performed seven hundred abortions a year. As a result, illegal abortion is very rare. Most hospitals in Japan have a room specifically used for abortions, and most patients are sent home as soon as they recover from the anesthetic. It is also interesting that Japanese doctors perform abortions up to the seventh month of pregnancy, which does not seem to worry them. By Western standards, the fee is extremely low—usually two thousand to three thousand yen—that is, between five and eight dollars. Moreover, this fee includes the cost of the operating room and the anesthetic, which means the Japanese doctor receives roughly two dollars for his work. It also means that Japanese doctors are most unhappy financially, for they earn from one hundred to one hundred and fifty dollars per month, little more than most Japanese workers.

Although Japan's law also applies to foreigners, some gynecologists felt hesitant about stretching it as far for them as they do for their own citizens. Others are willing to do abortions for foreigners under any circumstances. I talked with Dr. Shigeru Murakuni, attending gynecologist at the Sanno Clinic in Tokyo. He said that from a practical standpoint any person journeying to Japan could have an abortion carried out at a private hospital, but the cost would usually be a few hundred dollars. The reason the Japanese help foreigners in this way is because they find it totally impossible to understand our own abortion laws. They want to know why we have no laws to prevent unwanted children in families who are already living far beyond their means. And they ask why it is that we allow women who are morons to continue bearing children who will be morons and who will need institutional care? Furthermore, they argue that if the United States has more than one million illegal abortions yearly the laws are clearly not preventing women from having an abortion performed.

Nearly 100 percent of the people I talked with were convinced that the good points of legalized abortion far outweigh the bad ones. First and foremost, the law has been an effective means of controlling Japan's population. Its present growth is slightly less than 1 percent per year—the lowest in Asia—and much lower than either Canada or the United States. But in spite of this, the Japanese will continue to attempt to stabilize their population expansion. They know it is still increasing at an annual rate of one million people. Their cities are crowded, housing accommodation is difficult, and the arable land is 100 percent cultivated. Wherever there are no industries or homes in Japan, there are rice paddies. They are on the slopes of mountains where the land has been terraced for cultivation, and they are squeezed between industrial buildings on the outskirts of the cities. The land is a constant reminder to the Japanese of the necessity of limiting their population, for every increase is a further strain on their present standard of living and an obstruction to raising it to the much-coveted level of the West. Thus, in their view, legalized abortion goes hand and hand with economic progress. And as stated earlier, since they do not regard it as inconsistent with their moral or religious feelings, it is a socially acceptable procedure. As one taxicab philosopher stated, "It is only democratic that we should have the right to govern the size of our own family. There are some people who just don't want any children. Others want a dozen. Furthermore, I have a choice of who I marry and where I live, so why not the same freedom with one's family?" Most Japanese feel that abortion has done little to change the country's moral standards, and they feel that abolition of the present law would mean a return to illegal abortions performed by incompetent people. I would like to emphasize, however, that none of them believe abortion is the ideal alternative. Nearly all of the doctors I spoke with thought that young women should bear a few children before undergoing abortion, and what they all hope for is the creation of a safe, cheap, and effective means of birth control. Until that time, however, they hope and believe the law will remain.

Legalized Abortion in Great Britain

The Abortion Act, which applies to England, Wales, and Scotland, but not to Northern Ireland, came into effect in April of 1968. Compared to Japan the British Abortion Act is really the same song with a slightly different tune. Basically it states that a pregnancy may be terminated if two registered practitioners believe it will be either a threat to the life of the patient or involves substantial risk to the patient's physical or mental health. It is also noteworthy that an abortion may be done if the pregnancy is a greater risk to the physical or mental health of the existing children than the termination of the pregnancy. And last it permits abortion if there is a reasonable risk that the child will be born with physical or mental abnormalities which will result in a severe handicap to the child.

In the debate in Parliament that preceded the adoption of the abortion bill it was repeatedly stated that the provisions of the Act would not mean that abortion was available on demand. Yet in actual practice this is really what it amounts to. In any legal document it's often possible to interpret the wording one way or another. And in the case of legalized abortion this usually means either a conservative or liberal interpretation. For example, there are some British physicians who are of the opinion that the wording of the Act does permit abortion on demand. They argue that since the mortality rate of abortion carried out in a hospital is lower than that of normal childbirth, the continuation of a normal pregnancy is therefore more dangerous than its termination. So it is often the personal feeling and philosophy of the particular doctor that determines whether an abortion is performed.

It was originally feared that the liberalization of abortion in

England would result in an increased demand for hospital beds. This is exactly what has happened. And some gynecologists believe that because of it other patients who need gynecological surgery have to wait in line too long to get into hospital. It's also quite obvious that abortions can be obtained more easily in certain areas of Britain than in others. London, for instance, has twenty private clinics and tops the list in doing abortions. Liverpool, on the other hand, which is a predominantly Catholic area is at the bottom of the list.

A great number of the abortions in England are carried out in private nursing homes. It is because of these private clinics that London has developed the reputation for being the abortion capital of the world. Several thousand women have come to London from Canada, the United States, Germany, and other countries to have their pregnancies terminated in these private clinics. Foreign women have no choice, because persons who come to Great Britain specifically for medical treatment are not entitled to free care under the National Health Service. Most patients who travel to England for an abortion fly in one day and return home one or two days later. The fee is usually around five hundred dollars, and it's been said that some doctors in London are doing twenty-five abortions a day. It's hardly necessary to have a slide rule to conclude that these doctors are making rather large sums of money. And British doctors who resent the widescale abortions may in part dislike seeing their colleagues getting rich.

Legalized Abortion in the United States

There are few problems in the United States today that are causing more controversy than those surrounding legalized abortion. It is however not something new; it has been smoldering for a long time.

There have been two diverging forces at work both among doctors and the laity. At one end of the pole is a truly "liberal" group that views abortion as simply another means of birth control. But at the other end of the pole there has always been a large conservative group that considers interruption of pregnancy under any circumstances as murder. There is no doubt that this spectrum of views will continue regardless of what the law states. But in recent years there has been an increasing number of groups and individuals who accept the philosophy that a more liberal approach to abortion is one of the great social needs of our time. Like Montaigne they believe that "desperate diseases require desperate cures." It is their feeling that uncontrolled population growth is too monstrous a problem to treat with simple aspirin. They also believe that in a democratic society such as the United States it would not seem appropriate that the proponents of either position be allowed to impose their moral beliefs on the rest of the citizens. Yet they argue that until the present this has been the case with regard to legal abortions. Furthermore, they question why any group should require state law to insure that its members adhere to its moral, ethical, or religious code. And last they point out that they have no intention of trying to force a woman to have an abortion against her will. I, too, share this liberal view.

The Roman Catholic Church has and continues to be the major outspoken critic of abortion on any grounds. This has had a marked effect on formulating the policy of the American Medical Association, which for 96 years has been opposed to easing the restrictions on this procedure except for strict medical reasons. Yet other powerful and persistent forces have been setting the stage for change. One of the foremost organizations has been the Planned Parenthood Association, which follows the philosophy of its president—namely children should result from choice rather than from chance. And other groups such as the American Public Health Association, the American Baptist Convention and other church organizations have also been pressing for change. Some physicians have also played a vital role in bringing this matter to a head by open defiance of the law. One Washington State doctor made the headlines in December of 1969 when he announced in a letter to the Governor that he had performed 140 abortions in direct violation of the state's restrictive laws on this procedure. He finally decided to send this letter after the state legislature killed a bill to ease the legal restrictions on abortion. Then to add more fuel to the fire he hung a "Reproductive Crisis Clinic" sign on his door. Since then the publicity surrounding this letter has resulted in an invitation to the state legislature and also a referendum bill that will be voted on in November of 1970. This bill, like others, would allow termination of pregnancy up to the twentieth week. Other medical organizations such as the American College of Obstetricians and Gynecologists have come out in favor of looking at the patient's total environment in determining whether or not an abortion should be done.

And recently the American Medical Association has finally followed this trend. On June 25, 1970, following hours of debate and despite warnings of mass resignations from thousands of Catholic members, the powerful AMA went on record as condoning abortions on the following grounds. First, the abortion must be performed by a physician in an accredited hospital. Second, two other doctors must sanction the procedure. Thus in a sweeping statement the AMA flatly stated that time had finally come when the decision to do an abortion was basically a decision between the patient and her doctor. Carrying it a step further, it implied that social and economic considerations for the family would be evaluated in determining whether an abortion would be in the best interest of the patient and her family. In other words the issue of whether an additional child would cause unwarranted hardship on the "total family" in terms of either psychological stresses or dollar problems was to be considered. It is noteworthy that this approach has been endorsed by the Student American Medical Association, our future doctors.

History has repeatedly shown that once the pendulum of chance starts to swing it rarely stops halfway. This will undoubtedly happen with legalized abortion because the middle-of-the-road approach or the so-called "reform abortion laws" have proven to be a dismal failure. This is because in some cases reform laws have, for practical purposes, meant no change at all. And in cases where there has been a significant change in policy, it has often resulted in a double standard of justice. In short, usually the rich were looked after and the poor, the very ones who needed help the most, were left without care. Why? Basically because the cost was prohibitive. Most of these reforms were cluttered by regulations that bogged down the solution to a problem which needed quick attention. For example, most states insisted that the patient be seen by one or more psychiatrists, which automatically meant a fee of one hundred dollars. Then added to this were the anesthetists, surgeons, and hospital charges, which brought the total to between five hundred and eight hundred dollars.

Middle-of-the-road abortion laws have also had the subtle effect of making a patient feel like a part-time criminal. Doctors are not immune to it either, for there often were raised eyebrows from their medical confreres or other hospital personnel. In short, the procedure of an elaborate evaluation by psychiatrists, and the appraisal by the hospital abortion committee, conveyed to all the participants that they were doing something morally wrong. But halfway measures also contributed to gross injustice for many women, because it was very difficult to know where one should draw the line. In earlier years the indications for therapeutic abortion were quite specific. Women with severe heart disease, kidney infection, or tuberculosis were looked on as justifiable candidates for the operation. Without an abortion some would have undoubtedly died from the extra burden of a pregnancy. But today it is a different story, for most women do not have such clear-cut problems. This is because medicine has made phenomenal progress in the conquest of many diseases during the last thirty years. The danger has now been removed from tuberculosis; kidney infection can usually be cleared by antibiotics; and surgery can repair many damaged hearts. However, modern medical findings have also made us aware of problems that we were unaware of in the past. For example, in 1941 an Australian eye doctor noted that a large number of children in his district had been born with congenital cataracts. He related this to an outbreak of German measles among the wives of soldiers who lived in two large army camps nearby. When his findings became known to the medical world, other doctors discovered that heart defects, impairment of hearing, and mental retardation could also be caused by this disease, particularly if a woman came down with it in the first three months of pregnancy. But the trouble is that not all women who develop German measles have defective babies, although further research now indicates that there may be a higher incidence of long-term cardiac abnormalities than previously thought. Who will and who won't be affected by the disease is still an unresolved question. This makes it difficult for doctors and patients to decide what to do. Should patients accept the statistics quoted (some estimates run as high as 50 percent) by some doctors, and take a 10 to 30 percent chance that their child may be born with some congenital defect.

Such uncertain odds may be fine if you are betting on a ball game, but many people feel that it is a totally unreasonable approach to the game of life. But so important a decision can only be made after an extremely thorough discussion with your doctor, at which time all the various angles should be discussed. And it is well to bear in mind that what may be a sound approach for one couple may not work at all with another. For example, a thirty-five-year-old woman, who finally becomes pregnant after fifteen years of marriage is hardly a candidate for a therapeutic abortion. On the other hand a twenty-five-year-old woman with four children, who can become pregnant anytime she wishes, presents an entirely different problem. Another difficulty is that it is not easy to diagnose German measles, so there is often an element of doubt as to whether the patient has actually had this infection. This is even more true if the patient does not bother to see the doctor early in the course of the disease. I might say that some women have the mistaken impression that just walking by someone with German measles automatically means something will go wrong with the pregnancy. This is a fallacy, and contacts such as this mean nothing unless the patient actually comes down with the infection. No doubt the whole problem will eventually be resolved, for in all probability a vaccine will be developed that will give life-long immunity to this infection. Until that time comes, however, all doctors agree that young girls should, if possible, be exposed to German measles, since one attack will give life-long immunity. But if a girl is not lucky enough to develop the disease early in life and is exposed to it during a pregnancy, doctors usually advise gamma globulin, in the hope that this will provide temporary immunity. If, in spite of this, German measles makes its appearance, then both the patient and the doctor have to make the difficult decision as to whether or not an abortion should be done.

The majority of legal abortions that are being done today are being performed for psychiatric reasons. A mother with seven children, inadequate finances to run the household, and a husband who comes home drunk several times a week, may have reached the end of the line, and may threaten suicide if she can find no one to help her. Doctors know that this type of woman has no underlying psychiatric disease in the true sense of the word, since a Mediterranean cruise and a million dollars would solve all her problems. But as this kind of prescription is unavailable, an abortion may be the only alternative. Such a patient is in sharp contrast to a woman suffering from a genuine psychiatric disorder, whose only hope is long-term treatment rather than a world cruise. In some cases, patients of this type cannot cope with even one child, and an abortion may be advised either to help the individual or to stop the inheritance of a mental disease. But most women are not in this category, and the abortion is actually done for emotional reasons. Yet although these women do not have mental disease in the true sense of the word, having them seen by a psychiatrist gives it the stamp of authority, particularly when he writes a diagnosis on her record of "reactive depressive state." But the point is how upset does a woman have to be before she is allowed to have a legal abortion for emotional reasons? On the other hand if the abortion is being sought because of bad varicose veins, chronic back trouble, or kidney disease, how bad do these conditions have to be before the patient is allowed this procedure? It's easy to see that man-made arbitrary dividing lines present very perplexing problems.

And there is one other very important variable—who happens to be on the abortion committee at that particular time. In most hospitals the committee consists of a psychiatrist, internist, and a general practitioner. Yet it makes little difference whether the members of the committee are specialists or general practitioners or what their particular specialty happens to be. This is because it is usually their personal philosophy that governs whether or not an abortion should be done. For example, one year patients may be extremely lucky in having a committee composed of very sympathetic doctors. But the next year it may be a different story when the committee is composed of staid, somewhat sanctimonious physicians who have a deeply conditioned prejudice against abortions. And this strong bias against abortions is not limited to the Roman Catholic physicians. In fact, the writer has known a number of Roman Catholic doctors who are more in favor of carrying out a legalized abortion than their Protestant counterparts. But the point I want to get across is that at present, getting the go-ahead with an abortion depends, in part, on luck.

There is another aspect of the abortion committee that is also open to severe criticism. One of the basic principles in the practice of medicine is that doctors should never diagnose a patient's ailment without seeing the patient. It would be just as illogical to try and fix a car without taking it to the mechanic. But when these committees meet, all they do is read a report from the patient's doctor which gives the reasons why she should be allowed to have an abortion. If they turn the request down, in effect they are saying that they are more capable of evaluating the patient from a paper examination than from a medical one. This is poor medicine, in fact it could be looked upon as malpractice, and one would expect doctors to have better sense. If doctors are going to assume the function of gatekeepers in deciding who should and should not have abortion, then they must also assume the responsibility of seeing the patient. But what if they did see the unfortunate patient? The law is still asking the doctors to put on the collar of a clergyman, the wig of a judge, the robe of a philosopher, and assume the stance of a sociologist. An increasing number of doctors resent this pluralistic role when their only desire is to wear a surgical gown. Furthermore, it's been aptly pointed out that the decision of a committee is usually a decision that nobody believes and for which no one is responsible. And lastly, there is ample justification to ask why the civil rights of a woman is dependent on her state of health?

More American doctors therefore feel that the only logical solution to this complex problem is to take the simple approach—let the patient and her doctor decide on the pros and cons of an abortion without the hindrance of any third party. But behind this approach lies the deeper feeling—why should a woman be pregnant when she does not want to be? Is it not her fundamental right to decide for herself whether or not she wants a child?

Many American doctors also point out that it was not until the nineteenth century that the matter of an abortion was covered by any statutory law in any country in the world. The first law was actually passed in England in 1803. And in the United States it was not until 1829 that New York State passed a law to the effect an abortion could be carried out for the preservation of the life of a mother. Doctors argue that these early laws were not meant to prevent the procuring of abortion, but rather to guard the health and life of the mother against the hazards of abortions in those days. In short the risk to the pregnant woman was too great to allow an abortion in most cases. One must remember that it was not until the mid-nineteenth century that anesthesia and bacteria were discovered, and blood banks and antibiotics were not available until after 1900. So one can argue that these early abortion laws restricting abortions except to protect the life of a mother did make good sense. But now in view of the advances in medicine, many American doctors believe they make no sense at all. In other words American women no longer need to be protected from the dangers of terminating a pregnancy.

The courts of the United States sensing both the public's changing attitude and restlessness on this matter are now acting to implement changes in the existing legislation. In the past three years, sixty new laws have gone through the state legislatures and five of these occurred in the first four months of 1970. It means that over the next few years many states will revise their laws on abortion and the present differences among the various states will eventually disappear. But at the moment major variations do occur and for practical reasons one can classify the states into three different groups.

In three states—Hawaii, Alaska, and New York—abortion is virtually on demand with only minor variations among these states. For instance, in New York an abortion may be performed by any licensed physician within the first twenty-four weeks of pregnancy, and there are no residency requirements. In Hawaii and Alaska abortions can be terminated up to approximately six months, but in both states there is a ninety-day residency requirement.

Approximately nineteen other states have gone further than requiring merely a threat to the mother's life. They will allow an abortion if the mother's physical or mental health would be impaired. Then, depending on the state, other provisos are added. For example, some allow abortion if there is reason to believe the baby will be born with a physical or mental defect. Others allow abortion if the pergnancy results from rape or incest. Still others have a residency requirement that is sometimes as long as 120 days. And one state, Georgia, requires a bona fide legal residence certified under oath. Finally nearly all of these states require that two or three doctors approve the procedure.

Of the remaining states, about twenty-eight of them permit abortion only when there is a threat to the mother's life. Yet many American doctors believe that in the foreseeable future these states will also change toward more liberalized laws. And it is the writer's opinion that it is only a matter of time before every woman in every state of the United States will be able to have an abortion on demand. Therefore let us take a more detailed look at one of the states where abortion is currently available on demand.

New York State knocked down virtually every prohibitive control on abortion on July 1, 1970. The new law meant that any woman could request an abortion prior to the twenty-fourth week of pregnancy. It also implied that women own their own bodies and did not require the consent of their husbands. Yet most doctors that I've spoken to feel that at least for the sake of marital harmony it would be advisable to have both parties consent. Similarly, although any girl over seventeen could sign on her own, it seemed sensible to most doctors that the parent should also consent to it if they were aware of the pregnancy. Actually from a practical, economic standpoint many seventeen-year-old girls would have to inform their parents anyway, unless they had the means to pay the hospital and other expenses themselves. What about the girl under seventeen years of age? Even here it is not mandatory that the doctor inform the parents if the girl wishes it that way. But at this age it was the feeling of the majority of physicians that a psychiatrist should interview the girl to make certain she was mentally competent to make up her own mind. Yet nearly all doctors felt that if the girl was old enough to get pregnant she was also old enough to have an abortion. Consultations among doctors also went out the window with the New York law. Furthermore, there is nothing that states the abortion must be done in a hospital. Yet from a practical standpoint there is every reason to believe all legalized abortions for the present will be done in hospitals. First, the state medical society and the health code recommends that it be done in an area with supportive measures, namely where blood transfusions and anesthesia are available. Second, doctor's malpractice insurance may not cover the physician unless he performs it in a hospital. Third, it appears that health insurance payments will be paid only if the doctor uses hospital facilities.

Just what effect this will have on existing hospital facilities in New York State and eventually in other areas is impossible to predict at the moment. Some of the most outspoken critics of abortion have flatly stated it will simply turn the hospitals into abortion mills. Other American doctors feel that it will merely create an initial strain on the hospital beds until a more efficient system is developed to handle abortions. It is also apparent that some hospitals will bear the burden, since there is nothing in the law to force either Catholic hospitals or doctors to perform therapeutic abortions. So at the moment there are differing opinions as to how long residents of New York State will have to wait for a hospital bed. And there is also the question of the fate of those women from other parts of the United States and Canada who endeavor to seek abortions in this state which has no residency requirements. Again it's an imponderable question. I suppose in the final analysis much will depend on the ingenuity of the patient. Those who arrange for their own doctor to refer them to a New York physician will have an obvious advantage. Yet it's quite likely that resourceful and persistent patients who telephone enough doctors will sooner or later find one who will acquiesce to their request. But the acquiring of an abortion should not become a hit-or-miss affair when legislatures have made a law allowing its citizens the right of this operation. It is here that American medicine faces a great and urgent challenge. Surely it is a rather lame argument that there are not enough beds or doctors to do it. Countries like Japan, Russia, and other

Communist nations have been able to do it. And if untrained backroom abortionists can do an estimated one million abortions a year, surely America's 250,000 physicians can find the means of accomplishing the same thing. It will merely take some creative thinking on the part of the nation's doctors to develop a new approach to abortion. At the Battle of Trafalgar Admiral Nelson told his commanders to forget the rule in the Admiralties rule book that said battle line must always run parallel to the enemies' fleet. Instead he attacked at right angles, thereby cutting Villeneuve's line into three sections, which he then destroyed. It is people with imagination and ability to try new approaches who change history and get things done.

One can also ask: Is the abortion problem and solution really that difficult? Some centers have already changed their traditional approach to abortion with excellent results. For instance, Johns Hopkins and the University of California Medical Center in San Francisco have started outpatient clinics. These "come-and-go" facilities mean that patients leave the recovery room in about three and a half hours, rather than the usual thirty-seven-hour hospital stay. This simple routine of arriving for an abortion in the morning and leaving in the afternoon saves everyone a great deal of time and money. For the mother with six children and no one to help out, it solves the home crisis. But more important, it will insure that no one requesting an abortion gets left out in the cold because of lack of hospital beds. The time factor is also vital. An abortion is not like an acute appendix that must be removed in a few hours. But on the other hand, it can't be left like varicose veins for many months. All too frequently women procrastinate in consulting a doctor until the third month of the pregnancy. In these cases every additional day makes the procedure a much more difficult technical task, and waiting to be admitted for a hospital bed could mean the difference between having it done and not doing it. Outpatient clinics could be the answer to this problem.

It would be irresponsible if both the public and doctors did not take a hard look at the cost factor for abortions. It is just bad economics to pay more for anything than is necessary, and in the case of abortions the current high costs of five hundred to eight hundred dollars for a few minutes work seems out of proportion and, as mentioned earlier, too often results in a double standard of justice. Until now abortions, by and large, have been the privilege of the well-to-do. If you had enough money to fly to London or Japan the abortion was a *fait accompli.* Or in some cases it meant merely sufficient funds for the opinion of two private psychiatrists. Just whether those states such as New York will see to it that along with the liberalization of its laws it will also insure that lack of money is no barrier to abortion is still problematical. In reply to my question on this point, one professor of gynecology stated that in many of the large city hospitals there were actually more beds available for indigent patients than for private patients and that social insurance of one kind or another was available to all. Consequently on the surface it would appear that those who need abortions the most will have access to them. Whether it works out in practice remains to be seen. But in an era when American scientists can put men on the moon, one would logically think American medicine can find the ways and means to develop a fair and speedy solution to legalized abortion. It has taken too long a time for the passage of this legislation for them to fumble the ball.

On the other hand it may well be that worrying about the availability of abortions is merely wasting one's time. I say this because many Canadian doctors have already received notices telling them where they can send their patients for abortions in New York State. The doctors sending them say they will charge anywhere from nothing to eight hundred dollars. But one must question whether this blatant advertising for business by a few American physicians is because of their deep convictions on this matter or is related to the great profit that can ensue to them? At any rate it does point up the urgent need for the standardization of laws both in the United States and Canada so that women do not become somewhat like wandering minstrels in the search of abortions. In addition, uniformity of laws throughout the United States would obviously ease the hospital pressures in those states that will bear the brunt of the attack. It is not an understatement to say that hospitals in New York State are frankly worried as to whether or not they can adequately handle the demand. In fact one Buffalo hospital, predicting a marked increase in the number of Canadians crossing the border, stated it would only accept those east of the Welland Canal (a waterway connecting Lake Erie with Lake Ontario). So it looks as though Canadian women will have to quickly find convenient addresses east of the Welland Canal. And just as important as geography, they will have to be smart enough to get to the doctor early in the pregnancy.

At this point the reader might be interested in knowing how abortions are terminated. During early pregnancy (up to about fourteen weeks) a therapeutic abortion is achieved by D and C (Dilatation and Curettage), an operation which has already been described elsewhere in this book. A newer method of termination consists of removing the contents of the uterus by means of a vacuum-suction apparatus. The stay in the hospital after either procedure is usually no more than twenty-four hours, and it is not unknown for the patient to return home on the day of the D and C. Some doctors are not in favor of such a short hospital stay, but there are social considerations to take into account. With newer, wider abortion laws, it is sometimes necessary for a single woman to conceal her operation from her family circle and business, and this means that she cannot be away from home for too long. These patients are advised to consult the doctor if they feel feverish or develop pain, heavy bleeding, or a troublesome vaginal discharge. Between the fourteenth and twentieth weeks of pregnancy, therapeutic abortion is sometimes carried out by injecting a special saline solution into the uterine cavity. Other doctors prefer to carry out an operation called a hysterotomy. In this procedure after any incision is made in the abdomen a second cut is made through the uterus and the baby removed in the same manner as if a caesarean section were being done. This method is particularly desirable if the patient also wishes to be sterilized at the same time. Like all operations any type of termination of pregnancy has a certain amount of risk, even when carried out in the right surroundings by trained doctors. But this risk is extremely small and should not stop women from having it carried out when there are good indications for doing so.

In addition to the technical details of abortion, much attention and time will have to be spent on the educational aspects. For instance, one of America's foremost gynecologists has stressed that many Negroes in New York State are not happy with the new law. To them it represents a form of genocide, a sinister plot by the white population to diminish their numbers. It is problems like this which will take much more time and effort to solve than the simple act of doing the abortion.

But regardless of the above problems, this major shift in abortion policy is well on its way to becoming a reality in many states. And much more will be shortly clarified when the United States Supreme Court rules on the constitutional rights of the states in this matter. For example, the Supreme Court of one state has ruled that the phrase in their statute which allows for an abortion only when "necessary to preserve" the mother's life was unconstitutional because it was too vague and uncertain. Yet the court of another state with a large Catholic population has upheld the constitutionality of its state law against a charge of vagueness. How the United States Supreme Court will handle this matter is not known. But it is generally believed they will rule it unconstitutional for any state to refuse an abortion. It is difficult to imagine any other decision in view of the public's present attitude that whether or not a woman wishes a child is a fundamental right. But coupled with this individual freedom is the public's awareness that unless we stabilize the world's population, even modern technology cannot solve the pressing problems of pollution, adequate housing, and education. And it is also becoming increasingly apparent that we do not live on a large planet with unlimited resources. Shortages of fresh water, electricity, natural gas, and oil are the first rumblings of a problem that could become a major crisis in the decades ahead. It is all of these factors that are presently swaying both legislators and physicians to look at the abortion problem, not as a moral, ethical, religious, or even possibly a medical one, but rather a social need of our time.

It would be wrong, of course, to consider abortion a good thing for all. Doctors who advocate abortion realize it is not a utopian approach, and must be looked on as a stop-gap measure. Admittedly the ideal and most effective way to control the population explosion is by continuing research to find a safe, cheap, and effective contraceptive. But even with improved methods of contraception, there will always be some women who fail to take these precautions. And at the moment, contraception does not work 100 percent of the time. In this practical world we have to accept things as they are, not as we wish they were, and, therefore, use abortion as a second line of defense against unwanted pregnancies. Yet the opponents to abortion refuse to see any good in it, and are much like the reporter who interviewed Winston Churchill while he was building a wall around his Chartwell home. During the conversation the reporter pointed out that the wall was crooked. Churchill replied, "Of course it's crooked, any fool can see what's wrong. But can't you see what's right?"

These powerful forces, however, will continue their relentless fight against the rights of women to have an abortion. They will decry the procedures as a murderous act that infringes on the rights of the unborn child. Perhaps those who carry on a seemingly endless debate about the fine points of religion and morality might be well advised to consider Joseph Stalin's attitude toward religion when considering a very practical problem. During the Second World War, when things were going badly, Churchill and Roosevelt met with Stalin, not only to assess the situation, but also to reassure Stalin of the eventual success of the Allied cause. They argued that right would eventually win and that, after all, the Pope was on their side. Stalin quickly asked, "How many divisions does the Pope have?" Stalin, although he had few virtues, could nevertheless quickly pinpoint the realities of a situation that required more troops and less prayer. It is also somewhat paradoxical that most of the people who want to scuttle this procedure are men who neither bear these children, nor look after their infinite daily needs for so many years. I have often thought that if the tables were turned and the theologians, doctors, and politicians were in that unenviable position that the laws would be changed overnight. Fortunately it takes little foresight to see that the tide of history is moving toward total freedom of choice in limiting the size of families. In fact the day is not far off when society will take the next step and rule that pregnancy is a privilege and not a natural right. This means that the size of the family will be strictly limited by law, and couples who could pass on a severe inherited disease to their children will not be allowed to do so. But in the meantime unwanted children and sometimes diseased children are going to be born, and their mothers and families will suffer needlessly because of it. It's unfortunate that much of this will result merely because of bad luck. For instance, many women will live in states that still have very restricted laws on abortion. Others, even though they live in one of the very liberal states, will find it inconvenient, difficult, and sometimes impossible to get an abortion. This may be due to lack of hospital beds or a shortage of sympathetic doctors. It takes more than merely passing a law to get things done. In fact, the true spirit of these liberal laws may not come into being for a few years until our current medical students, who are much more aware of the priorities of our society, graduate. It will seem ludicrous to them that there seems to be more respect for the rights of the unborn fetus than the inherent rights of those neglected children who are already with us.

The writer is not naive enough to think that unlimited abortion on demand and greater utilization of contraception will quickly alleviate all of our problems. But it will at least help to slow our population growth and give us a breathing spell and a chance to catch up on problems that have been long in the making. It would be equally naive if the opponents of abortion thought that there would be no more fires in the slums of our cities and that unwanted, unloved, and uncared for children will not help to kindle the flames. Surely when law enforcement officers and town planners state that for security reasons future generations may be forced to live in guarded, walled apartment complexes, it is time to start curing the ills that will make this necessary. Since man has a great desire to survive, there is still good reason to speculate that he will finally rise to the occasion and endeavor to make this a better world for more people. In making such a decision he will have to realize that one cannot be all things to all men and that abortion, although distasteful to some, is merely one of the practical ways to reach that goal. But, if bigotry and ignorance overcome these forces of change, he will race more quickly to his doom. And when nuclear war, famine, or civil strife occurs there will be no point in his looking for a scapegoat on which to lay the blame. Rather he will have to conclude that man and not his environment caused his downfall. In *Julius Caesar*, Cassius hammered this most basic fact home to Brutus when he counseled him, "The fault, dear Brutus, is not in our stars, but in ourselves."

Legalized Abortion in Canada

Canada, as the United States, is currently witnessing some heated debates on abortion, and major changes have already taken place. But I would strongly suggest that you first read the section on therapeutic abortion in the United States. This is because I covered the philosophical and practical aspects of this subject in detail at that time, and since this applies to both countries it would be repetitious to repeat them here. I did so in that section, not because of the size of the United States, but because the American problem is more complicated and encompasses the entire range of thinking on this matter. For example, some states have very restrictive laws. Other states are extremely liberal. Still others have middle-of-the-road laws. This gave me the opportunity to show the reader the various pros and cons of the different approaches to abortion in that country and equally important, to emphasize why I and an increasing number of doctors feel that abortion-on-demand is the only simple and effective way to handle this problem. But some Canadian doctors believe the patient should not be able to demand an abortion anymore than they should be allowed to demand a hysterectomy or that you amputate one leg. Yet a closer look would indicate that this is not a good comparison. Admittedly an unnecessary hysterectomy is subjecting the person to an unwarranted surgical risk, but this is not so with a therapeutic abortion, which is such a relatively safe procedure and which also relieves the patient of unnecessary worry. Possibly it would be a good idea if we all started to use the term abortion-on-request, rather than abortion-on-demand. Everyone, including doctors, tends to get his fur a bit ruffled by anyone demanding anything. A polite request would undoubtedly be a better approach for all parties.

The Canadian stand on this sensitive subject is much more standard than that existing in the United States. The one big exception is French Canada, where to all intents and purposes there are no abortions carried out in Quebec's French-speaking hospitals. This has resulted in a great strain being put on the few English hospitals that do them. It should also be pointed out to the American reader that Canada has a large Catholic population and therefore the political situation in this country is more complicated than in the United States. Yet Canadian doctors are quite similar to their U.S. colleagues, in that they, too, are very divided in their opinion on this hot issue. At the moment a relatively small minority supports the principle that abortion is the fundamental right of all women. These doctors are rarely applauded and usually draw criticism in this nation of diverse religious doctrines. This is, of course, to be expected; for Canadians, as all people, resent change—even in noncontroversial matters. And the doctors who feel this procedure has great merits for controlling population growth and protecting the rights of women, are, nevertheless, taking a risky position. Yet often one has to accept an element of risk in this life if one believes he is working toward a justifiable goal. Possibly one seasoned Canadian business man summed that position up as well as anyone when he said that if he were presented with a suggestion that did not have a bit of risk associated with it, it was most likely a poor idea.

Prior to the amendment of the criminal code in Canada doctors performed a very limited number of therapeutic abortions. This was because there was no law to guide them as to what they could do or could not do. Caught in such a no-man's land, most doctors did the obvious thing and played it safe by not doing them. And the few doctors who did an occasional one always kept the Alek Bourne case of 1938 in mind. Doctor Bourne, a prominent English gynecologist, intentionally carried out an abortion on a fourteen-year-old girl who had become pregnant as the result of rape. Mr. Justice MacNaughten held that the crown had to prove whether the abortion had been done in good faith to preserve the life of the mother. The learned justice concluded on page 619 of Volume 3 of the 1938 *All England Reports:* "If the doctor is of opinion on reasonable grounds and with adequate knowledge, that the probable consequent of the continuance of the pregnancy will be to make the woman a physical or mental wreck, the jury are quite entitled to take the view that the doctor who, in those circumstances, and in that honest belief, operates, is operating for the purpose of preserving the life of the woman." In short, in the Bourne case the necessity of preserving the mother's life was held to be a defense to procuring an abortion, although such a defense was in no way mentioned in the relevant English statute.

The amendment to Section 237 of the Criminal Code of Canada, which came into effect in August 1969 has had two major results. First, it put into statutory law a policy that had actually been followed since 1938. Second, having finally become a law rather than a loose policy, it has put doctors on more solid ground; and, therefore, some physicians have become more adventuresome in doing them. The law also spells out the steps that must be taken before the doctor can perform an abortion. For instance, an abortion must be performed by a qualified doctor and only in an approved hospital. Furthermore, the abortion must also be approved by the majority of a therapeutic abortion committee consisting of at least three physicians. These doctors must decide that an abortion is in the interests of a patient's physical and/or mental health.

These regulations are basically the same as those in those U.S. states that have middle-of-the-road abortion laws. In essence it's neither fish nor fowl and results in a grossly unjust and inefficient system. In one sense, however, this law could be effective in spite of its faults, if Canadian doctors would look after their own morals, rather than those of their colleagues. In a Canada with two major cultures one could hardly expect the French Canadians to march down the street waving banners favoring abortion-on-demand. But conversely non-Catholic groups have descended on Ottawa demanding that abortion should be a decision reached by the patient and her doctor. Diverse as these viewpoints are, the Canadian law can still satisfy both camps. Those patients who do not wish an abortion are not compelled to have one, anymore than they are forced to live in a particular city or marry a blond or a brunet. Similarly those doctors who decry the operation need not perform it. But those patients and doctors who see it as a humanitarian act are well covered by the law. Yet to think that people would accept such a utopian approach to this controversial subject is obviously unrealistic. The main obstacle is the refusal of the antiabortionists to let the proabortionists organize an efficient system for performing them. Let's take a look at some of the obstacles that are currently making a mockery of abortion in Canada.

The writer unfortunately has to direct a good deal of the criticism at the medical profession. This is because many doctors who are not opposed to abortion are nevertheless afraid to rock the boat for fear of personal criticism. It is well to remember that most physicians in non-Catholic hospitals are Protestants and could very easily endorse a liberal abortion policy for their hospital. Yet in many instances this silent majority has sat on the fence and said nothing. Another problem is that hospital administrators (the great majority are not doctors) have always been in a difficult situation when dealing with physicians. In most instances, whether they are giving advice on a new addition to the hospital or changing the color of a hospital chart, they are damned if they do and damned if they don't. Consequently, for their own survival, they try to steer a middle course in their attempt to keep as many doctors happy as is humanly possible. This means that they, too, do not push for more efficient systems to handle the increased demand for this procedure simply because it will surely produce some form of reaction from the staff doctors.

What about the hospital's board of governors, for this is actually the final high court that dictates hospital policy? These boards are composed of respected members of the community and come from all walks of life. They receive no compensation for their services and are to be congratulated for spending long hours on hospital affairs. And certainly a number of these boards did move quickly to go through the necessary steps to set up an abortion committee so that they could look after the needs of the community. But many others have been slow to act, partly because many of its elder members still consider abortion a somewhat nefarious act. Thus large numbers of women flock to the large cities and in particular to the university-affiliated hospitals. The result has been too many people for too few beds.

Large numbers of women are therefore given the disquieting news that the quota is full and advised to come back in six weeks' time. This is rather impractical advice, for when a patient is ten weeks pregnant she requires immediate attention, not a delay of six weeks. The result is that women frantically begin to look for other hospitals and other doctors. They are often helped by the Planned Parenthood Association, which points them in the right direction.

It is a mockery of justice that Canadian women should have to wander like gypsies in search of an abortion. Particularly when the public conscience of this nation has manifested itself in a change in the law, and, equally as important, when the answer is so simple. The problem could be solved overnight by appointing only those physicians who believe it is a woman's fundamental right to decide whether or not she wants a child to abortion committees. It would admittedly be a sham committee, but it would solve the dilemma in a country with divided religious opinions. Furthermore, even now the committee is a ritualistic farce, for 99 percent of the time, after all the red tape has been gone through, they allow the doctor to perform it. It much reminds me of the story of the Zuni tribe who realized that the rain dance didn't bring on the rain, but it at least made the tribe feel better. In a similar vein there is little doubt that Canada's pseudoconscience will require a somewhat similar rain dance, namely a therapeutic abortion committee, to make everyone feel better. But it is vital that at least they pick sympathetic doctors to sit on that committee. It is equally paramount that Canada and the United States develop come-and-go abortion facilities to alleviate the acute bed shortage. These come-and-go centers will also help to fend off the attacks of criticism from the antiabortionists who contend that abortion cases cause a delay for patients having other surgery done. The writer is somewhat sympathetic to that approach, for it can be argued that irresponsible patients who repeatedly become pregnant should not inconvenience responsible citizens who need surgery to repair varicose veins and hernias. But looking at it from another angle one could argue that population control and human rights are much more important than varicose veins. Furthermore,there is equal justification for suggesting that irresponsible girls who repeatedly become pregnant take precedent over responsible citizens, for these people will bring up irresponsible children putting an even greater strain on our already overburdened social services. But regardless of the pros and cons as to who has first right to any bed, the basic point remains that it is illogical for most abortion patients to stay in a hospital overnight. If patients can return home after having all their teeth extracted and if children can be sent home immediately after a tonsilectomy, then it is equally logical that therapeutic abortion cases can return home after a few hours.

It is often argued that Canada, a vast country with relatively few people, needs a larger population to ensure its own survival for both economic and military reasons. In fact France has recently decided that it requires fifty million more people for the same reasons. It would appear that old-wives' tales are not limited to medical problems. One has only to look at India and South America to realize that the sheer numbers game does not necessarily mean either affluence or power. Furthermore, atomic weapons have also dealt the numbers theory a final military blow. Certainly if one has the awesome potential to kill three hundred million Chinese, such a blow will also send the other three hundred million on the long walk. It should also be pointed out that not all nations of the world should develop their full population potential. If this happens how can countries send excess food to already overpopulated areas? Canada and all nations should take a hard look at the world's population clock, not just their own old-fashioned time-piece. It could be that Canada, which is well-respected in international circles, should stress upon its own population and that of the world community that nations should pursue quality rather than quantity. No nation is in greater balance than when its own individual members are happy enjoying the pleasures of a balanced family.

CHAPTER IX

Sterility

IT WAS ONCE ASKED, "How many angels can dance on the point of a very fine needle without jostling each other?" Just as there is no good answer to this question, there is a similar lack of adequate answers to some of the puzzles of infertility. Childless marriages present doctors with one of the most frustrating enigmas in gynecology. The enormity of the problem becomes clear when you realize that one in ten marriages are childless. Or to put it another way—there are over three million infertile couples in Canada and the United States.

One of life's worst tragedies occurs when a child is born into a family that does not want it. This happens all too often in our society, and is undoubtedly a major cause of juvenile delinquency and the increasing violence in our cities. Children, like apples, can become rotten if they do not receive the proper attention. But it is enormously satisfying to bring a child into the world knowing that it will at least start its life being loved and cared for. So to compensate for the occasional disappointments of working on fertility cases, there are fortunately many occasions when one achieves the reward of a much-desired pregnancy. Of course, when a doctor starts to treat a sterile patient, he can never be sure of the outcome. A woman who has a benign fibroid or ovarian cyst can be told without any reservation that surgery will solve her problem, but there can be no such guarantee for the successful outcome of a sterility case. In addition, patients must realize that the time required for adequate treatment can take many months. It may appear to the reader that I am painting a rather bleak picture of this subject, but this is not my intention. What I want to emphasize is that no doctor can wave a magic wand, and be certain of achieving either quick results or ultimate success. But the fact remains that many such stories do have happy endings in the form of one or more bouncing babies, and I trust this chapter will show how the correction of certain conditions can help accomplish this.

Yet it must also be admitted that sometimes the outcome is the result of a little luck. Even the street dog has its lucky days, and doctors and others are no exception. Napoleon Bonaparte was once asked by his commanders to promote a particularly brilliant officer. After being informed of all the man's excellent qualifications at the military academies Napoleon replied "Fine, but *est-il chanceux?*" (Is he lucky?) A little luck doesn't do any of us any harm.

What are the ingredients essential to a pregnancy? So far as we know three conditions must be met. First, the wife must produce the egg around the mid-point of her cycle—that is, halfway between periods at about the fourteenth day. Second, the husband must have an adequate number of sperm. Third, there must be a free passageway, so that the sperm and egg can reach each other. It sounds simple, and usually is a fairly straightforward process. Most couples can have a child within the first year of marriage if they decide to start their family immediately.

Why is it, then, that some healthy young couples fail to have a child? Not infrequently doctors see distraught young people who think something must be terribly wrong because they are getting no results. Fortunately, in the majority of cases nothing is seriously amiss. They have simply failed to remember a few important points about conception. For instance, the two important ingredients, the sperm and egg, must come together at the proper time, and there is only one chance each month. And not only is there just this single opportunity, but also it only lasts for a few hours. The sperm appears to be the hardier of the two, because it can be seen in the vagina for as long as five days after intercourse, although by this time its numbers may be so reduced that they are incapable of starting a pregnancy. The egg, in contrast, only lasts about twelve hours, and if it does not meet the sperm during this time it dies. Is it so strange, then, that it can take a number of months, or even a year or two, for a pregnancy to occur? There are about 720 hours in a month, and during only 12 of these is it possible for the sperm and egg to get together. Furthermore, although most women ovulate (produce an egg) regularly each month, a few women do not. Usually, failure to ovulate is a temporary affair, but if it lasts a number of months there is absolutely no way that a woman can become pregnant during that time. I have described this process in detail to show that pregnancy cannot be achieved as easily and surely as flicking on a light switch. Husbands who are on shift work or who spend a considerable amount of time away from home on business, with wives who also have jobs, frequently cannot manage to get together at the right time for a period of many months. This means that patients frequently push the panic button too soon. Whereas, with a bit more planning and patience, a pregnancy would eventually occur.

Many women have the mistaken idea that failure to become pregnant is always due to some deficiency in them. But this is not so, since about one-third of such cases are caused by the husband. Frequently, the realization of this fact comes as a shock, not so much to the woman, as to the man, who seems to consider himself far removed from such a stigma of failure. Some women seem quite reluctant even to discuss this possibility with their husbands. And indeed, when the subject is finally broached to the man of the family, it seems to come as a terrible blow to his ego. But it is extremely important to first rule out the husband as the possible cause of infertility, for there is little point in subjecting a woman to extensive tests if it is later shown that the husband is the responsible partner. Consequently, let's first talk about the husband and then later discuss the common reasons for infertility in women.

The Husband

To determine whether anything is wrong with the male partner is a fairly simple thing. Doctors merely have to find out whether he is producing an adequate amount of sperm. This can be done in several ways, but one of the most frequent tests used is referred to as the "post-coital test," which means that the sperm is tested following intercourse. The husband and wife are asked to have relations anywhere from three to six hours before the wife visits her doctor. The mucous just inside the cervical canal (opening into the uterus) is then placed on a glass slide, and examined microscopically to see whether or not sperm are present. This is certainly the most important part of the test, for without sperm there can be no pregnancy. Yet many doctors also place a great deal of emphasis on whether the sperm are active, how long they live, and whether or not most of the sperm appear normal. (My readers may be interested to know that at the time of ejaculation the husband deposits about *five hundred million sperm* in the vaginal canal. And yet it takes only one of these sperm to fertilize the egg!)

Why are some men unable to produce sperm or adequate amounts of sperm? Some men are either born without organs of reproduction or with defective ones. The testicles, which produce the sperm and the male hormones, are normally present in the scrotum. Some men are born without them, which makes them permanently sterile. Another difficulty is the undescended testicle. Before birth, the testicles gradually descend from the abdominal cavity into the scrotum. In a few men they fail to reach the scrotum and either stay in the abdomen or stop somewhere between the abdomen and scrotum. Sometimes only one testicle is involved, at other times both may fail to descend. This will be apparent at birth, but fortunately, in most cases, the testicles will frequently continue to descend during the first year of life, and then finally reach their normal position in the scrotum. If they do not, surgery is advised, because the increased temperature inside the abdomen appears to harm the ability of the testicles to produce sperm. But normal location does not necessarily imply normal function. For instance, the testicles may be in the scrotum and still fail to manufacture adequate numbers of sperm. Why this is the case is still a puzzle.

But there are many other reasons for male sterility beside birth abnormalities. Infections, such as gonorrhea, used to constitute a major problem, but in recent years, with the wide use of antibiotics and penicillin, the disease less frequently reaches an acute form, and is therefore less likely to cause permanent damage. Another infection, mumps, may cause infertility if the germ localizes in the testicles. Such diseases as diabetes and an underactive thyroid may also be responsible for male sterility. Injury to the male reproductive organs may occur in various ways and may result in damage to either the testicles which manufacture the sperm, the ducts that transport the sperm to the outside, or to the penis. Whether permanent sterility results will, of course, depend on the severity of the injury. As the reader might suspect, severe war injuries can result in extensive damage which is often irreparable.

In the event that a specimen of male semen fails to show any sperm, one of two things may be at fault. First, the male testicles may not be manufacturing sperm; and if this is the case there is nothing that can be done to change the situation. Second, the male testicles may be producing adequate numbers of sperm, but there may be a blockage in the tube called the vas deferens that carries the seminal fluid away from the testicles. This may have become blocked by a previous disease, such as gonorrhea, or by a congenital defect. In order to determine what is at fault, doctors then do a testicular biopsy in which a small piece of the testicle is removed and examined microscopically to see whether the gland is normal. If it is normal, the fault must be in the vas deferens, and surgery may be advised to cure the obstruction. In most of the cases, however, sperm are present but are just not being produced in adequate numbers.

Exactly what "adequate numbers" means is a debatable point, for men vary in their production of sperm, sometimes by many millions. For example, most men will produce about one hundred million sperm per cubic centimeter, and since the total ejaculate may reach anywhere from five to ten centimeters, a single act of intercourse may then be responsible for one billion sperm. For several years the average lower limit of good fertility has been looked on as sixty million sperm per cubic centimeter, but in recent years doctors have lowered this limit to about thirty million sperm. In the case of individuals whose sperm production is low, the reader might justifiably ask whether there is any way to increase the male production of spermatozoa. I can only reply that many drugs and other methods have been tried, but up to the present day there has been no method found to achieve this. On the other hand, the reader should remember that it takes only one sperm to fertilize an egg. Therefore, so long as the male partner is producing even a limited amount of sperm, there is always some hope of pregnancy. I mention this because doctors see men whose sperm counts are high and whose wives are quite healthy, but who still cannot achieve a pregnancy. Conversely, they also see men with low sperm counts whose wives sooner or later become pregnant. But let us now discuss some of the female causes of infertility and what can frequently be done to correct them.

The Wife

As I have already said, approximately two thirds of the problems of infertility are due to women. Tracking down the causes is done in a very systematic way. During his patient's first visit, the doctor will take a detailed history and will ask questions regarding her present and past health, which may help to pinpoint the diagnosis. For example, a history of a ruptured appendix at the age of ten may mean blocked tubes. Current symptoms, such as painful periods or abnormal bleeding, may mean trouble with the female organs, such as infection or endometriosis. But frequently nothing is found in the patient's story to indicate where the trouble lies. Consequently, the next step is the physical and pelvic examination, but here again the majority of patients will be found to be quite healthy. Other tests follow, such as routine urinalysis, blood determinations, chest X rays and, lastly, tests to determine whether the tubes are open and whether the patient is ovulating. We will talk more about these later as we discuss the various problems that commonly cause infertility.

Congenital Problems

One of the doctor's first steps in evaluating the infertile woman is to do a pelvic examination to determine whether the female organs are present and, if so, whether they are normal. Congenital (birth) defects occur because during the development of the unborn child the female organs are bilateral, that is, there are two halves of each organ on either side of the body. During the course of prenatal development these structures come together, so that at birth there is only one vagina, one cervix, one uterus. The tubes and ovaries, however, remain double.

Various types of problems may arise from incomplete fusion

of the pelvic organs. For example some women will have a double vagina with a complete septum, a partition of tissue down the middle. Sometimes this septum is off to one side, resulting in one small vagina and one normal-sized vagina. Other women may have a double cervix (opening into the uterus). Still others may have a double uterus, or a single uterus with a thick septum dividing the uterus into two parts. Not infrequently these variations in the anatomical structure of the female organs are of no importance, for women will become pregnant just the same, and deliver a normal child. At other times, however, a septum which divides the uterus in half will be responsible for repeated miscarriages. When this occurs, surgical removal of the septum will frequently result in the patient carrying the child to term.

On rare occasions women may be born without some of the female organs. For example the uterus or ovaries may be absent, and when this happens pregnancy is impossible. As the reader will recall pregnancy is the result of a number of factors, and if one important link of the chain is missing, it is impossible for a pregnancy to occur. For example, if the ovaries are present and producing eggs, but the uterus is absent, there is no place for the pregnancy to develop. Conversely, if the uterus is present but the ovaries are absent, there are no eggs being developed; and without eggs there can be no pregnancy. Fortunately, absence of the female organs is an extremely rare happening, and I mention such a possibility merely for the reader's information.

Ovarian Problems

Since the production of the egg each month (ovulation) is carried out by the ovaries, it is essential that they remain in a healthy state to function properly. Doctors therefore have to determine whether or not ovulation is taking place. In general, if the periods are fairly regular, it is safe to go on the assumption that ovulation is occurring. On the other hand, when the periods are very irregular ovulation may not be taking place, and various tests have to be carried out to see if this is the case. Some doctors will perform an endometrial biopsy, which means removing a small piece of tissue from inside the uterus. This can be done in the doctor's office, just before an expected period begins. Following ovulation the glandular pattern of the endometrium changes, and therefore it's possible to determine if ovulation has taken place by miscroscopic study of this tissue. Other doctors will elect to do a D and C for the same reason. Still others will advise the use of temperature charts. Patients are asked to take either their oral or rectal temperature as soon as they awaken in the morning. Since the temperature increases slightly following ovulation, and remains elevated until the period occurs, the exact time of ovulation can sometimes be determined. Planned intercourse at this time may result in a pregnancy.

Ovarian cysts may now and then stop ovulation. When a doctor finds an ovarian cyst about the size of an orange in a young girl, he usually waits a few weeks before he decides whether an operation is necessary. This is because occasionally a cyst of this size will form during the normal course of a monthly cycle, and a few weeks later will entirely disappear. If it does not, surgery may be advised to remove it, leaving the rest of the ovary intact. This usually clears up the trouble and ovulation returns.

What else can doctors do when ovulation fails, and the ovary seems normal? Sometimes the problem and its answer are both apparent. A girl I had known for years as a slim and striking young lady came to my office a few months after her marriage. It was immediately obvious that once the wedding ring had been slipped on her finger, she had thrown caution and good sense to the wind. Now, many tea parties later, she was a plump, unattractive woman, fifty pounds heavier, and was only having a period every few months. In some way obesity upsets the finely balanced hormonal applecart and not only do the periods become infrequent and irregular, but ovulation stops. In the case of this young woman, it was only when she checked her desire to constantly nibble at food and managed to lose weight that she eventually became pregnant.

Emotional problems can also have a profound impact on the menstrual cycle. One has to admit, however, there are large numbers of women with multiple problems who nevertheless continue to ovulate and have repeated pregnancies. Yet now and then doctors do see patients with irregular periods and apparent lack of ovulation who go away on a vacation with their husbands and manage to come back pregnant. Whether they would have also become pregnant at home is hard to say.

But the most perplexing problem of all has always been the big question of why some women's bodies consistently refuse to produce an egg when none of these other problems are present? What to do in these circumstances has always taxed the ingenuity of doctors. Usually they try a variety of drugs in an endeavor to stimulate the ovaries. Frequently, patients are given the female hormones, estrogen and progesterone, for a few months. Other patients, who have a low metabolic rate, get thyroid to speed up the body's metabolism. Still others, whose adrenal glands are producing too much male hormone, receive cortisone to slow the gland down. Yet, all too often, everything proves an exercise in futility.

Thousands of these women may now be helped by a new drug, "clomiphene citrate," which is a chemical compound. Some women who have never before produced an egg are now doing so with its assistance. Just how many women it has helped is still a partial question mark. But since 1967, when the United States Food and Drug Administration granted approval to market clomiphene citrate, many women using it have become pregnant. In fact, sometimes it produces eggs so well that women who have hoped for one child have unexpectedly given birth to triplets and quadruplets. Fortunately, most multiple births, should they occur at all, only result in twins. And since doctors are finding out more about this drug each day, they will undoubtedly soon find a way to stop multiple births from occurring.

How clomiphene citrate produces an egg is still not known, but some facts are clear. Women with poorly developed ovaries that are producing very little of the female hormone, usually do not react to the drug. This is what one would expect, for it's logical that you can't stimulate a very weak ovary any more easily than you can make a tired horse run. But most researchers believe that the pituitary gland is usually the main reason why ovulation fails in the first place. A weak pituitary just can't prod the ovaries sufficiently to make them ovulate. In some way clomiphene citrate manages to give this gland the necessary shot in the arm.

Yet regardless of how clomiphene works, there's no point in using it if less potent drugs will do the trick. Doctors don't prescribe morphine for headaches. Similarly, they reserve clomiphene for those women who do not respond to other drugs, such as thyroid, cortisone, or the female hormones, estrogen and progesterone. Before it is given, doctors also have to be certain that the infertility is due to a failure of ovulation—not to something else. And even clomiphene will do nothing for the woman who earlier in life had a ruptured appendix, with severe peritonitis, that blocked both Fallopian tubes. It also goes without saying that the drug is useless if the husband is sterile. In fact, it is only when all the ground rules for giving clomiphene have been satisfied that doctors will use it. Usually, patients start taking it on the fifth day of the period every day for five days. If ovulation occurs, it normally does so about six to twelve days after stopping the drug. If it does not, the drug can be tried for another couple of months. If still nothing happens, the present opinion is that there is no point in continuing its use.

One problem that seems to be made to order for clomiphene is the so-called "Stein-Leventhal Syndrome." In 1935, these two doctors made an interesting discovery. During surgery they noticed that some infertile women with a long history of infrequent, irregular periods and sterility, had a much thicker outer covering to the ovaries than those who had borne children. The doctors reasoned correctly that although this was neither a painful nor dangerous problem, it was causing infertility, because the egg could not become fertilized, since it was unable to break through this tough fibrous layer. Then when Stein cut into these ovaries he clinched their diagnosis when he saw numerous small cysts containing the eggs lined up underneath the ovarian surface. This was the proof he needed that the eggs were literally trapped inside the ovary and had no chance of ever being fertilized. Since these swollen ovaries looked as though they were bursting at the seams, Stein and Leventhal did the next logical thing. They cut out a pie-shaped segment in each ovary and then stitched the ovaries back together. Not only did this release the pressure, it also released some eggs, although doctors are still not certain why this is the case. And with the initiation of regular periods and ovulation, about eight out of ten of these women became pregnant. Now doctors use clomiphene citrate for patients with this complication, and reserve surgery for those who fail to respond to the drug. There is little doubt that research will unlock the door to many of the other problems of sterility. But in the meantime, the discovery of clomiphene citrate has brought hope and happiness to thousands of couples who previously had no chance of ever having children.

Blocked Tubes

This is one of the common causes of infertility and may result from a variety of problems such as pelvic infections, endometriosis (internal bleeding), ruptured appendix, and previous surgery. For centuries the main cause was pelvic infection due to gonorrhea, but today, due to the widespread use of penicillin and other antibiotics, this condition is seen much less frequently.

In order to determine whether the Fallopian tubes are open, doctors do a test called a "tubal insufflation," which is an attempt to pass air through the tubes. This is done by inserting a small plastic tube into the cervix and then introducing small amounts of air into the uterus, using various degrees of pressure. When patients are told they are going to have air passed through the Fallopian tubes they usually worry that it is going to be quite painful and are then surprised to find out that it causes little, if any, discomfort. Some patients may find that following the test they have slight pain in the stomach or in one shoulder. This is because the air in the abdominal cavity rises and collects under the diaphragm, which sometimes irritates the phrenic nerve, resulting in shoulder pain. However, it is usually not severe, and even if present, only lasts a few hours. Actually, the presence of a little shoulder pain is encouraging, since it confirms, along with the gauges on the gas machine, that the tubes are definitely open. Not infrequently, it is necessary to carry out this test on more than one occasion since, with extremely nervous patients, the tubes may go into a temporary spasm and the air will not pass through them. But if after repeated attempts, the air still fails to pass through the tubes, the doctor will inject a "contrast liquid" (a dye which is put into the tubes, so that X rays will show up) into the uterus, to see if they can find the area of obstruction. This test is carried out in the radiology department of a hospital, and it is possible to follow the course of the dye by both fluorscope technique, and by X rays. If the tubes are open, X rays will show dye in the general abdominal cavity. If, on the other hand, one or both tubes are blocked, the X rays will show the point of obstruction. In some cases, only one tube will be shown to be blocked, so that pregnancy can still occur through the other tube. But should both tubes be obstructed, surgery may be advised in an attempt to open them.

Other Problems

Up until now we have been talking about difficulties which if not corrected, totally preclude a pregnancy. But there are many problems in gynecology which are far from being a matter of black and white, and which may or may not have some bearing on whether a woman becomes pregnant.

Chronic Cervicitis, for instance, refers to a rawness around the opening into the uterus. This is an extremely common problem, and about 30 percent of the women who suffer from it are born with the condition. The remainder acquire it following a pregnancy. As we mentioned earlier, at the time of delivery the cervix becomes greatly dilated to allow for the birth of the infant. It is this stretching that may injure the cervix slightly, which may leave the area reddened and raw-looking. It is highly unlikely that this problem has much, if any, bearing on future pregnancies but, during the course of an infertility workup, doctors will usually cauterize the area to insure adequate healing.

Endometriosis (internal bleeding), on the other hand, does seem to have some connection with infertility. The reader will recall that the menstrual bleeding results from the sloughing off of the inside lining of the uterus and, under normal conditions, this endometrial lining is present only in the cavity of the uterus. Patients with endometriosis, however, have endometrium not only in the uterus but also outside it. Consequently, when the normally placed endometrium bleeds from stimulation by the ovaries, the endometrium abnormally placed outside of the uterus also bleeds. The problem is simply this: the blood inside the uterus escapes normally by way of the vagina, whereas the blood on the *outside* of the uterus is literally trapped inside the abdomen. It is this trapped blood that causes scarring around the pelvic organs which may be very mild, or quite extensive. Sometimes the scarring causes kinking and blockage of the tubes. At other times the tubes are totally normal, but the patient still fails to get pregnant for reasons which are not always known. Although endometriosis was formerly thought to be a rare disease, doctors now know it is extremely common. In fact, gynecologists state that 20 percent of the patients on whom they operate have endometriosis. They have also made one other interesting observation. Women who married late, or who postpone having children, are more likely to have endometriosis than those women who marry early and have children at a younger age. It appears that in some way early interruption of the periods by a pregnancy seems to decrease the overall chance of getting endometriosis. Fortunately, the majority of women with endometriosis have no trouble becoming pregnant, but about 25 percent do, and when this happens treatment is required. Sometimes hormones are given in large enough doses to stop the menstrual periods for a number of months. This is advisable because by stopping the periods no internal bleeding can occur and the areas of endometriosis will have a chance to heal. Other patients who have extensive endometriosis may require surgery to correct it, which involves cauterizing or cutting away the areas of endometriosis, removing adhesions from around the tubes, suspending the uterus in its proper position, and doing a "presacral and uterosacral neurectomy," which involves cutting the nerves that run from the uterus, thus decreasing the possibility of period pain. As a result of this procedure, a large number of patients do become pregnant.

Fibroid Tumors are a less common cause of infertility since they are more apt to occur after the child-bearing years are finished. But when these benign growths occur in young women they may, in some cases, distort the normal contour of the uterus and result in either infertility or repeated miscarriages. But there are exceptions to every rule, and all surgeons will recall patients who had massive fibroids and yet went through their pregnancy without any complications. If, on the other hand, repeated miscarriages occur, an operation called a "myomectomy" will be advised, in which the growths are removed and the uterus left intact.

Ineffectual Sexual Technique is an infrequent cause of sterility, but it is occasionally responsible for it. I recall one patient who consulted me after ten years of marriage, in which pregnancy had never been achieved. Both husband and wife stated that they had normal sexual relations. But examination of the wife showed a nearly complete closure of the vaginal opening by the hymen which made it impossible to have normal intercourse. For ten years the only contact had been between the thighs. An operation was performed to remove the hymen, along with an adequate explanation of their problem, and a pregnancy resulted within a few months.

In a large number of patients the doctor fails to find any reason for the infertility. The tubes are open, the patient is ovulating, and the sperm appear healthy. In addition, none of the other problems that I have just mentioned are present, and why a pregnancy does not occur is unknown. Fortunately, in many cases continued patience will sooner or later bring results. If it does not, the question of whether or not to adopt a baby usually comes up. This of course is an individual problem, but I think it is fair to say that most couples finally decide to adopt a child if they are getting along in years and realize that they should start their family as soon as possible. I don't believe there is much point in discussing adoption in detail, except to stress one aspect of it which I think most couples overlook. When such a decision is taken, 99 percent of women want to adopt an infant who is either a few weeks or a few months old. There is no doubt that adoption agencies now do a tremendously good job in trying to fit the right couple with the right child, but it has always been the writer's opinion that it is totally impossible to assess a child until he reaches somewhere between one and two years of age. By this time, the personality of the child begins to become apparent, along with certain physical features. Consequently, adopting a child at this age involves less risk, and I am sure that over the long run it will prove just as satisfying. And yet the writer is not naive enough to believe that women will quickly change their opinions in this matter.

CHAPTER X

Common Symptoms in Female Diseases

Before I start to discuss the various complaints of women I would like to tell the reader a story to help emphasize how this particular chapter should be interpreted. During my final year at the Harvard Medical School, one renowned surgeon drove home a point I have never forgotten, and I hope the reader will be equally impressed by this incident. This much-respected teacher was conducting surgical rounds with a few of us would-be doctors when he came across a patient who had recently undergone surgery. None of us knew what had been done, but we were told she had been admitted to hospital with low right-sided abdominal pain, vomiting and moderate fever. He then asked one of the students to list the various diseases that could cause these symptoms and no doubt trying to impress the professor with his wealth of knowledge, the first disease the student mentioned was cancer of the large bowel. Before he could proceed further he was abruptly interrupted. "If you walked outside your house and saw water on the road what would you think had happened?" the professor asked him. The student, whose ego was a little ruffled by this question, thought a moment and replied that it must have rained. "Right," answered the surgeon, "Ninety-nine percent of the time you would be correct in assuming it had rained, not that a water truck had passed by to clean the road. Therefore," he continued, "why don't you apply the same common-sense logic to this case? The most common cause of right lower quadrant pain in a patient of this age is appendicitis, not a cancer of the bowel. Always think of the common things first."

This student made the mistake of letting his mind jump immediately to the thought of a rare and serious disease. He would find out later on that cancer patients would constitute only a small fraction of his practice, and that most doctors would starve if they had to rely on malignancies to make a living. It is no wonder, therefore, that women who have not had the benefit of years of medical training and experience should make the same error as this student. But being forewarned is forearmed, so I hope those of you who read this chapter will bear this story in mind and remember that the majority of symptoms are due to minor, not major diseases.

It is equally important to remember that not only do these minor problems occur more frequently, but also they have the same set of symptoms as the more serious diseases. It has to be this way, because there are many diseases, but relatively few symptoms; so it is impossible to have a group of symptoms for minor diseases and another group for major diseases. There are just not enough symptoms to go around. For example, the "big three" symptoms, pelvic pain, abnormal bleeding, and discharge can be present in the most simple trivial problem, or in the most serious one. And as I have been repeatedly saying —*don't* compare your symptoms with those of another woman. And lastly, remember that symptoms are only part of the story. The final diagnosis depends on what your doctor finds during pelvic examination.

Before I leave the subject of symptoms, there is one other "don't" I would like to stress: When a symptom occurs, *don't* take several months to make up your mind to see the doctor. That does not mean you should run to the office for every small variation that occurs. Obviously if the period lasts one day longer on just one occasion or if it's slightly more painful for a month or two there is no point in getting yourself tied up in a knot about it. These minor changes can be considered as well within normal limits. After all if you don't pass urine every four hours or have a bowel movement every twenty-four hours you don't start worrying about it. So there is also no need to fret about the occasional slight alteration in the menstrual period. But if suddenly bleeding lasts for several more days than it normally does, or if the periods are consistently heavier, longer, or more frequent, get the doctor's opinion about it. And remember that there are some things that should be looked into even if they happen just once. For example, if bleeding occurs after intercourse and this has never happened before, don't wait for a second time. If you think you have a significant symptom, a quick decision to see the doctor is the only realistic approach. I say this for two reasons. First, if the symptom is bothersome and causing tension, failure to see the doctor will result in continued worry. This is unfortunate because most of the problems will turn out to be ones that are of no importance and are easily cured. Second, on those rare occasions when the condition is found to be serious, the longer it's left, the more difficult it will be to treat. Yet I've known some very intelligent women who procrastinate for months because they can't get down to the business of making up their mind. This common human trait of putting things off to tomorrow has always been the path of least resistance, but it's also well known that indecision may get you into a pile of trouble. Jean Buridan, a fourteenth-century philosopher, told the story of a certain jackass with a high intelligence quotient that was placed midway between two equally attractive bundles of hay; he died of starvation because he couldn't choose between them. It's important for patients not to fall into the same foolish trap.

What about the women who don't have any symptoms? Your best safeguard here is a regular yearly checkup. Through the activities of the Cancer Society and other organizations, the new generation of women has become more conditioned to the concept of an annual examination. But when I ask some of the older women when they had their last pelvic examination, they frequently reply, "When I had my last baby, Doctor, twenty years ago." Fortunately, most of these women have been lucky and nothing serious has happened to them. But frequently one finds bothersome minor problems which, if treated, could have made their lives much more pleasant.

The routine, yearly checkup, whether or not symptoms are present, provides one additional benefit. Benign problems, such as fibroids, may gradually increase in size over a period of years. If this happens, and your doctor is aware of the growth's presence, it is much easier to remove it before it attains a large size. But women who procrastinate about seeing their doctor, may find when an examination is eventually done that even though they have no symptoms, a large fibroid or ovarian cyst is present, which would have been much easier to remove earlier.

A few women complain of the inconvenience of a yearly checkup, but they would be well advised to follow the philosophy of the streetcorner merchant who once said, "What I lose on the bananas I make up for on the peanuts."

Pelvic Pain

Throughout this book I have been emphasizing that pelvic pain, which is a very common symptom in gynecology, is often a most confusing and difficult condition to evaluate. Many years ago, while I was vacationing at a summer resort, a patient of mine checked into the same hotel. I had been seeing this particular woman for a number of years and treating her for a variety of rather nonspecific complaints, foremost of which was an almost constant nagging backache. Yet during her stay at the hotel I frequently saw her on the golf course, swinging her clubs far more vigorously than most of her companions. It became obvious, as I had long suspected, that most of her pain was due to the boring routine of her daily chores.

"Housewife's Battle-Fatigue" is a syndrome well known by an doctors. Yet doctors not only see variations in the severity of pain in the same individual, but also from patient to patient. Some women complain bitterly about a small amount of pain, while others can tolerate a reasonably large amount with relative ease. One of the main problems that confronts gynecologists are those women who complain of severe pelvic pain, and yet on repeated pelvic examination nothing can be found wrong with them. Most of these women have been to different doctors and in and out of several hospitals, without ever finding a cause for their trouble. In addition, quite a number have had one or more operations, and usually, on checking the operative report, it is apparent that the surgeon discovered nothing of significance. These women have what doctors refer to as a "low pain threshold," that is, they do not tolerate pain very well. Just what produces this particular type of pain is often impossible to say. At times, it may be due to muscle or bowel spasm that triggers the sensation of pain, yet there is little doubt that in the majority of cases the cause of the pain is largely above the neck.

Like anyone else, patients who suffer from a low pain threshold can develop a condition which requires surgery. And when this happens, doctors proceed with the operation knowing full well that they will be sailing into rough waters. I say this because every doctor is aware that once the operation is over he will more than earn his fees listening to his patient's multiple complaints.

Let me give you some idea of what can happen. A couple of years ago, a patient came to my office with her oversolicitous husband. She had just moved to our city and a month earlier had been discharged from hospital following a hysterectomy for a fibroid uterus. Now she was complaining of abdominal pain. I examined her and found absolutely nothing wrong except that a small dressing still covered her incision. I gently removed it, and during this process she fiercely clutched the sides of the table and clenched her teeth. She was the perfect example of a patient who could not stand even a small amount of pain. I don't doubt that after her operation her doctor must have wished that he had taken a slow boat to China.

On another occasion, a patient of mine following an operation for the removal of an ovarian cyst was complaining of much more discomfort than one would normally expect to run into. I had always suspected that she had a low pain threshold, and my opinion was confirmed when she insisted on an injection of morphine before allowing removal of her stitches. Luckily, the majority of patients are not like this; but these two cases at least will show the reader the other side of the coin. The sad part is that these women have about as much chance of changing their personality as the leopard has of getting rid of his spots. Shakespeare was even more explicit when he wrote in *Twelfth Night*, "such as we are made of, such we be."

Another type of patient who is hard to diagnose is the woman who does have some minor pelvic trouble, but the pain seems totally out of proportion to the findings on pelvic examination. For instance, a mild inflammation of the tubes may be present, which should cause little if any discomfort. After seeing this type of patient for a few weeks, the doctor often comes to the conclusion that 25 percent of the pain is in the pelvic region, but 75 percent is certainly somewhere else. And although it is often difficult to know what specifically is troubling these women, sooner or later most will tell the doctor what is really bothering them. And as I have said before, it usually boils down to too much work and too little fun in their lives.

Some patients, on the other hand, are quite happy, well-adjusted women with genuine pain which may be caused by any one of the conditions described in this book. Some of the problems, such as internal bleeding (endometriosis), are more likely to cause pain during the period. Others, like chronic infection, may result in constant pain which is increased during the bleeding. Still others, like large ovarian cysts, may produce a constant feeling of pressure in the lower abdomen. And it may be well to again repeat that 99 percent of pelvic pain, is *not* due to cancer. When cancer pain does occur it is usually a late sign, for early cancer is quite painless. Waiting for pain to occur before consulting a doctor is therefore one of the worst mistakes a patient can make, should a malignancy be present. It is much the same as closing the barn door after the horse has already bolted.

Painful periods are discussed in a separate chapter, so I'll only mention them briefly here. Most women realize that it is quite common and normal to have slight discomfort at this time. Even moderate cramps may be of little significance if they have been present for years without getting worse. But, should pain develop when previously there was none, or should it gradually or suddenly increase, it may be a signal that something is wrong with the pelvic organs and an examination should be done.

Ovulation pain is discussed in more detail in Chapter I, so I'll merely remind the reader that a few women notice slight pain, usually on one side about halfway between the periods. Sometimes it is on the right side one month, and the left side the following month, but there may be many months when there is absolutely no pain. Normally, the discomfort lasts a few hours and occurs because when the egg escapes from the ovary the small amount of fluid in the sac surrounding the egg is also discharged, and temporarily irritates the sensitive inside lining of the pelvic cavity. It produces a mild localized peritonitis.

Another fairly common sensation, which can hardly be called a pain, is a heavy, or bearing-down feeling in the vagina, as if something were falling out. Elderly women are more likely to complain about feeling it when they stand or at the end of a busy day. On questioning them one finds they have had either large babies, difficult labors, or numerous pregnancies. This sensation is usually the result of a fallen bladder, less frequently a fallen uterus, or a combination of both. As we will see later, many of these women also complain that when they cough, sneeze, or perform any strenuous activity they lose a small amount of urine.

I trust the reader will now understand that pain can be a most elusive symptom to nail down, for no two people react the same way to the same amount of pain. Furthermore, there is no way to measure pain, and it is therefore much more difficult to interpret than abnormal bleeding or discharge, which doctors can see with their own eyes.

Abnormal Bleeding

Since this is another of the major female disorders and one which all women experience at some stage of their lives, I have dealt with it exhaustively in other sections of this book. Therefore, for a detailed description of the various types of abnormal bleeding I refer you to the two chapters on the subject (XIII and XIV), as well as Chapters III and IV, which deal with both menstruation and the menopause.

Discharge

Vaginal discharge is by far the most common pelvic complaint; but although it causes a great deal of annoyance, it is usually not due to serious disease. Many women fail to realize it is quite normal to have an average amount of discharge for, without it, the vaginal lining would dry up, and intercourse would be impossible. Furthermore, no two women have the same amount of discharge, just as some men are bald and others have large amounts of hair. Equally important, no two women react to it in the same way. Doctors frequently see patients who have copious amounts of discharge but are completely unaware of its presence. Conversely, they also see women with scanty, normal discharge who complain bitterly about it.

When is discharge normal and when is it abnormal? Normal discharge is usually colorless or white, without any significant odor, and does not cause itching either in the vagina or at the vaginal entrance. Some women frequently notice slight staining on their underclothing, but if it is not bothersome, it is usually of no significance. On the other hand women who, after a number of years, suddenly notice a discharge for the first time, or an increase in the amount of discharge, should have it checked. So should patients who notice a change in its color or who develop troublesome irritation. The problems that commonly cause discharge are discussed in Chapter XVII, so I'll merely give the reader a bird's-eye view of it here.

Chronic Cervicitis, a rawness at the opening into the uterus, is one of the major causes of discharge. During childbirth the cervix undergoes tremendous stretching and although it gradually shrinks back to normal size it is frequently left with varying amounts of raw tissue at its opening. It is not serious, and a simple cauterization of the cervix, which takes about one minute in your doctor's office, will clear it up.

Vaginal Infections are the other main reasons for increased discharge, and there is also a much greater chance that there will be varying degrees of itching and irritation associated with it. The main offender is a small unicellular organism which goes by the technical name "trichomonas"; and, although it is not a serious infection, there is no doubt that it is the most annoying one that doctors treat. It is still not certain how women become infected, but the condition is so common that hardly a day goes by without seeing one or more women suffering from it. It is also a bit of an enigma, since some women have this infection and are in no way bothered by its presence. Yet the majority of women do have some troublesome discharge and itching. Treatment consists of either taking drugs by mouth, or inserting either creams or suppositories into the vagina. Unfortunately, the infection is one that often recurs, and repeated courses of treatment are then needed to cure it. Another less common infection is due to a yeastlike fungus called *monilia albicans,* which results in marked vaginal irritation. Fortunately, this infection quickly responds to treatment and is much less likely to recur. Lastly, bacterial infections are responsible for a few cases of vaginal discharge.

Now and then doctors see more unusual reasons for vaginal discharge. An elderly patient once arrived at my office complaining of vaginal pain and discharge of several years duration. Examination revealed an old ring pessary that had been placed in her vagina ten years previously. She had then moved to another city, and had completely forgotten about it. On another occasion, the cause for excessive, foul-smelling discharge was found to be a lost tampon. And this happened to a graduate nurse!

Doctors may suggest douches, depending on the reason for the discharge as well as on their own personal attitudes toward this form of treatment. For instance, following an office cauterization of the cervix, douches are frequently advised for a number of weeks while the area is healing. This helps to remove excessive discharge and many doctors believe it also speeds up the healing. Vaginal infections, conversely, can be adequately treated by drugs without resorting to douches. The reader is advised to read Chapter XVIII, on "Personal Hygiene" which discusses this topic in more detail.

Painful Intercourse

In Chapter V, I pointed out that some women enter marriage very poorly prepared for the physical side of married life. Some come from strict homes where discussion of sex has been taboo. Others have repeatedly been told by their mothers that sex is hateful and something they have to endure. Still others have either heard various old wives' tales about sex or have been the victim of an unpleasant sexual encounter early in life. Sometimes it is possible to get these women to accept and enjoy the sexual side of their marriage, once they can be made to understand why they have developed a fear of it. But every doctor sees cases where their ingrained prejudices are so deep that it is impossible to remove them, even with prolonged psychiatric care. And when this happens, such women have to learn to live with their difficulty, just as other people may have to put up with rheumatism or any other chronic annoyance. Fortunately, since prudishness is largely a thing of the past, an increasing number of girls receive a more logical explanation of sex prior to their marriage than in former years. One might also argue that nowadays we have erred in the other direction, and may be talking a little bit too much about the subject. In fact, when one takes a long look at much of contemporary literature, and such entertainment media as film and TV, one wonders if we are not developing an almost pathological obsession with the subject.

Doctors also see patients who suddenly start to complain about physical relations after many years of marriage. In the majority of cases, it is fairly easy to pinpoint the trouble, but some people have so many troubles in this area that it would take a carload of psychiatrists, marriage counselors, and economists to attempt to straighten them out. In talking to some women, it becomes quite obvious that they have been indifferent to sex all their married lives, and eventually their experience of it reaches the point where it psychologically starts to produce pain. Certainly, one difficulty in trying to determine the cause of such trouble is that most women are rather loath to talk about it. Most will vehemently deny that anything is wrong with their marriage during the initial interview. Nevertheless, a great number will admit after a few visits that they are experiencing marital difficulties. Some women have merely become tired of their husbands and the responsibility of marriage and wish they had not become tied down at so early an age. Others will tell a long tale of woe about either drunken husbands or suspected infidelity. Yet sometimes the cause of the trouble is extremely obscure, and it is only after repeated visits that finally the doctor can put his finger on it. For instance, I vividly recall a patient who repeatedly denied that anything was wrong with her marriage. But after numerous interviews she happened to mention that she was worried about her ten-year-old son, who had failed his year at school. She went on to recall that her husband flew into a rage when he heard about it. He had given the boy a beating and, since then, had refused to talk to him. As the reader would suspect, it was just after this incident that the woman found intercourse painful. Such a story points up the fact that what may be extremely obvious to an outsider may be totally unapparent to the person involved.

At other times, though, from the moment a patient walks into one's office, an instant diagnosis is possible. For example, take a twenty-five-year-old girl who looks forty years of age, who has borne five children in rapid succession, and who is living in constant fear of another pregnancy. But all such cases point to a single diagnosis. There is nothing wrong with the patient concerned except what could be (literally) cured by a change of life and an alleviation of her responsibilities. Such a prescription would make painful intercourse a thing of the past. But let us now turn our attention to those cases where the problems are truly of a physical nature.

The Rigid Hymen. A friend of mine, who is a gynecologist in a well-known honeymoon city, once told me that during the course of a year he sees a good number of couples who are distraught because of their inability to have intercourse. Their first night has been a nightmare, and after repeated unsuccessful attempts at penetration they have finally given up and sought help. By this time, the entrance of the vagina is bruised and sore because the fibrous ring at the vaginal entrance, called the hymen, is too rigid. Fortunately this does not happen often, because in 99 percent of cases the hymen is quite soft and pliable, and easily pushed out of the way.

But it does point out the need for premarital examination so that, should it be necessary, the hymenal ring can be cut a few weeks before the marriage. Most gynecologists could count on one hand the number of times this has been necessary, because even the most rigid hymen can usually be gradually dilated by just inserting the second finger into the vagina and pushing back towards the rectum. Repeating this a few times is normally all that is required. But it is much better to have explanations of this kind before marriage rather than after it. For further information on this subject, see Chapter V.

Vaginal Infections can also cause varying degrees of pain on intercourse depending on the type and severity of the infection. For instance, the most common infection, which is called "trichomonas," only causes pain when a particularly bad infection is present. But there are some infections, such as fungus, which almost always cause not only marked pain on intercourse, but also intense itching. This is because the vaginal walls become quite inflamed, and any irritation, such as that produced by intercourse, just adds additional trouble. A cut finger certainly heals quicker and with less pain if it is not constantly rubbed. Chapter XVII provides a more detailed rescription of these infections.

The Aging Vagina can also be the culprit in causing pain during intercourse, particularly in women past the menopause. A full description of this condition, and of its treatment and cure will be found in Chapter III and Chapters X and XVII.

Pelvic Infection and Pelvic Endometriosis can also be the cause of pain during intercourse. Although they are two entirely different diseases, they nevertheless cause many identical symptoms. In addition, both diseases frequently cause injury to the ligaments that lie at the very end of the vagina, so that any pressure on them, such as would occur in intercourse, will produce pain. It is not necessary for me to enter into a discussion regarding these two diseases here, since full details regarding them will be found in Chapter XIV.

Backache

Most women with backache do not suffer from it because of pelvic disease. It is important to realize this point, since so many women who visit a doctor because of this trouble are convinced something is wrong with the female organs. Sometimes the examination will show that a pelvic disease is present, but nine times out of ten it is still not causing the back pain. Rather, the symptoms are due to some muscular or bony trouble in the back, obesity, poor posture, or pressure on a nerve. And while we're talking about misconceptions, we may as well throw some cold water on another one. Backache can result from kidney disease, but for every woman who ends up with this diagnosis, a thousand other women do not have anything wrong with the kidneys.

Pelvic Disease. Let's first talk about the one woman in ten who has a backache that may in part result from pelvic disease. And again, contrary to what most women believe, a tipped uterus does not, on its own, cause backache. A tipped uterus is no more physically important than whether a woman has brown or red hair. It is only when a tipped uterus is associated with pelvic infections or endometriosis (internal bleeding), that it produces adhesions, pulling the uterus backwards, so that backache may occur. But it is the adhesions and scarring that produce the pain, not the tipped uterus. Other problems, such as large fibroids, may cause a nagging sensation in the low back. But unlike regular backaches that can occur at any time, the backache of pelvic disease is much more likely to be associated with a menstrual period. But it is also important for the reader to remember that most women with menstrual backache do not have any serious pelvic disease. Once again it points to the wisdom of submitting to a pelvic examination to ascertain what pains are important and what pains are of no significance. Now we will turn our attention to that large group of patients who do have backache but no pelvic disease.

Osteoporosis. Gynecologists in recent years have become particularly interested in a problem called "osteoporosis," because it occurs four times more frequently in women than in men, and may be partly related to lack of the female hormone estrogen. Most women used to die before this condition had a chance to develop, but now, with her increasing life span, it has been estimated that one woman in four over fifty years of age has osteoporosis which may cause backache, a decrease in height, and some curvature of the spine. Each day of our lives, our bones are constantly producing new bone, but also losing old bone. Usually this process is in a state of equilibrium, so that the hardness and strength of the bones remain the same. In later life, however, this process gets out of balance, and more bone is lost than is built up, so that the bones, particularly the long vertebrae of the back, become thin, more transparent on X-ray examination and, equally important, more brittle. Old ladies with fractured hips are ample evidence of this fact.

The biggest puzzle is to find out what triggers this loss of calcium from the bones, and here there is considerable debate. Some believe it may be related to dietary intake of calcium or to the fact that we do not absorb calcium from the bowel so easily as we age. Many others believe this negative calcium balance is due to lack of estrogen, since patients receiving estrogen have shown a progressive increase in the density of the spinal bones. This, along with the improved sense of well-being that occurs with estrogen, frequently removes the nagging pain in the lower back. But an ounce of prevention is still worth a pound of cure, so many doctors now automatically advise women at the menopause to take a hormone pill of estrogen every day for three weeks out of every month for the rest of their lives. There is little doubt that this helps to prevent the hunchback, stooping appearance that many aging women develop. And as the reader will see in Chapter III, there are also many additional advantages to long-term estrogen therapy.

Arthritis is another problem that is often responsible for a dull nagging sensation in the lower back, particularly in women who weigh one hundred pounds on their wedding day and later tip the scales at two hundred. Arthritis is a word that, possibly second to cancer, strikes fear in the hearts of most people, for they immediately envision themselves sitting in a wheelchair. It is wrong to think this way, for many people fail to realize there are two kinds of arthritis. The less common one, "rheumatoid arthritis," is the inflammatory type, and although it occasionally cripples, early treatment and new drugs can now usually handle even this difficult problem. The more common type, "osteoarthritis," is the one we are concerned with here. As we age, our skin wrinkles, the teeth decay, and everyone develops some arthritis in the bones we move most and the ones which bear the most weight. The low back is therefore a favorite spot for this wear-and-tear arthritis, but normally the small amount present does not cause pain, and unless an X ray was taken no one would be aware of its presence. But should it cause a troublesome ache, weight reduction, exercise, heat, massage, and an occasional aspirin will usually ease it.

A *Lumbo-Sacral Strain* is another fairly common cause of backache. Sometimes it comes on quite suddenly while lifting a garage door or moving heavy furniture. Its effect is to make it difficult for the person to either bend over or straighten up. In fact the rather rigid, fixed, and slightly bent over position in which such patients walk has prompted doctors to use the term "poker spine" when describing this condition. A few days of bed-rest, hot tub baths, and drugs, to relieve the muscle spasm and pain will generally ease the patient over the acute period. But more frequently doctors see patients who cannot recall injuring their back, yet nevertheless complain of an almost constant, dull, aching sensation in the low back. Nearly all have been overweight for some time. To make matters worse, they usually have poor posture. Sooner or later something has to give, and the lumbo-sacral spine, one of the crucial pivot points of the body, starts to break down. And when this happens, patients have to realize that a planned program of weight reduction and exercises to strengthen the back muscles is essential for a successful cure. Heat and aspirin will relieve some of the discomfort, but the reason for the difficulty must also be corrected to obtain good long-term results.

Disk Trouble. This is a less common cause of back-ache, and is frequently referred to as disk trouble. It occurs when one of the shock absorbers between the bony vertebrae is injured by either a sudden strain or from repeated injuries. Since each pliable disk sits between two bony vertebrae any severe pressure on the spine is more likely to injure the softer disk. Consequently, when the disk is squeezed too hard, a small part of it may rupture and produce pressure on the nerves going out of the spine, particularly the sciatic nerve. And since this nerve runs down the leg, patients with a ruptured disk frequently complain of not only back pain but also of pain, numbness or a tingling sensation, usually in one leg. Sometimes coughing or sneezing will increase the pain. A neurological examination normally shows a decreased or absent ankle jerk on the affected side, and sometimes a little wasting of the muscles in the affected leg. But to pinpoint the exact location of the rupture, it is necessary to use various X ray techniques. Fortunately 95 percent of the patients with disk trouble respond to rest on a hard bed, which may be necessary for anywhere from one to six weeks. The other 5 percent sooner or later need surgery.

Kidney Trouble. I will mention this disease just to round out the picture, but, as I said earlier, it is a rare cause of backache. When it does occur because of infection, stones, or dropped kidneys, the diagnosis is quite easy to separate from the other reasons for backache. First, the pain is much higher in the back. Second, nearly all patients with kidney trouble have symptoms other than pain. Not infrequently an associated urinary infection will cause increased frequency of urination or a burning sensation on voiding, and this, along with an examination of the urine, usually clinches the diagnosis. Then to pinpoint the cause of the trouble, X rays are done.

Loss of Urine (Stress Incontinence)

Loss of urine is a complaint that may be of little or great annoyance. Most women first notice it on coughing or sneezing. Others may be aware of it even without any increased stress of this sort. For instance, some women after sitting quietly in a chair will be embarrassed to find it quite wet. On other occasions it may be noticeable while walking down the street. And finally some patients are damp all the time. In short it runs all the way from being a very minor complaint that only now and then results in a small loss of urine to a very major trouble which tends to make some women social outcasts. I've known some reasonable young women who were so afraid of being noticed with this complaint that they have literally given up most of their social activities. I would suggest that women read the section on "Prolapse of the Bladder and of the Uterus," in

Chapter XVI which discusses why women develop this problem and what can be done about it.

Breast Lumps

There is little doubt that women worry more about
lumps in the breast than in any other part of the body. In fact,
there has been so much talk about breast lumps in recent years
that women have gotten the impression that any lump in the
breast is automatically a cancer. This is far from the truth,
for most lumps are benign and of little significance. Yet, it is
of the utmost importance to immediately consult the doctor
when any lump is noted, because this allows for early diagnosis
and treatment of possible cancer.

Since the breast is such a readily accessible organ, and since
patients are being told by doctors and others to regularly
examine their breasts for lumps, a good deal of confusion
and unnecessary worry frequently results. Patients are always
more concerned when they see their blood flowing after a cut
than when it happens to someone else, and it is also true when
a patient feels for breast lumps. A small thickened area of
normal tissue, which would be easily passed over if the patient
was feeling the breast of another person, becomes a definite
lump in her own breast. That we should be more sensitive
and cognizant of our own body is of course quite natural, but
it sometimes produces imaginary lumps where none actually
exist. Self-examination is therefore at times, and in certain
patients, a mixed blessing, and one has to balance the benefits
of potential early diagnosis against the hazards of creating
undue worry by self-examination. Certainly for those women
who are inclined to be a bit hypochondriacal, a visit to the
doctor once or twice a year for a general checkup is the wiser
approach, and they should forget about their breasts in the
meantime. For others, less inclined to be worriers, a monthly

self-examination does no harm, and may result in earlier diagnosis should a lump appear. In this regard, however, there is one point I would like to make. A few women become either so enthusiastic (or so neurotic) about examining their breasts that it becomes almost a daily ritual. This is utter nonsense. Plain common sense should prevail in this matter, as in other things; but unfortunately this is too often not the case.

Over the years, a number of women have consulted me because one breast was larger than the other and they were fearful this might be due to a malignancy. What had happened is that the patient had suddenly noticed that one breast was larger than the other when, in fact, this condition had existed for years, and is quite normal. Usually the left breast is larger than the right, but in a few women the reverse is true, and it is of no significance. It is therefore important for women to know what the normal breast is like before looking for the abnormal, otherwise they may fall into a number of traps. For example, in evaluating breast lumps and painful breasts one must bear in mind that the breasts are vastly different from most other organs of the body, such as the heart and lungs, which remain the same in appearance and function day after day. The breasts, on the other hand, do change during the course of the menstrual cycle, and some become quite tender and bumpy (particularly in the upper outer areas of the breasts just before the period starts) and again this is quite normal. But this breast soreness may focus the patient's attention on a particular area and, in examining the breasts, one or more lumps may be felt, causing undue concern. Usually, following the onset of the period the pain subsides, and so may the lump. Many women develop painful breasts before their period, which may or may not be associated with a slight degree of lumpiness. This is also perfectly normal.

There are also women who have a nodularity of their breasts nearly all the time, as if there were BB shot or marbles scattered throughout the breast tissue. Doctors refer to this condition as "cystic" disease of the breasts, and use terms such as "chronic cystic mastitis" and "fibro cystic disease" in describing it. About one woman in fifteen will have this condition at some time during her reproductive life, but usually following the menopause it gradually subsides. In most cases, both breasts are involved, and the lumps may be single or multiple and also vary from the size of a pea to that of a walnut. In general it is of little significance, but may cause intermittent, annoying pain. Sometimes the discomfort occurs prior to the period. At other times, it can be constant for a few months, and then disappear for long periods of time. In fact, the majority of patients are not only without pain, but also completely unaware of the existence of the lumps unless they are pointed out to them. The manner in which the lumps come and go, or change in size, and the fact that the tenderness and pain usually bear some relationship to the menstrual period helps to point to the correct diagnosis.

What causes cystic disease of the breast is not known, consequently there is no single specific form of treatment. A good brassiere, which may be worn at night by women with large breasts, may ease the pain. At other times, drugs to get rid of the excess fluid are helpful, since the body tends to collect more fluid in the week to ten days before the period begins. The breasts share in the absorption of this water, and part of the pain at this time is thought to be due to this. Some doctors may prescribe hormones for a short period, since some physicians believe a temporary hormonal imbalance is responsible for the symptoms. Other doctors may freeze the area, if one lump is particularly large and painful, following which a small needle can remove the fluid from within the cyst. Once removed, the fluid frequently fails to recur, and doctors are not certain of the reasons for this. But sometimes the diagnosis is not certain, and in cases where any element of doubt exists the surgeon will advise removal of the lumps, and microscopic examination of its tissue, to be certain that a malignancy is not present.

CHAPTER XI

Venereal Disease

IT HAS BEEN SAID THAT "Sex is here to stay, but venereal disease need not be." Whether this is true remains to be seen, for although much of its sting has been removed since the discovery of antibiotics, in particular penicillin, the problem of venereal disease is still far from being solved at the moment. In fact, it is a rather sad commentary on our civilization that in an age in which man is solving the problems of space, these diseases continue to flourish when they could be completely eradicated by extensive public health measures.

At a recent world forum on venereal disease it was pointed out by many experts that, rather than decreasing, venereal disease was making a decided comeback. This resurgence of VD was in part due to the miscalculation by many people that penicillin, which cures the early cases so easily, would quickly wipe out the disease. For many years it looked as though this was happening, as fewer and fewer cases were seen. Then, in the early 1950's, when these diseases appeared to have been conquered, the public funds to fight them were drastically reduced, and the knockout blow never came. For when patients receive the proper dosage of penicillin, venereal disease can be cured. Yet, the revival of VD is not merely an economic problem, for the historic, hush-hush Victorian attitude towards venereal disease still exists and will not quickly change. Lack of education both in homes and schools is largely responsible for the pseudowise, know-it-all attitude of many teenagers who account for a good deal of the increase of these diseases. Furthermore, it is now being spread as much by the "good-time bar girl," as by professional prostitutes.

These easy pickups deserve to be evaluated with as much care as the porcupine makes love—very, very carefully. The Italians have often said that "the buyer needs a hundred eyes, the seller but one." Yet, unfortunately this wise advice is rarely heeded when people are out doing the town. This is because there is a fairly direct correlation between the amount of alcohol consumed and how attractive a girl appears to be. But it's also true that even without the stimulating effect of alcohol many of these girls are not only attractive, but also well groomed, which tends to convey the false impression that they are similarly free from disease. This surface pureness is also exuded by young teenagers who are currently experiencing more sexual freedom than at any other time. I pointed out in the chapter on contraception that one bad aspect of the pill is that it has made people forget, not only about pregnancy, but also about venereal disease. A promiscuous high-school student who has a different bed companion every few weeks is an excellent candidate for venereal disease. But being a teenager and surrounded by the pseudorespectability of a high-school atmosphere, it's hard to think of these girls as having venereal disease. They simply do not appear to be the type of girl that one normally thinks of when talking about syphilis and gonorrhea. Unfortunately one cannot tell whether or not a girl has venereal disease merely by looking at her, any more than you can tell the egg by its shell. This deceptiveness of external appearance is nothing new. Long ago Cervantes stressed this in Don Quixote when he cautioned "All that glistens is not gold." It's even more valid in today's society, because with expanding sexual freedom the old hazards of venereal disease are still very much with us. To irradicate all these carriers of the disease will take a tremendous amount of money, time, and public education. And unlike the efforts of the 1950's, the attack must be pushed until VD is completely irradicated in our country. A. W. Hare in *Guesses At Truth* wrote in 1827 that half the failures in life arise from pulling in one's horse just as he is leaping. So until we live in a world free of venereal disease, we have to logically conclude that whether we are purchasing a stock or looking for a bed companion proper, selectivity is just as important today as it has always been in the past.

How many people have venereal disease becomes more of a guess than an estimate, for many cases are never diagnosed, and those that are found are frequently not reported to the Public Health Authorities. Yet some facts are known, insofar as each year over one hundred thousand cases of syphilis are reported in the United States, of which twenty thousand are thought to be new cases. There are also more than four thousand babies born with this disease, and at least four thousand people die from it annually. Adding it all up, just for syphilis alone, a staggering nine million Americans are thought either to have this disease, or to have had it at some time in their lives. But gonorrhea does not have to take a back seat, for it is believed there are one million new cases of it each year. It seems quite likely, therefore, that until we stop burying our head in the sand, and begin an all-out effort to stamp out VD, there will be little change in these statistics.

Gonorrhea

This disease is due to a bacterial germ, the gonococcus, which is transmitted by sexual intercourse; and, although it is common in all parts of the world, some areas have a much higher incidence of the disease than others. A number of years ago during a trip to South America as a ship's surgeon, I treated a high percentage of the crew for this problem following their nightly sojourns to the local cafés. It was quite easy to foretell when I would be most in demand, since sailors with this infection would appear at sick call with amazing regularity a few days after the ship had left port. Certainly these waterfront areas, and the slums of crowded cities are hotbeds of this infection, yet it can also occur in higher levels of society.

Patients sometimes worry in case they pick up this disease from a toilet seat. Actually, it is only a million to one chance, since the germ is quickly killed by either heat or drying. One day while I was making rounds with one of Harvard's gynecologists we came across a patient whom he had seen many times in the clinic for repeated gonorrheal infection. After the usual greetings, this woman, who had none of the earmarks of a virtuous lady, stated that she must have picked it up on a toilet seat. The professor, a rather quick-witted fellow and no doubt somewhat bored by this worn-out story, shot back, "that is a rather strange place to have intercourse." Women like this, who are repeatedly infected with gonorrhea, accept it in much the same way as many of us look on the common cold. But for other girls it represents an overwhelming tragedy. I recall a young, bright-eyed schoolteacher who tearfully told me about her first sexual experience while on a vacation. More carefree than usual, she had indulged in too much wine, after which she allowed herself to be romanced under a Caribbean sky by the hotel musician. A few days after her arrival home it became very evident that she had returned with more than just memories of a good time. Fortunately, she was wise enough to seek immediate treatment, and was quickly cured.

The Acute Stage. The symptoms of gonorrhea fall into two distinct categories: the acute symptoms and, later, the chronic stage. The acute stage is usually ushered in about the fourth to tenth day after exposure, but the degree of the symptoms may vary considerably. Some gonorrheal infections may be so mild as to pass unnoticed, with either no symptoms, or ones so mild that the patient is completely unaware of the presence of an infection. But in most cases there are increased amounts of vaginal discharge, frequency of and burning on urination, soreness and swelling of the vaginal entrance, abdominal pain, fever, chills, and sometimes nausea and vomiting. One or more of these symptoms may occur, and at this stage the infection has been referred to by some doctors as "downstairs gonorrhea." This is because in the early acute stages the disease is limited to the lower parts of the female organs before it starts to attack the structures deep inside the pelvis, primarily the tubes and ovaries, and when this happens it could be conveniently called "upstairs gonorrhea." In the early stages, the increased vaginal discharge results from irritation of the cervix (the lower part and opening of the uterus) which becomes quite reddened and inflamed, sometimes producing copious amounts of discharge. Similarly, the burning on urination is due to irritation of the lining of the urethra, which is the tube connecting the urinary bladder to the outside.

The treatment of this "downstairs gonorrhea" has been totally revolutionized in recent years by penicillin, since a single injection completely cures the great majority of patients. Serious reactions to penicillin are rare, but patients who have developed a rash or other problems following its administration should inform the doctor, so that he can use other effective antibiotics. In addition, bedrest and the temporary avoidance of alcohol and intercourse are advisable during the course of treatment.

In the event the patient does not seek medical attention, what happens largely depends on the strength of the gonococcus germ. Usually, the infection goes upstairs, traveling through the uterus, and infecting the tubes and ovaries to varying degrees. In some cases, this extension of the disease may produce only a minor discomfort for a few days, but in other instances there may be severe low abdominal pain, high temperature, and some swelling of the abdomen. Again, depending on the strength of the germ, varying amounts of pus may form in the tubes, and some of it may drop out of the ends of the tubes entering the general pelvic cavity, and resulting in a pelvic peritonitis. At other times, the ends of the tubes close off, the pus becomes trapped and the tube, which is normally about the size of a piece of spaghetti, becomes greatly distended, reaching the size of a banana or larger. This inflammatory process also involves the ovaries to a greater or lesser extent, since the ovaries are closely attached to the tubes. Not infrequently, the tubes and ovaries may become so swollen that it is impossible to tell one from the other. This is usually the worst that can happen and, even in these cases, once antibiotics are given the tubes and ovaries start to heal and gradually return to their normal size.

In the most severe infections, which do not receive prompt treatment, one further complication may occur: the tubes and ovaries become part of a large pelvic abscess, frequently the size of a grapefruit, that develops deep inside the pelvic cavity. Frequently, this abscess forms behind the uterus, and the surgeon is able to drain pus from it by making a small incision through the end of the vagina. I vividly recall one patient whom I operated on during my residency training who had enough pus to fill a gallon jar. An abdominal operation is done only during the acute stage, when the pelvic abscess is in a situation where it cannot be drained easily through the vagina, and where there is no improvement in the patient's condition from day to day, or when, on rare occasions, the abscess suddenly ruptures on its own.

Patients who have had severe infections, particularly those that developed into a pelvic abscess, frequently require surgery either months or years later because of the damage done to the tubes and ovaries. This is because these structures were so badly infected that in the process of healing a good deal of scar tissue formed around them, resulting in chronic pelvic pain, and various types of abnormal bleeding. And, as one would suspect, many of these young women become permanently sterile, because of blocked tubes from the scar tissue that forms not only inside the tubes, but also from adhesions on the outside that block off the tubal opening. This brings up the problem of chronic infection of the tubes and ovaries, which may or may not follow the acute stage.

Chronic Stage. Chronic infection of the tubes and ovaries may occur in a number of ways. First, the infection may be so mild with so little in the way of symptoms that the disease goes unnoticed and slowly develops into a chronic infection without passing through the initial acute stage. Second, where an acute infection does not receive prompt treatment it may result in a chronic infection. Third, patients who repeatedly reinfect themselves invariably end up with chronic infection.

Women with chronic gonorrheal infection may be affected in a number of ways. Some are lucky and have relatively few complaints, but sooner or later it usually makes its presence felt. Just as a chronic infection of the gall bladder can suddenly erupt into an acute infection, so can chronic pelvic infection suddenly flare up into an acute infection, producing all the symptoms that I mentioned earlier. But this is the exception rather than the rule, for the great majority of chronic pelvic infections remain chronic, and usually cause varying degrees of pelvic pain and abnormal bleeding. Sometimes the pain is limited to the period, but it may also cause a dull gnawing, aching sensation in the low abdomen between periods. And if adhesions have pulled the uterus backwards, and are holding it rigidly in that position, backache and pain on intercourse may also be present. The abnormal bleeding may take many different forms—being either prolonged, heavy, frequent, irregular, or a combination of one or more of these problems. At this point, I would like to remind the reader that many other kinds of infection and other diseases also cause these same symptoms. Similarly, the inability to become pregnant may also be the result of a previous gonorrheal infection, but much more frequently it is due to other problems completely unrelated to venereal disease.

Diagnosis. The diagnosis of gonorrhea can be either very simple or quite difficult. For example, during the acute stage, not only does the overall condition of the patient point to the diagnosis, but also by taking discharge or pus from the cervix (opening into the uterus) the gonococcus germ can be seen under the microscope. Another way is to place some of the discharge on a special culture plate, which is then incubated at a certain temperature for a couple of days. If the gonococcus bacteria is present, large numbers will grow in this favorable climate.

The chronic stage of gonorrhea is much more difficult to diagnose, since in most cases the gonococcus germ has done damage to the tubes and ovaries, but then has entirely disappeared. Doctors often refer to this condition as burnt-out gonorrhea. The symptoms which prompt the visit to the doctor are therefore due to the extensive adhesions and scarring around the pelvic organs; not because of the presence of any germ. The diagnosis in these patients is therefore made on the basis of the patient's complaints, the finding of tender thickened tubes and ovaries on pelvic examination, and finally the adhesions which a surgeon finds, should an operation be necessary. Yet it must be admitted that in a great many cases all the doctor can say is that a chronic infection occurred at an earlier date, but it is impossible to know whether it was due to gonorrhea or to other nonvenereal bacteria, such as the staphlococcus, streptococcus, or other germs. It would be the same as trying to determine what the color of the horse was after it has escaped from the barn.

Treatment. "Hurry," the Russians say, "is good only for catching flies," but in catching the gonococcus, haste is indeed vitally important. As soon as the patient is examined and the diagnosis suspected, penicillin or other antibiotics should be given immediately, for at no other time will there be a better chance to completely eradicate the disease. One injection of penicillin will cure the majority of cases. If the patient is sensitive to this drug, then other antibiotics can usually be given by mouth.

In the event surgery is required, the type of operation depends on a number of factors. Those women who are young and desire children can sometimes be helped by a conservative surgical approach in which an attempt is made to remove adhesions from the pelvic organs, suspend the uterus in its correct position, cut nerves to aid in removing the pain from the periods. Occasionally extensive plastic repairs are done on the tubes if they are blocked at some point. But sometimes the disease is so extensive that this approach is neither practical nor possible. In these instances, or where women are beyond their reproductive life, a hysterectomy, with removal of the tubes and ovaries, is the best approach.

Syphilis

For many years people believed the false story that syphilis was brought to Europe by Columbus' sailors, who were supposed to have contracted it from the Indian maidens. Whatever the true origin of this disease, syphilis was first mentioned in European writings in the latter part of the fifteenth century. Since then this disease, frequently referred to as the "Great Pox," has continued to ravage mankind, with Canadians and Americans being infected at the estimated rate of ten thousand cases a month. As mentioned earlier, it looked as though syphilis was on the way out a few years ago, but now, according to public health authorities, it is making a decided comeback. And whereas in former years it was largely confined to the lower-class groups, it now appears to be infecting more of the well-educated and well-heeled citizens. The late President Kennedy, recognizing the problem, asked for plans to eradicate syphilis in the United States by 1972, and such a plan is cur-

rently being developed by the United States Public Health
Service.

One of the most ironic aspects of this disease is that the
syphilitic germ called *treponema pallidum* is an extremely feeble
germ, easily destroyed by a little heat and, unlike many germs
which can survive in other animals, this one can survive only
in the human body. At one time, before antibiotics became
available, artificial heat was used as a treatment for syphilis.
Furthermore, unlike some germs that get from one person to
another by means of water, food or air, syphilis can only affect
a person through sexual contact. Yet in spite of the fragile
nature of the germ it has crippled, blinded, deafened, and
made insane millions of people throughout history.

The "pickup," whether it be male or female, is now the
main source of infection, and infection is largely due to sexual
intercourse. Many patients worry whether drinking from an
infected cup, eating utensils, or public washrooms could be
responsible for the infection. This is practically impossible since,
as mentioned before, the syphilitic germ dies immediately once
it leaves the human body.

First Stage. Doctors usually talk about the three
stages of syphilis. The first stage occurs from three or four
weeks after intercourse with the infected person. At this time
a highly infectious sore called the "chancre" (pronounced
shanker) occurs at the site of the entrance of the germ. This
sore may form on the outside of the vagina, but more frequently it starts on the inside and the patient may not notice it.
But there is one further reason why women so frequently miss
this early lesion: invariably the sore is painless. This is an
important stage, for not only are women extremely contagious
while the open sore is present, but also it is the best time to
start treatment. Along with the development of the ulcer,
patients may also notice that the glands in the groin become
swollen and tender. The main thing for women to remember

is that any sores that appear around the vagina following intercourse must be considered as syphilis until proven otherwise by various tests. And since chancres can also appear on the lips, tongue, or in fact anywhere, prompt attention is required for any of these sores.

The Second Stage starts four to eight weeks after the original sore appeared, at which time there is evidence of invasion of the whole body. Now the patient may notice skin rashes, sores around the mouth or vagina, various eye inflammations, painful bones, swollen glands, or falling out of the hair. Any combination of these symptoms may occur, and again, since they can be mistaken for other diseases, the real condition may not be diagnosed. This secondary syphilis is also very contagious, but adequate treatment can still arrest and cure the disease.

The Third Stage includes all the late problems that may or may not occur, even if the patient does not receive treatment. Just why some patients who have never been treated fail to develop these later problems is not known. Yet many untreated patients are not that lucky, and anywhere from three to thirty years later develop major complications of the disease. Again, it is not known why syphilis should go into hiding for such a long period, during which time patients may feel perfectly well, and be totally unaware that the disease will later strike them down. When it does reappear there are three principal areas of the body that are injured, but no organ is exempt. For example, large masses called "gummas" may form in various parts and organs of the body, such as the liver, bones, skin, stomach, and brain. But gummas are not as common as the degenerative lesions that affect the heart and blood vessels, the brain and spinal cord, and the eye. The main lesions affecting the heart and blood vessels occur in what is known as the "aorta." This is the largest blood vessel in the body, carrying blood away from the heart to the more distant parts. What happens is that the elastic tissue in the wall of this major vessel is gradually destroyed, and in this weakened area a large herniation occurs, which may become so tremendously dilated that it eventually ruptures, causing sudden death. When syphilis involves the nervous system it tends to concentrate its attack primarily on the spinal cord, sometimes resulting in a complete paralysis from the waist down. Not infrequently, the degeneration is limited to the brain, causing confusion, progressive lack of memory, and ending in insanity. The eye is another major area of late involvement, resulting in either inflammation of the eye, paralysis of the ocular muscles, or degeneration of the main nerve of the eye. In this latter instance, the degeneration of the optic nerve initially results in dimness of vision, which may progress to complete blindness.

The Diagnosis of syphilis is in part dependent on a high incidence of suspicion by both the patient and the doctor that syphilis might be present. Obviously, the most skilled doctor cannot detect syphilis unless the patient is willing to consult him for any sores that are present. Unfortunately, patients rarely see the physician during this early first stage, and it is not until the generalized symptoms of the second stage occur that they seek help. Many cases are first diagnosed when a routine blood test is done. This blood test is extremely accurate, but when the primary sore first appears only 25 percent of these blood tests will show that syphilis is present. Stated another way, it takes about four weeks after the initial appearance of the sore before all of the blood tests will be positive for syphilis. Should the patient consult the doctor early, when the sore first appears, there is one further way to diagnose syphilis. Doctors at this time can scrape the surface of the sore and, by a special staining technique, identify the corkscrew syphilitic germ under the microscope.

The Treatment of Syphilis used to be extremely lengthy and painful, requiring repeated injections of arsenical and bismuth compounds. Now the treatment has been completely revolutionized by the discovery of penicillin. A few million units of penicillin will cure the disease in its early stages, and even in a large number of those who receive treatment when the disease is further advanced.

CHAPTER XII

Common Operations

IN RECENT YEARS there has been a general feeling among the laity that too much surgery is being done, which implies that much of it is unnecessary. What people forget is that in former years operations were performed primarily as life-saving procedures, because the risk of carrying out elective surgery was too great. Now it is an entirely different story, for with improved surgical techniques, antibiotics, blood transfusions, and well-trained anesthetists, the chances of something going wrong are extremely small. This means that women no longer hemorrhage to death from large fibroids, ruptured tubal pregnancies, or die during childbirth after days of exhausting but unproductive labor. And just as important, women who are suffering from chronic annoyances can now be helped by surgery rather than having to live out the rest of their lives with bothersome problems. This is why more surgery is done today, and it doesn't appear that this trend is going to stop in the immediate future. This is not surprising when one considers the tremendous advances in the field of heart surgery, and the transplantation of organs such as the kidney. These new operative approaches are still in their infancy, but they have opened up new, exciting frontiers in surgery.

Another reason for the longer lists of surgery at hospitals

is that women are living longer, and are therefore more prone to develop problems of one sort or another. In earlier years, the patient's age was a major consideration, and often proved to be the decisive factor in a doctor's decision. But now the reverse has happened, and surgeons now look more at the disease than at their patient's age in deciding whether or not something should be done. Women who have reached seventy are usually made of pretty good material to have lasted that long, and very frequently come through surgery just as well as a twenty-year-old girl, if they are adequately prepared for it. This does not mean that there is anything really special about operating on elderly patients, because the same basic preoperative workup applies to all age groups. However, it is only logical that old patients, like old cars, require a little more care. This means that a low blood count should be corrected by iron before surgery takes place. A chronic cough should also be looked into, and if possible cured before an elective operation is advised. And women suffering from heart disease, hypertension, diabetes, asthma, or kidney disease, just to name a few, require a thorough evaluation of these problems.

Lastly, every effort should be made to get obese patients to lose weight, although on most occasions it is, admittedly, a lost cause. I have, on occasion, said somewhat facetiously, that "Surgeons should charge by the pound!" This statement smacks of commercialism, but there is more than an element of truth in it. And no doubt if this proviso *was* added to the surgical fee schedule, surgeons would be accused of being Wall Street barons. But surgeons, by and large, have proved themselves dismal failures when it comes to persuading their patients to lose weight, and it may be that by failing to "charge by the pound," doctors are not utilizing the one sure way to persuade obese women to push themselves away from the table. And it would most surely be for the patient's benefit, rather than the financial gain of a doctor, for obese patients present surgeons with a host of problems. Most patients consider obesity more a cosmetic problem than a medical one, or they don't bother to think about it at all. Those that do briefly consider it, no doubt quickly come to the conclusion that it is twice as difficult to operate on a two-hundred-and-fifty-pound woman as on a one-hundred-and-twenty-five pounder. This is far from the truth. They would be more correct to multiply the technical problems by ten. And the complications do not stop once the surgery is over, for such women are also more prone to develop poor healing of the incision, infections, and pneumonia. The cold, blunt fact is that obese patients are more prone to everything from flat feet, diabetes, and hypertension, to arthritis and a host of other medical diseases. They don't seem to have that tiger in their tank, the get-up-and-go that is present in slim patients.

I would be the first to admit that overeating is not the only cause of obesity, but it is certainly an important one. After all, there were no fat people in the concentration camps of Nazi Germany! The two-hundred-and-fifty-pounder who says she never eats anything, nevertheless seems to lose weight during a week of close observation in a hospital. I hasten to add this does have to be very close observation, otherwise her relatives will bring in food, or she obtains it by other devious methods. I recall one patient, during my early years of practice, with whom I unsuccessfully pleaded to lose weight in preparation for her surgery. Finally, it was necessary to do it because of an emergency, and when making the rounds the following day I cautioned her to just take fluids for the next twenty-four hours, and things apparently went along very well. However, about a month later, another patient of mine, who happened to be in the same ward at that time, came into the office for her postoperative visit. She confided that this patient had consumed a pound box of chocolates a visitor had brought her later that same day! Irresponsible patients like this cause surgeons a great deal of blood, sweat, and tears in the operating room, and no doubt in the process add a few more scars to their coronary arteries. The knowing smile they give you when you stress that their extra weight is going to complicate the procedure seems to indicate they take a bit of pleasure in the knowledge. From others, you get the feeling they consider they are presenting you with an interesting challenge, which should inspire you to rise to great surgical heights. It all adds up to the fact that overweight patients have, for years, been getting something for nothing, and it has been proven time and time again that when people do get something free, they value it less. Possibly, the economics of medicine has failed to keep up with this increasing problem of obesity in our affluent society, and it may be that charging by the pound might do more for patients than all the fancy diets of the past.

Before we proceed to talk about the common operations in gynecology, there is one other topic I would like to discuss. During the past few years there has been a good deal of irresponsible talk about lost instruments and sponges. The sensational newspaper headlines that informed the public of these mistakes certainly sell newspapers, but they never give a balanced account of the facts, and unfortunately raise doubt in the minds of patients where there should be none. During all the hullabaloo, no one bothers to mention that for every sponge left in the abdomen, there are five hundred thousand operations carried out without this happening. Most hospitals have now instituted not only sponge counts, but also instrument counts, which hopefully will do away with both problems. And one world-famous clinic now automatically takes an X ray before the patient leaves the operating room, to make sure that no "foreign bodies" remain inside them!

The patient becomes aware that the operation is over when she wakes in the recovery room to find a nurse checking her pulse, blood pressure, and breathing. At this point, some patients may become aware of a needle in their arm that feeds in a solution of sugar and water. Others may be receiving a bottle of blood, but this does not imply anything has gone wrong. And since, after most gynecological operations, a catheter is inserted to drain the bladder for a short while, most women will also be conscious of the presence of this tube. Usually after a few hours the majority of patients have forgotten that it is present.

The care of the postoperative patient is just as important as the preparation for surgery. In former years, patients were kept in bed for as long as two weeks before being allowed up and about. Now doctors recommend the very opposite, and most women will be out of bed either on the day of surgery or the next. This is because early activity keeps the circulation better, the lungs expanded, and decreases the chance of complications. So when doctors and nurses ask patients to turn from side to side in bed, move their legs, take deep, deep breaths, and encourage them to take a few steps around the room, they have a good reason for doing so. Now let's take a look at some common pelvic operations, and start our discussion with the most frequent one of all, the D and C.

D and C

This is the most common and useful operation that a gynecologist has at his disposal for the accurate diagnosis and treatment of many common pelvic problems. Certainly it is a rare day when a number of these are not carried out in most hospitals across the country. The term "D and C" stands for dilatation and curettage, and is also frequently spoken of as a scraping out of the uterus after the cervix has been slightly dilated. The tissue is then sent to the pathologist, who examines it under the microscope to see if it is normal.

The present popularity of the D and C is not without good reason, since the early diagnosis of pelvic disease is being stressed more and more in recent years. The old saying that "a stitch in time saves nine" certainly applies here, because today nearly all pelvic disease, if diagnosed early, can be totally cured.

The great majority of D and C's are done because of some change in the patient's bleeding pattern. The periods may be more frequent, heavier, longer, or irregular. At other times there may be bleeding between periods, which may or may not be related to intercourse or douching. Other patients may have spotting, or bright red bleeding, following the menopause. But whatever the type of bleeding, the main point is that it represents a departure from what the patient normally expects, and 99 percent of the time it is a change to more bleeding rather than less.

Usually the D and C shows that either a minor problem such as a polyp accounts for the bleeding, or it is just a temporary upset in the menstrual cycle which the D and C quickly corrects. Less frequently, a small fibroid will be found inside the uterus, or the lining of the uterus is discovered to be thicker than normal. But most important of all, it is very rarely that a malignancy is detected by the D and C. I can't stress this point enough, because most women with either abnormal bleeding, discharge, or pain immediately jump to the wrong conclusion that a cancer is causing it, and spend many sleepless nights of unnecessary worry, certain that their days are now numbered.

The D and C also gives the doctor a chance to examine thoroughly not only the inside of the uterus when it is scraped out, but also to feel adequately the outside of the uterus, and the size of the tubes and ovaries, particularly in patients who are either quite obese, or who find it difficult to relax in the doctor's office. Most women, of course, can be easily examined in the office without an anesthetic, but for the occasional patient it is essential to make certain there are no fibroids, ovarian cysts, infection, or other problems present.

Another major reason for doing a D and C is following a miscarriage (see Chapter VIII), when it is necessary to remove whatever is left of the pregnancy. Nearly always some of the placenta (afterbirth) remains, and unless a D and C is carried out, excessive bleeding may occur later.

Doctors are frequently asked, following a D and C, whether anything serious was found. As mentioned above, a polyp, a fibroid, or other problem may have been diagnosed, but in the great majority of cases the female organs were found to be normal on examination, and the tissue which has been scraped out of the uterus looks normal to the naked eye. It is therefore impossible for the surgeon to give a definite answer until the tissue is examined further by the pathologist. During the next few days the tissue is stained by various dyes, embedded in wax, cut into fine sections by delicate instruments, and finally examined microscopically. Only then can the answer be given with any final assurance, and in most cases it will be good news.

How inconvenient is it to have a D and C? Usually the patient has to put aside a couple of days, since she is required to enter the hospital a day before surgery, and will be able to go home the day after. The evening before surgery doctors may or may not ask the nurse to shave off the hair around the vagina, the blood and the urine will be tested, and a sleeping pill given to insure a good night's rest. Then, the next day, the patient is quickly put to sleep in a few seconds by injecting a drug called "pentothal" into an arm vein. The actual D and C takes just a few minutes.

Patients frequently ask whether a D and C is dangerous, and how long it will be before they can resume their normal activities. In experienced hands, the operation is completely safe, and most women can return to normal home life, or to work, as soon as they leave the hospital. This operation only becomes dangerous when criminal abortionists attempt to perform one to remove a normal pregnancy. These unskilled people usually work under the worst possible conditions, and have no knowledge of the human anatomy, as is explained in the section on criminal abortion in Chapter VIII. Obviously such an "operation" as this bears no relation to a properly performed D and C, carried out by a capable surgeon in one of our modern hospitals.

What should the patient be aware of after the D and C? Usually there is a reddish-brown discharge for a few days, which gradually decreases in amount. There may also be a slight aching sensation in the lower part of the abdomen, particularly if the patient is obese, and the doctor has had to push on the stomach a little more than usual in order to feel the pelvic organs. The pain is never severe, and goes away in a few hours, or at the most in a day or two.

The periods are the main thing that may or may not change, and if the patient is not aware of this fact it causes needless worry. For instance, if the periods have been irregular, profuse, prolonged, or frequent they may quickly revert to normal after the D and C. At other times, the periods may be heavier for a month or two, or the next period may be a little early, late, or entirely missed. The main point to remember is that any change in the amount of flow, or the pattern of bleeding, may temporarily occur following a D and C and there is no need for any concern. But it is also as well to know that the next period may also come at the expected time, and the blood loss may be the same as before.

In summary, the D and C is a simple, safe, and effective way to accurately diagnose many of the problems which confront the doctor. Consequently, if the doctor suggests having one done, patients should not make the mistake of waiting to see whether the trouble will go away on its own, for should a serious problem exist its early diagnosis will usually result in a complete cure. Fortunately, most of the time patients will be given good news following a D and C, and will then have the peace of mind that comes from having looked a problem squarely in the face rather than burying their heads in the sand.

Vaginal Repair

This is another quite common operation, although it obviously is not done as often as the D and C. Doctors refer to it as a "cystocele repair," and it is done because the bladder has fallen down. I discuss it in detail in the section on "Prolapse of the Bladder and of the Uterus," in Chapter

XVI. A number of factors may cause this condition. Difficult childbirth and repeated pregnancies are the most usual, although some women are born with weak tissues and when the patient gets older they begin to sag in the same way as some people get fallen arches in their feet.

Uterine Suspension (For a Tipped Uterus)

A tipped uterus is just as common as a crooked pair of legs and, in the majority of cases, of no more importance. There are, however, many women who have worried needlessly for years because they were told that their uterus was tipped, and their doctor, in the course of a busy day, had forgotten to mention that it was of no significance.

The reader will recall from Chapter I that the uterus is usually closer to the stomach wall than to the back. A tipped uterus, on the other hand, has gradually fallen back towards the spine. Some fall back only slightly and are called a "first degree retroversion" (this is the technical name doctors use when referring to a tipped uterus). Others fall back a little more and are called a "second degree retroversion," in which they are about halfway between the abdominal wall and the spine. Still others fall back until they almost rest on the spine itself, and this is known as a "third degree retroversion."

Why does the uterus change position? The most common cause is childbirth, when the ligaments supporting the uterus become stretched allowing it to fall backwards. Another large group of women is actually born with this condition. Yet regardless of how it develops, so long as it is not associated with any disease, all these types of retroversions are of no importance. They merely represent minor mechancial changes from the normal position.

Doctors did not always think this way. About one hundred years ago pessaries were in vogue to change the position of the uterus. It has been said that in those days fortunes were being made by two groups of gynecologists—those who inserted pessaries and those who removed them. This treatment, although it was not very effective, at least did no harm. A number of years later, surgeons frequently advised a suspension operation to correct the position of a tipped uterus in patients who complained of backache. It was soon discovered to be a poor solution. The majority of these women were not helped by the surgery, because in most instances the trouble was in the back; not in the pelvic organs. Many of these patients had a lumbo-sacral or sacro-iliac strain. A few had a slipped disk. Others were overweight and suffered from poor posture. Still others had home troubles that were causing a great deal of tension.

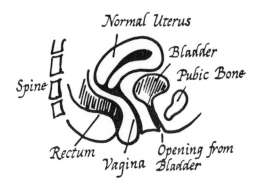

Normal Uterus

Spine / Bladder / Pubic Bone / Rectum / Vagina / Opening from Bladder

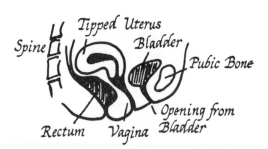

Tipped Uterus

Spine / Bladder / Pubic Bone / Rectum / Vagina / Opening from Bladder

Now doctors realize that a tipped uterus is important only when it is associated with a pelvic disease, such as pelvic infection or endometriosis. Both of these conditions tend to cause scarring and adhesions behind the uterus which pull the uterus backwards and may be responsible for pelvic pain, abnormal bleeding, backache, or pain during intercourse. But even in these cases it should be emphasized that the symptoms are not entirely due to the tipped uterus, but are primarily the result of the disease that is pulling the uterus backwards.

A tipped uterus may also be responsible for a condition which doctors refer to as "chronic pelvic congestion," although not all physicians agree that it is either important or that it represents a definite disease entity. On the other hand, some doctors believe that just as women can have varicose veins in the legs, so can they develop varicose veins and a bloody congestion of the pelvic organs. Usually, this condition is seen in patients who have had a large number of children and, on examination, not only is the uterus found to be tipped but it is also enlarged, boggy, and tender. And should an operation ever be required, it is then that the surgeon usually sees marked dilatation and congestion of the blood vessels which carry blood through the uterus. Yet I hasten to add that most women with a tipped uterus do not develop this further affliction. However, those few who do usually complain of a dull, aching, nagging pain in the lower pelvic area which has aptly been referred to as a "pelvic toothache." If you have ever stood on your head for a few minutes, you will remember the feeling of pressure that occurs from the increased amount of blood going to your brain. It may well be that the same sort of thing happens in the pelvis to a lesser degree. Other symptoms, such as backache, painful periods, pain on intercourse, and abnormal bleeding may also be present. Furthermore, these symptoms are usually worse just before the period, when some degree of pelvic congestion occurs even under the most normal conditions.

The reason some doctors are extremely skeptical about the

pelvic congestion syndrome is that so frequently they see women with a boggy, congested, tipped uterus who have absolutely no symptoms. Many physicians have therefore come to the conclusion that one can only make a borderline diagnosis in such cases, because many women who do complain of backache and pelvic pain with a congested uterus are also frequently unhappily married, and suffering from "housewife's battle fatigue." It therefore is often difficult for the doctor to know how much of the patient's pain is due to the congested uterus and how much is due to emotional factors.

Doctors have to face a similar problem in evaluating any disease, but in the case of pelvic difficulties it is even more of a dilemma, because even the most casual woman is more emotionally attached to her uterus than, for example, her gall bladder. This means that very frequently doctors who are handling such cases come to the conclusion that the source of the difficulty is in the head and not in the pelvis. A great deal of talking is then necessary to convince the patient that, just as most of the nation's headaches are due to tension, so are a great number of pelvic pains. The majority of patients, either with a tipped womb, or one that may be associated with a slight degree of congestion, therefore require absolutely no treatment other than the reassurance that nothing is wrong. Some may be advised to take warm daily douches. Others, whose symptoms only become annoying just before their period, will be relieved by taking diuretic pills, which help to remove the excess fluid that normally increases at that time. A few others may be given hormones for a number of months.

In the very rare cases where surgery is required for a tipped uterus, the type of treatment is determined by such factors as the patient's age, the number of children she has had, the severity of her symptoms, and the findings that result from a pelvic examination. In young women, the operation normally consists of a number of procedures, rather than just a suspension of the uterus, since the surgeon must correct not only the position of the uterus but also the disease that is causing the uterus to be tipped. For example, if a problem such as endometriosis (internal bleeding) is present, the surgeon will either burn or cut away these small blood-filled cysts that may be present in a variety of locations on the ovaries, uterus, bowel, or wall of the pelvic cavity. Sometimes this necessitates removing part of the ovary, or freeing adhesions that may bind parts of the bowel to the female organs. Then a presacral and uterosacral neurectomy may be done, in which the nerves are cut that carry painful sensations away from the uterus. This latter procedure will frequently relieve the menstrual pain that is often seen with these conditions. Finally the appendix is removed, should it still be present. This type of operation, in which the female organs are conserved, means that not only will the majority of women be cured of the condition, but they will also still be able to have children.

In the case of older women who have a tipped uterus with extensive pelvic disease a hysterectomy is usually in order. One last point. In the majority of cases, it is possible to be reasonably sure of the extent of the pelvic disease prior to the operation, but this is not always so. In certain situations it is sometimes impossible to be sure until the incision is actually made, and then, what was originally thought to be a fairly localized disease, is found to be a more extensive one. And it may be so marked that although the surgeon planned on preserving the uterus by a suspension operation, he now finds the only way to cure the disease and relieve the patient of her difficulties is by doing a hysterectomy. Fortunately this kind of problem occurs very rarely.

The Presacral Neurectomy

In Chapter XIV, in the section on endometriosis (internal bleeding) I point out that when some women menstruate they may also bleed internally and, since this trapped blood has no way of escaping, it causes scarring and adhesions to form behind the uterus. This results in the uterus being pulled backwards toward the spine by the adhesions, which may result in painful periods, pain on intercourse, or abnormal bleeding. In the event other treatment fails, and surgery is advised in an attempt to relieve the discomfort, it is imperative that the pelvic organs be left intact, since most of such women are still in their child-bearing years, and have not yet completed their family. To achieve this, surgeons carry out a multiple-type procedure in which the uterus is suspended in the proper position, areas of the endometriosis are cauterized, and the nerves that carry painful sensation away from the pelvic organs are cut. It is the severing of the nerves which doctors call the "presacral neurectomy." This particular group of nerves runs along the lower part of the spine and, by removing a piece of the nerve, painful periods are frequently cured. Another important nerve is present in the uterosacral ligament, an important structure which helps to hold the uterus in position. These nerves are also usually cut at the same time by doing a uterosacral neurectomy.

Hysterectomy

I recall hearing the story about the man who had a life-long ambition to work on the railroad. Finally, he was told that he could have the job, providing he could pass the necessary test. He was then given the following question: "Suppose you were at a railroad station with a single track, and you saw an express train coming east at sixty miles an hour. Then you looked the other way, and another train was coming west at sixty miles an hour. The trains were just one mile apart. What would you do?" The man thought for a minute, and then he said "I'd go and get my brother." The committee stared at him in astonishment, and one of them finally asked, "Why would you get your *brother* at such a critical time?" And the man replied, "Because he's always wanted to see a train wreck."

I very much doubt that this man got the job, but at least he had the wisdom to realize that some things are inevitable. Just as surely as those two trains would collide, doctors are equally certain that there is no operation which has been more discussed by the general public than a "hysterectomy."

Everyone who discusses it immediately becomes an expert on the subject, even though his knowledge is usually limited to pure hearsay, based on all kinds of false information from friends and neighbors. No doubt some of these people sincerely believe they know what they are talking about, but the fact remains that they are nearly always wholly censorious of this type of surgery. It is the rare patient indeed who, before or after the operation, receives any words of encouragement from her family and friends. Instead, dark pictures are painted of the bleak future in store, and of the trials that await her on her return from hospital. These foolish tales cause untold suffering and worry, and often succeed in transforming a normal, intelligent patient into one who distrusts her doctor's every move. In fact it's not unusual for patients to hear these stories the night before the hysterectomy while being visited by a friend. I'm sure it must be hard for the reader to believe that anyone would bring in this type of bedtime story a few hours before the operation, but unfortunately it happens all too often. It's been recommended that one should beware of the Greeks bearing gifts. One should also put this type of friend in that same category.

Why should this particular operation cause so much controversy and misunderstanding? Certainly, no such debate centers around other common operations, such as repair of a hernia, or removal of the appendix. But the uterus is after all the "woman's organ," and therefore both patients and their husbands tend to view it in an emotional manner. It was in this part of her body that the patient carried and nourished her children for nine long months. In addition, her monthly period, although somewhat of a nuisance, was nevertheless a constant reminder of her womanhood, and the possibility of pregnancy.

For years, therefore, the uterus occupies a place of special significance in a woman's mind. The fact remains however that both they and their husbands are making a considerable error when they mistakenly associate the uterus with sex and with their general well-being. It has absolutely nothing to do with either. The function of the uterus is to carry a baby for nine months. No one has ever proved it has any other role. Similarly, the monthly period is present merely for the purpose of a possible pregnancy. It does not, as some think, rid the body of poisons or other substances. Consequently, stopping the period by a hysterectomy does not result in injurious substances collecting in the body. The fear that a hysterectomy will cause adverse changes is entirely needless. What nearly everyone seems to forget is the important fact that the operation is done to *remove disease,* and thereby restore the patient's health. People also forget that less than a hundred years ago this type of surgery was impossible. In those days, women suffered for years from chronic ill-health, caused by pelvic pain and profuse bleeding. Others hemorrhaged to death. Still others, who developed cancers, had no hope of cure. What a different picture we see today, when surgery can quickly and safely relieve their problem, and within a few weeks time their health is restored to normal. Many patients, once their initial fears are overcome, are genuinely grateful for the surgery. But others tend to blame the operation, the doctor, or both, for any trouble that arises later. I therefore intend to discuss some of the most common misconceptions regarding this operation, in the hope that understanding will help to eliminate some of these unnecessary fears and confusions. It's unfortunate that some people go through life always convinced that the worst will surely happen to them. But I hope that after reading about this operation they will realize that the Portuguese expression, "The worst is never certain," is at least true about a hysterectomy.

Will a Hysterectomy Affect Your Sex Life? As I have already said, one of the most frequent old-wives' tales concerns the operation causing some change in sexual function. A number of women are afraid that they will lose their femininity following surgery. And even if a patient begins by believing that the operation will leave her the same as before, she is frequently convinced of the reverse by some "good friend." Why any person would suggest such an idea to a patient before a major operation is hard to understand. There are, of course, a few people who delight in worrying others. They are women who are usually themselves unhappy in their marriages, and in their general approach to living. To see someone else facing difficulties gives them a certain amount of satisfaction. Husbands, too, are sometimes at fault. Instead of giving comfort and moral support to their wives, they also on occasion fall prey to foolish rumors. One cannot help wondering if such men are more interested in their wives as companions in bed rather than as human beings whom they love. This is not true of the majority of husbands, who are sincere in their sympathy and concern, and ask genuine questions regarding their future sexual life with their wives. But a few men will, following surgery, accuse their wives of no longer being capable of performing their sexual "duties." They may even blame the doctor for ruining their married life, when in actuality they never had a sound relationship with their wives. It is the old story of finding a scapegoat on which to pin one's troubles, rather than facing one's own responsibility in the matter.

What are the real facts about sex and its relationship to hysterectomy? As I said in Chapter V, the enjoyment of the sexual act is a mental phenomenon and is in no way dependent on whether the uterus or ovaries are present. Thousands of women continue to live happy married lives after a hysterectomy. A few even find their marriage improved, because for the first time they are able to enjoy sex fully. Free of the constant fear of pregnancy, they can at last relax. But for most women there is no change. Those who enjoyed sex before surgery will continue to do so afterwards. Those who were never able to enjoy it will still face the same problem after the operation. One cannot change a person's attitude toward sex merely by removing an organ which has to do only with pregnancy, *and has nothing to do with sex*. But of course the woman who has never enjoyed sex, or who has fallen out of love with her husband, finds her hysterectomy represents an excellent excuse for pushing her husband away. And undoubtedly she will find friends to support her stand. It is this type of woman who helps to give the operation an unjustly bad reputation. Yet the normal woman, fortified by the proper knowledge, will continue to enjoy her life and her marriage, regardless of what her friends tell her.

Will a Hysterectomy Cause a Gain in Weight? Another common misconception is that women routinely become obese after the operation. This is also untrue. Admittedly, a few women do put on weight following a hysterectomy, but it is not because the uterus has been removed. One or more factors are responsible for it. The first and most common reason is overeating. Too much food or the wrong kind of food are the causes for increase in weight. Fancy desserts, for example, are not conducive to maintaining one's weight at a normal level. Second, inactivity may play a role. Third, as women grow older many of them gain a few pounds. In the years that follow a hysterectomy, it is wrong to blame the operation for changes which are due to advancing age. But again, the hysterectomy is made the pretext for all sorts of problems as said before. Why blame ourselves when there is a good excuse available?

Will a Hysterectomy Cause Insanity? This is another false rumor that causes considerable concern among some women. Yet a quick appraisal of the facts should immediately reassure any patient of the stupidity of such a suggestion. Would surgeons continue to *recommend* an operation that caused even a small number of patients to end up needing psychiatric care? Obviously they wouldn't even attempt this type of surgery if that were the case.

What, then, is the source of this ridiculous story? We know from the popular press that about one out of every ten people develops some form of mental disease, which may be either mild or serious. And unfortunately a considerable number of people with grave psychiatric troubles never receive proper medical care. From time to time, a few of these women will develop a pelvic disease that may require a hysterectomy. Doctors do not like to operate on emotionally unbalanced women, but occasionally a patient's condition leaves them no choice in the matter. In a few cases, the patient becomes even more emotionally disturbed for a short period following the operation. *But the operation is not the underlying cause of the problem.* It is the patient's basic mental imbalance that is at fault. These are the type of people who are unable to cope with any of the normal stresses of living. Any crisis, such as the death of a loved one, financial difficulties, or other upsetting situations causes them to collapse, because they are walking an emotional tightrope all the time. When one examines their lives one finds a continuous history of chronic worry, nervous hysteria, and other such symptoms; so that it is not at all surprising that any type of major operation would prove too much for them to handle.

Unfortunately, many people don't bother to examine the facts intelligently. Instead, their uninquiring minds immediately jump to the wrong conclusion: Mrs. X had a nervous collapse after her hysterectomy—therefore the operation was to blame—so why did the foolish doctor perform it in the first place? It is this type of incident combined with this type of reasoning that has contributed to the aura of fear and doubt which surrounds this particular operation. But to repeat, you must remember that an acute psychiatric difficulty arises only once in many hundreds of hysterectomies, and even then it is only triggered by the operation, not *caused* by it. It is an extremely rare occurrence in any case, so rare it does not even need to concern the average patient, or even the patient who is by nature extremely tense. To be concerned about a forthcoming operation is a normal reaction. All women worry to varying degrees, but this is an entirely different reaction than that associated with psychiatric disease. Women can therefore be assured that a hysterectomy neither causes insanity nor changes a patient's personality. Women who have been depressed and unhappy all their lives will no doubt remain the same following surgery. But those who take the ups and downs of living in their stride will continue to do so.

What is a Hysterectomy and why is it performed so frequently? The operation involves removal of the uterus, with or without the tubes and ovaries. A number of years ago, an operation called a "subtotal hysterectomy," was more frequently done. As the name implies, only the upper part of the uterus proper was removed. Its lower part, the cervix, was left in place. Removing the cervix is technically more difficult, because it lies -close to the tube (ureter) that carries urine from the kidney to the bladder. In the early days of hysterectomy doctors worried about injuring this structure. In addition, the loss of blood was usually greater when a total hysterectomy was done. But today surgeons are using better techniques and instruments, and they rarely leave in the cervix. There are two reasons for this. First, it may develop a cancer later on in life. Second, it is frequently infected and causes vaginal discharge if not removed. Doctors call this complete operation a "total hysterectomy," that is, when both the uterus and the cervix are removed. How the uterus is removed depends on the type of disease, the age of the patient, and other factors. The majority of surgeons do an abdominal hysterectomy, which means the operation is performed through an abdominal incision. But during recent years an increasing number of vaginal hysterectomies have been performed in which the uterus is removed through the vagina. In this case, the patient is unaware of any incision following the surgery. The doctor is the best judge of the proper operation to perform.

I mentioned earlier that the tubes and ovaries may or may

not be removed during the hysterectomy. Again the surgeon has to consider a number of factors. Are the ovaries diseased? How old is the patient? What diseases have necessitated the hysterectomy?

The Ovaries. Let us first discuss a few situations where the ovaries must be removed. Should the ovaries be infected or cystic, the decision is simple, they must be taken out. Leaving them in will result in future trouble. Sometimes only one ovary is diseased, in which event the surgeon can safely leave the other ovary in. Endometriosis (internal bleeding) is another problem which may require their removal. Here the ovaries may be entirely normal, but since they are responsible for producing the female hormones which cause

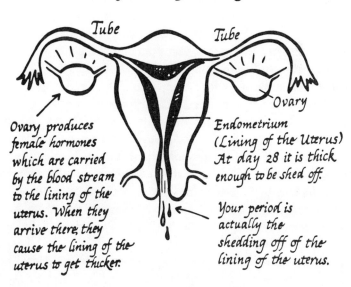

Before the Hysterectomy

Tube   Tube

Ovary

Ovary produces female hormones which are carried by the blood stream to the lining of the uterus. When they arrive there, they cause the lining of the uterus to get thicker.

Endometrium (Lining of the Uterus) At day 28 it is thick enough to be shed off.

Your period is actually the shedding off of the lining of the uterus.

endometriosis it may be necessary to remove them in severe cases of this disease. A hysterectomy is also performed for cancer of the cervix or uterus. In such cases, removal is clearly indicated, since the malignancy may have spread to one or both ovaries. This may be quite evident during surgery, when the ovaries are revealed as grossly enlarged from cancer. Yet even if they appear normal they must still be removed, for early cancer invasion is not visible to the naked eye. It is only after the surgery, when the ovaries are examined microscopically, that it can be determined whether or not the cancer has spread to them. One further point: Some surgeons habitually remove the ovaries during a hysterectomy, even when they are normal. They argue that during this operation the normal blood supply to the ovaries is affected, causing a small percentage of them to become cystic later on.

In what instances do some surgeons leave in the ovaries? A typical example is the young woman who has a hysterectomy because of fibroids. As the reader will recall, fibroids are benign (noncancerous) growths, limited to the uterus. Since the ovaries are usually normal in such cases, many surgeons will leave them in, because normal ovaries function for many years after a hysterectomy. Leaving in one or both ovaries will stop the patient from starting the menopause. The reader will recall that it is the ovaries that produce the female hormone, estrogen. Removing the ovaries stops the major source of production of the hormones and menopausal symptoms may occur. The patient's age is therefore an important factor in the decision as to whether normal ovaries are to be removed. If a woman is under forty-five, they may be left in. Over that age, they are more frequently removed, and most doctors will then advise a daily tablet of estrogen. Doctors may also advise a hysterectomy for various reasons which are discussed in detail in the separate chapters or sections which deal with these disorders.

The Fibroid Uterus (Chapter XIV), is one of the common reasons for a hysterectomy. These growths usually occur after thirty-five years of age, and are always benign (non-cancerous). One or more may be present, and they vary in size from being as small as a pea to becoming larger than a grapefruit. Whether they cause trouble depends on their size and location.

Infection of the Female Organs (Chapter XIV) is another frequent reason for hysterectomy. Infections primarily injure the tubes and ovaries, sometimes causing dense adhesions to form between the uterus and these structures. Today most of these infections are caused by bacteria such as the streptococcus, which produces severe throat infections, or the staphylococcus, which causes the common boil. Other bacteria may be involved, but the point I want to emphasize is that in the average person gonorrhea is a less common reason for the infection than it was a number of years ago. A great number of the infections appear to begin after delivery of a child, when the opening into the uterus is so dilated that any harmful bacteria in the vagina may more easily enter the uterus and reach the tubes and ovaries. This is particularly the case when labor has been longer than normal, or when a difficult forceps delivery has been required. Both of these conditions cause more injury to the pelvic tissues, and the greater the injury the more likelihood of an infection. Most of the infections that doctors see today are chronic ones—that is, they have been present for a long time, and furthermore they may not cause trouble for many years. Danger signals are usually abnormal bleeding of one sort or another, pelvic pain, painful periods, or pain with intercourse. One or more of these symptoms may be present. Often, the symptoms are not pronounced, and no treatment is required. But if the symptoms are severe, and if on pelvic examination there is a great deal of scarring around the pelvic organs, a hysterectomy is usually advised.

Pelvic Endometriosis (Chapter XIV) is another problem that has been diagnosed with increasing frequency during recent years. Once it was thought to be a rare occurrence, but it is now regarded as a common problem. It results from internal bleeding at the time of the period. The symptoms are very similar to pelvic infection, except that the pelvic pain is usually more cyclic in nature; that is, it recurs each month around the time of the period. Pelvic examination similarly shows scarring of the female organs, resulting from the irritation of the blood, since it is literally trapped in the abdomen without any way of escaping. Young women are most frequently treated by an operation that conserves the uterus. Since the uterus is frequently tipped and firmly held in that position by adhesions, the surgeon does a uterine suspension operation. Then a presacral and uterosacral neurectomy is done to stop the painful periods. (Both these operations are described in detail earlier in this chapter.) But women past the reproductive age are best treated by a hysterectomy, and in this instance the ovaries are usually removed.

Ovarian Cysts (Chapter XIV) may or may not require a hysterectomy. There are of course many different kinds of cysts, most of them about the size of an orange, but they may reach the size of a watermelon, weighing many pounds. Ovarian cysts usually grow slowly and since they hang freely from the tubes, like a trapeze artist hanging from a wire, they may reach a large size before they press on the surrounding organs and cause symptoms. Consequently, it is not rare for a patient to have a cyst the size of a nine-month pregnancy and still be free of symptoms.

Hyperplasia (Chapter XIV) is another reason for doing a hysterectomy. This term means the endometrial lining of the uterus has become much thicker than it is under normal conditions. In most cases it occurs because the ovary fails to ovulate, and without ovulation the endometrium may develop this abnormal thickness. Since the monthly period originates in the lining of the uterus, the thicker the lining, the greater the amount of bleeding. It is not unusual for women in their twenties or thirties to develop temporary hyperplasia. But toward the menopause it is more apt to become permanent and may require a hysterectomy to control the heavy, prolonged bleeding that accompanies it.

The Tipped Uterus has already been discussed earlier in this chapter.

Prolapse of the Bladder and of the Uterus is becoming a very frequent reason for hysterectomy, because women are living so much longer. This condition is also discussed in Chapter XVI.

Cancer of the Pelvic Organs (Chapter XV) may be treated by hysterectomy in some cases. But it is well to remember that the great majority of hysterectomies are done for reasons other than cancer. I have known so many patients who in the few days following the operation worry themselves into a state of nervous exhaustion believing that cancer was the reason for their surgery. It happens even when patients have been adequately reassured that the hysterectomy was done for a benign (noncancerous) reason. Then there is the woman who continues for years after the operation to mistakenly believe that the benign fibroid growth was a cancer. Many people worry away the best years of their lives! Let me repeat, most hysterectomies are not done for cancer.

When a patient is told a hysterectomy is required, both she and her husband may genuinely need convincing that it is absolutely essential. Their misgivings may be prompted by some old wives' tale, or they may have read a magazine article which criticizes the number of hysterectomies done each year. Often such articles refer to the hysterectomy as unnecessary surgery, which is performed because the doctor is more interested in the money than in the patient's welfare. Unfortunately, in any group of people, whether they be television repair men or doctors, there are those who are not honest. But this is the exception rather than the rule. The majority of doctors are hard-working and honest men who have their patient's interests at heart. Many patients who ask this question merely want to know if the operation can be postponed or whether it must be done immediately. This of course depends on the disease. If cancer is suspected, no delay is justified. But if the condition is a benign one, a postponement of a few weeks will not make any difference. Some people, of course, are terrible procrastinators, wanting to delay until the very last. Others, when they know the operation is required, are anxious to get it over with as soon as possible. Some problems such as heavy monthly bleeding from a fibroid uterus can be tolerated for a number of years. After all, chronic ill-health and annoyance will not kill a woman, and whether surgery is finally done may depend on how much discomfort is being experienced.

What Happens in the Hospital. What happens when you decide to go ahead with the surgery? Unless heart disease, diabetes, anemia, or some other problem is present, you will be admitted to the hospital on the day before the operation. This gives you a chance to settle in and familiarize yourself with your surroundings. It also enables the hospital staff to check your blood, urine, and obtain an X ray of the chest. Although the average hysterectomy does not require a blood transfusion, blood is always made ready in case it should be required in a hurry. The night before surgery, the surgeon and the anesthetist will drop by to see if there are any last-minute changes in your condition. Hospital surroundings on the first night, and the tension engendered by the thought of an operation in the morning, are not very conducive to a sound sleep. Therefore, to insure a more restful night, you will usually be given a sleeping pill.

The following morning you will be taken to the operating room. (Most patients recall being in a somewhat drowsy condition by this time.) And the days of dreading the anesthetist's

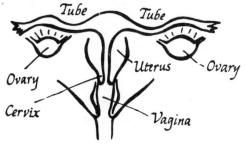

Normal Anatomy Before Hysterectomy

Tube — Tube

Ovary — Uterus — Ovary

Cervix — Vagina

After Subtotal Hysterectomy

Only the
cervix is left.
Ovaries may remain.

Vagina

After Total Hysterectomy

Cervix, too, has gone
and top of vagina
has been closed.
Ovaries may remain.

Vagina

mask are over. Now doctors inject a small amount of pentothal into your vein and in ten seconds you will be asleep. Most hysterectomies take from one to two hours to perform, during which time you may or may not receive a blood transfusion. Usually the next thing you will remember is slowly coming out of the anesthetic in the recovery room where nurses are in constant attendance. It is only when you have become fully conscious that you will be returned to your room. There are two other things you may worry about at this time unless you have been prepared for them. First, a needle may be present in one of your arms. The needle is attached to a bottle at the side of the bed. This is just a sugar solution to give you temporary nourishment and will be discontinued after a few hours. Second, a small rubber tube (catheter) will have been inserted into your bladder through the urethra, which is the passageway through which one normally voids. The purpose of the tube is to keep the bladder empty, as most patients have difficulty passing urine initially without its help. Most surgeons remove it within twenty-four to forty-eight hours, by which time you will be able to void normally.

What about the next few days? During this time you will be given adequate amounts of medicine to control any abdominal discomfort. Some of the pain results from the incision. But the so-called "gas pains" cause varying degrees of trouble. Usually the pain is mild and easily controlled by injections. Yet women should remember that the amount of discomfort varies from patient to patient. Sometimes two women who have had a hysterectomy will be placed in the same room. Usually one will have a little more pain than the other. There are two reasons why this is perfectly natural. First, the hysterectomies have usually been done for different problems. The second, and most important, point is that no two people react the same way to pain. You should also remember that following any abdominal surgery, the discomfort varies from day to day. Naturally it is worse during the first few days than at any other time, yet it is wrong to assume that the pain invariably gets better with each passing day. For instance, frequently the second day after the surgery is worse than the first, which makes many patients think something has gone wrong. This is not the case, for usually improvement occurs a day later. During the first few days your stomach is usually slightly distended and tender to touch.

This swelling of the stomach is quite normal and results from the collection of gas in the bowel. After a few days the bowel becomes active, gas is passed from the rectum, and the abdomen returns to normal size. Certainly these few days after the operation are nothing to be feared.

In the early days of convalescence many patients also worry because they do not have much appetite, and they are afraid that if they don't manage to eat their body will not function properly. But this is not the case. All of us have excess body food that we can adequately draw upon for a number of days without any trouble developing. Sometimes nurses or nurses aides mistakenly encourage patients to eat, even though they are not hungry. In an effort to be cooperative, their charges frequently force themselves to eat and become nauseated or vomit as a result. Therefore, you should not eat until you feel hungry, and it is unusual for most people to want a heavy meal until a few days have passed. After all, even if we are merely suffering from a common cold our desire for food is less. Is it not logical to assume it will be even more reduced after a major operation?

Also, following an abdominal operation, the bowel is normally partially paralyzed for a day or two, and it is not wise to overload a sluggish bowel, since most of the food will remain in the stomach. There are two signs which show doctors that the bowel is returned to normal activity. First, placing a stethoscope on the abdomen will determine whether bowel sounds have returned. (If present, these sounds indicate the intestines are now working.) Second, the passage of gas from the rectum is another good omen. When either of these two signs are present, doctors will advise a more liberal diet. But for the first one or two days most patients will probably prefer liquids, and water is still the best fluid there is. If you are unable to drink adequate amounts, the doctor may supplement it with a sugar solution into the vein for a day or two.

Not too many years ago doctors kept patients in bed for one or two weeks following a hysterectomy. This is in marked contrast to today when you will find yourself sitting in a chair on the first or second day after the operation. Doctors have found that getting patients out of bed earlier results in fewer postoperative complications. Early activity improves the circulation in the legs, which means fewer cases of phlebitis (inflammation of the veins in the legs) are seen. It also aids the circulation and activity of the lungs, which again means that postoperative problems, such as pneumonia, are now a rarity. So when the doctor insists on getting you out of bed, remember it is for your own good. Patients, like ships, get rusty if they are tied up for too long.

A reddish-brown discharge or slight amounts of bleeding are present to varying degrees for the first few weeks after a hysterectomy. This is because the end of the vagina has been opened to remove the uterus, and then stitched up again. Usually, the bleeding is small in amount, and gradually decreases during the hospital stay. At other times, enough blood will collect to form a blood clot the size of an egg which will be expelled from the vagina. This may unduly alarm the patient, who may immediately assume she is going to bleed to death or require another operation. This is not the case, for once the clot has been expelled usually nothing further happens. It is only on extremely rare occasions that the bleeding will persist and require treatment, such as temporarily packing the vagina, or putting in another stitch. A pack can be placed in the vagina painlessly without an anesthetic. Should a stitch be needed to control the bleeding area, an anesthetic is given and the area is sutured (stitched) by the way of the vagina. But let me repeat, a suture is required only on rare occasions when the bleeding persists or is profuse in amount.

When you arrive home, intermittent discharge and slight bleeding may occur for the next few weeks and is of no importance. This is because it takes a number of weeks for the end of the vagina to heal, and in the process of doing so granulation tissue commonly referred to as "proud flesh" may form. This tissue is soft, red and bleeds very easily. Should pelvic examination reveal granulation tissue, it is painlessly cauterized with silver nitrate about six weeks after the operation. Unless told about it by the doctor, you would not even know it was being done during your visit to his office.

The abdominal incision is closed by either silk stitches or small metal clips depending on the choice of the surgeon. Sometimes a combination of both are used, but regardless of kind, their removal is feared by a good many patients. Some worry about the pain. Others fear the incision will open up. The trouble is patients place too much emphasis on the only part of the operation they can see with their own eyes. They should remember that these stitches are only to fasten the skin edges together, and are of no use in supporting the important layers under the skin. Consequently, removing the stitches will in no way weaken the incision. What about pain? Actually if one approaches the experience calmly and sensibly, there is very little pain and most patients agree on this point. But occasionally a woman works herself into such a state of apprehension that when it is time to remove the stitches the pain is magnified many times beyond normal. (Patients who have had a vaginal hysterectomy do not have an abdominal incision and hence there are no stitches to remove.)

The length of hospital stay following a hysterectomy varies from patient to patient. Some women are ready for discharge at the end of a week. Others, who have a number of children to care for on their return home, are usually advised to stay a few days longer. Your own doctor, who knows both you and your home surroundings, is the best judge as to the length of your hospital stay.

Some Advice After Leaving the Hospital. There are some do's and dont's to follow for the two months following a hysterectomy, and they all center primarily around the word "moderation." By the time you arrive home you will be able to be up and about most of the time, and your normal activities can be carried out with complete safety. This includes cooking meals, dusting, going up and down stairs, and anything

else that could be classified as light work. Heavy lifting, such
as moving furniture is obviously out. So is excessive stretching
such as is required for washing walls or ceilings. In other
words, take it as easy as is practicably possible for the first
two months. Many women want to know when they can safely
bathe or shower. This should be all right about one week after
you get home, providing you don't try to use a douche. It has
been recently proved that water does not enter the vagina
during an ordinary bath.

Most women will find that they tire easily, and should therefore take a short nap or two during the day and retire early
at night. Adequate sleep and rest are certainly important during
these early weeks, but nevertheless you should get back into
a routine of light activities as soon as possible. It is just as
wrong to do too little as too much! And conversely it's also
wise not to do too much, as it's been demonstrated many times
that too much of anything is worse than none at all. So at this
stage of the convalescence follow Aristotle's doctrine of the
golden mean: Not too much and not too little. Since cars are
now so much a part of our daily lives most patients are eager
to know when they can either be taken for a drive or get
behind the wheel themselves. It does no harm for you to be
taken for short drives anytime after your arrival home, but it is
as well to wait for a month before you do any driving yourself.
More strenuous activities, such as bowling, golf, tennis, or
skiing, should not be attempted until three months from the
time of surgery.

When will you be able to return to work? Here again it
depends on the type of activity. As I have already said, if you
are a housewife, light housework can be started immediately on
your return home, but there should be a two-month delay before attempting anything strenuous. Ideally, some extra help
in the house for a couple of weeks is desirable, particularly
when the family is a large one. Women in the business world
are usually able to return to work in six weeks' time, as long
as their activities do not involve heavy lifting. I've known

many secretaries who are back at their typewriters in four weeks. Women who work in factories may need two or three months before they are able to resume their duties.

What about the return to normal sexual activities? The reader will recall that when either a vaginal or abdominal hysterectomy is done, the innermost end of the vagina is opened so the uterus can be removed. At the end of the operation it is stitched together again but it does not heal completely for about six weeks. Consequently, patients should refrain from sexual intercourse until a pelvic examination shows everything is healed. Usually normal marital activities can be resumed in about two months' time. Should a slight amount of reddish spotting or bleeding occur at that time, it is the result of small pieces of proud flesh that may still be present at the end of the vagina. As was mentioned earlier, the doctor can correct this problem painlessly in a few minutes by cauterizing the areas of proud flesh with a chemical called silver nitrate.

Caesarean Section

About four or five women in every hundred will have their babies by caesarean section. Should this happen to one of my readers, she should realize that it is certainly nothing to despair about. Rather, she should be grateful she was born in the twentieth century, when this operation can be done with safety. Less than a hundred years ago, half the women who underwent this surgery died from hemorrhage or infection; and before that time nearly all such women died, because doctors had not then developed a technique for closing the uterus after the incision had been made in it and the baby removed. There are probably few individuals in history who have suffered more than women in childbirth. When the first obstetrical hospital was opened in Vienna, just a few hundred years ago, one woman in six who entered never left it alive. This was because doctors in those days knew nothing about germs, and how they could transmit them from one patient to another. It was not unusual for them to go from the autopsy room to the delivery room without even washing their hands prior to a child's birth. If they had been examining a patient who had died of infection, they would carry these germs to the mother, who would herself die as a result. But dying from infection was not nearly as painful as the death of the woman who was endeavoring to give birth to a child through a pelvis that was too small to allow its passage. After days spent in fruitless labor, she would finally die in exhaustion along with her child. What a different situation today, when doctors can easily and safely perform a caesarean section with usually happy results for both mother and child.

Difficult Deliveries. There are many reasons for doing a caesarean operation. The most common is because of difficulty in the mechanical delivery of the baby. This can be due to many different causes, and often more than one cause is present. For instance, the woman's bony pelvis may be small or deformed. Years ago, rickets used to cause severe deformities of the pelvis, making it impossible to deliver a baby normally. On the other hand, the pelvis may be average size, but the baby extremely large. Then there are those situations where the baby's head is pointed in the wrong direction so that it does not descend as quickly or as easily as it should. Another problem may be a breech delivery. Here the baby is turned completely around so that the head, which normally is the first to be delivered, becomes the last. This means that the buttocks or feet are the first parts of the baby to push against the muscles and bones of the pelvis. Since they are not as hard or round as the baby's head, delivery may be slow or literally impossible, particularly if it is the patient's first child. Fortunately, tumors are rarely seen among the younger age group who are most likely to have pregnancies. But now and then a benign fibroid tumor, growing near the entrance of the uterus, will block the passage and prevent a normal delivery. There is one further mechanical reason which should be mentioned. The baby may be normal in size, and the bony pelvis adequate for its delivery, and yet labor becomes unduly prolonged. Here the fault lies with the muscles of the uterus, which are not able to push the baby downward with as much force as is necessary. But as mentioned earlier, a combination of factors may be present. The pelvis may be small, the baby large or in the wrong position, and after a prolonged labor the muscles of the uterus tire.

Hemorrhage is also another common reason for surgery. Usually this occurs in the last two months of pregnancy, and there are two primary reasons for it. The first condition is called "placenta previa," which means the placenta, or "afterbirth," as it is commonly called, is situated at the opening of the uterus rather than high up on its wall. Sometimes the placenta completely covers the opening, making it impossible for the baby to get out. But usually only part of the opening is covered, and in many cases the placenta has just grown up to the side of the opening of the uterus, but not over it. The important point here is that a placenta in this situation is more likely to bleed, either before labor or when it begins. Usually the bleeding is quite sudden and painless and may be extremely profuse. The second problem is a partial separation of the placenta, even though it is situated in a normal position inside the uterus. What causes it is in most cases unknown, but it seems that patients with high blood pressure, diabetes, or a condition called toxemia are more prone to develop it. Here the bleeding may be painless or associated with extreme sudden pain in the abdomen. All degrees of separation may occur. Many are what doctors refer to as "marginal separation," whereby a small part of the outer side of the placenta pulls away from the uterus and bleeding occurs. Less frequently, only the central part of the placenta separates, trapping the blood behind it and causing severe pain. Whether a caesarean section is required for these conditions depends on many factors such as the amount of bleeding, the number of pregnancies, condition of the baby's heart, the amount of pain present, and how far labor has advanced. If the bleeding is minimal and it appears that the labor will be short, surgery may temporarily be postponed. But if both pain and bleeding are severe, an emergency operation may be needed to save the lives of the mother and child.

Toxemia. A less common problem today is a disease which doctors call "toxemia of pregnancy." Not too many years ago this was frequently encountered and was usually the result of inadequate supervision during the pregnancy. Doctors have debated for years as to the cause of this problem, and there is still a great deal of controversy. But all agree that excessive weight gain is most frequently the forerunner of the hypertension and urinary changes that follow. Women who gain over twenty pounds are most likely to develop it. The common symptoms are a gradual progressive swelling of the ankles, increasing blood pressure, and the passage of albumin in the urine which normally is not present. Should the patient still fail to see the doctor these symptoms progress, the face becomes swollen, and spots appear before the eyes, along with a severe headache. In the latter stages, convulsions occur. Doctors rarely see symptoms which have gone as far as that today, since they keep a careful watch on their patients; and should any signs of toxemia appear, they start treatment at once. Normally, the use of drugs to get rid of excess fluid, combined with weight control, and a low-salt diet will quickly correct any problems. But some patients who are seen by a doctor very late in the course of the disease or who fail to respond well to treatment may require a caesarean section.

The Prolapsed Cord. This is one of the less common reasons for a caesarean. It happens when a patient develops what doctors call a "prolapsed cord" during their labor. This means that the umbilical cord, which carried blood from the mother to the baby and normally remains inside the uterus until the baby is born, may suddenly fall through the opening of the uterus. This can happen only when the mother's membranes have broken and the amniotic fluid has escaped. When it does fall down into the narrow vagina, pressure on it from the baby's head may shut off the blood supply and, if this is not corrected immediately by caesarean section, the child may die from lack of oxygen.

Chronic Diseases, such as diabetes, may prompt some doctors to advise a patient that an operation is the safest way to deliver the baby. They argue that diabetic babies are larger than others and should be taken from the mother three or four weeks before their due date. This, however, is a controversial point, as other doctors prefer to deliver a diabetic patient normally. Kidney disease is another occasion when surgery may be indicated. The kidney may work adequately during the greater part of the pregnancy; but as the term nears its end, the load becomes too much for it and trouble begins. In order to preserve the mother's health it becomes necessary to perform a caesarean section. A further situation that may require surgery occurs with the woman in her late thirties or forties who becomes pregnant for the first time. It may be that she married late or, after years of infertility, is finally pregnant. Some of these women may be advised to have their babies normally. But a good number of doctors will advise an operation. This is because childbearing is a young woman's occupation, for as women age the tissues of the pelvis become less elastic and more rigid. Furthermore, the expulsive powers of the uterus that push the baby to the outside are not as strong. Labor is therefore more likely to be unduly prolonged, and in order to prevent injury to the baby surgery is commonly advised.

The Rh Problem

The Rh problem may occasionally necessitate a caesarean section, but I want to talk about it here for two other reasons. First, there has been a dramatic scientific breakthrough in recent months which will eliminate this disease in the oncoming generation. Second, there is a great deal of confusion and misinformation surrounding this topic in the minds of most people. One day I received a semifrantic call from a husband who had just learned his wife was Rh negative. I could hear her crying in the background as he asked how long it would take to adopt a child, now that his wife could never have a family. Asked how he had arrived at such a dead-end conclusion, he related how a friend at work had told him about Rh babies dying inside the mother. Why should he put his wife through such an ordeal when there was no hope? Later that day, after hearing the real facts, they wondered how they could have been so far wrong. This couple went on to have three healthy babies without any difficulty. Fortunately, the above story is not an unusual or isolated case, because the presence of Rh does not always mean trouble. And the reader will see that the new method of treating Rh will take away all fear of this problem.

Let me explain what Rh means. It is fairly common knowledge that we all have different blood groups, such as A, B, AB, or O. Should we require a transfusion, it is important that we receive blood of our own group. Before doctors realized this, many people were given the wrong blood group and died. Not too long ago it was also discovered that eighty-five people in every hundred had blood that contained something called the rhesus or "Rh factor." The remaining fifteen people did not. Consequently, those who have it are called Rh positive and those without it are Rh negative. Now, about thirteen of every hundred marriages bring together an Rh negative wife and an Rh positive husband. This is the potentially trouble-making

combination, but what most people don't realize is that sometimes nothing untoward happens. Put another way, not all Rh
positive husbands cause trouble, as there are two different
types of positivity. Some men for instance, are "homozygous,"
which means they always give their wife an Rh positive baby,
which may present a problem. But others are "heterozygous,"
in which case they are capable of giving their wife either an
Rh positive baby or an Rh negative one. If the wheel of chance
comes up with the negative baby, then no trouble results,
because the baby is of the same Rh as the mother.

Now let us look at the dark side of the picture—that is, when
the wife is given an Rh positive baby. As I have just explained,
this happens because her husband is either homozygous and
that is all he can provide, or he is heterozygous, and for this
particular pregnancy he comes up with an Rh positive baby
The following sequence of events *may* take place; and the
reason it does so is because some of the baby's Rh positive
blood cells, which normally stay inside the baby, work their
way into the circulation of its Rh-negative mother. If this is a
first pregnancy, usually nothing happens, unless the mother
has been previously sensitized by receiving an Rh positive blood
transfusion at some earlier date. As her pregnancy progresses
some doctors believe that a few of the baby's red cells break
through the placental barrier which separates the two circula-
tions, and these positive cells invade the mother's blood stream.
These cells, as we will see shortly, stimulate the mother to
produce antibodies, but at this point there are not enough of
them to cause any trouble.

But the wheels of trouble are set in motion at the time of
delivery. What happens then is that as the placenta (afterbirth) pulls away from its attachment to the uterus, more of
the baby's Rh positive blood cells get into the mother's circulation. This adds something new to her system that it doesn't
want and triggers the production of antibodies in an effort to
destroy these foreign blood cells, in much the same way that a
family of lions would toss out even a friendly tiger that wan-

dered by. But for the first baby these antibodies are of no particular consequence, as by the time they have been manufactured in sufficient quantities to be harmful, the baby is safe in the outside world. But later babies may not be so lucky, because these antibodies are there at the very start of the pregnancy and are easily revitalized by an Rh positive baby. During the subsequent nine months the antibodies not only increase in the mother's blood, but may also pass through the placental barrier into the baby's circulation, because the placental barrier is a two-way street. In the first instance the reader will recall the baby's red cells pass from the baby into the mother's circulation, but now these antibodies go the other way from mother to baby. Once inside the baby's circulation they attack and destroy many of its red cells, resulting in anemia. This in turn means that the circulation cannot carry sufficient oxygen to important organs such as the brain, liver, and heart. Whether the baby survives is strictly dependent on the severity of the Rh problem. Fortunately, many Rh difficulties are so mild that once the baby is delivered no treatment is required. But babies who are severely affected by Rh must receive an exchange transfusion for two reasons. First, they need new blood to correct the anemia. Second, the destruction of the red cells results in the formation of a chemical called "bilirubin," which in turn produces jaundice. It has been shown that too much jaundice causes severe injury to the baby, particularly the brain. Consequently to insure that this does not happen, an exchange transfusion is done whereby nearly all of the baby's blood is replaced by new blood. This has resulted in saving the lives of many infants.

I trust the above gives you some idea of the problem that faces doctors when they are confronted by an Rh pregnancy. I should also mention that somewhere along the line doctors have to decide when to remove the baby from the uterus if they suspect it may be getting into trouble. Sometimes the mother is allowed to continue to term, and then labor is induced. But if doctors have reason to believe the baby may not last that long, they may elect to carry out an earlier induction or caesarean section a few weeks before term. The trick is to time it correctly. Too early a removal may mean a premature baby that may not survive. On the other hand, waiting too long may result in the death of the baby in the uterus. How to remove the baby once the decision has been made rests on two choices. If the cervical opening into the uterus is what doctors refer to as "ripe," they will consider stimulating the patient into labor. But if the cervix is not ripe, then a caesarean section is performed.

However, for those women who today are Rh negative and about to get married, all the above is past history. Rh problems are now preventable, because there is a substance called anti-Rh immune globulin. During the pregnancy the mother is tested to see if she is Rh negative. Then if she happens to deliver an Rh positive baby, this substance is given to protect her from becoming sensitized to any of the baby's Rh positive blood cells that may have escaped into her circulation. This agent will result in the virtual elimination of the Rh problem in the next generation of mothers.

CHAPTER XIII

Common Causes of Abnormal Bleeding without Pain

THE GROUP OF DISEASES we are about to discuss usually cause abnormal bleeding unassociated with pain in the majority of cases. This is not, however, a 100 percent rule, but for the convenience of the reader these cases are grouped together.

Chronic Cervicitis

There is a section in Chapter XVII dealing with this most common gynecological problem, and I would recommend that all women read it. Suffice to say here that chronic cervicitis refers to a rawness of the cervical opening, which is the opening into the uterus. Since it is raw, it bleeds easily, particularly after intercourse. In addition, it usually causes increased amounts of vaginal discharge. But it never causes pain. Fortunately, it is easily corrected by cauterizing the raw area, and this along with daily douches will result in healing in about six weeks' time.

Polyps

Just as polyps can occur in the nose, they can also arise in the cervix or uterus. It is an extremely common problem, and luckily nearly all polyps are benign. The great majority of these soft, red growths are called "cervical polyps," since they arise in the cervical canal (opening into the uterus). The other type, are known as "endometrial polyps," because they are an outgrowth from the endometrial lining and are present inside the uterus. Most of the polyps are less than an inch in length and about as round as a piece of spaghetti. But some are longer and may occur on the outside of the vagina. Most patients develop only one polyp, but some women may have many. But whether they are single or multiple, long or thin, patients should not spend any sleepless nights worrying about them.

A good number of polyps never cause any symptoms and are first detected only when a pelvic examination is done. But when they do cause trouble, the most common sign is intermittent spotting or bleeding between periods. Since polyps bleed easily when touched, this is usually first noticed after douching or intercourse. At other times polyps may cause staining for a few days following the period. Yet patients should remember that the majority of women who spot for an extra day or two do not have a polyp. And it is only on rare occasions that polyps cause prolonged episodes of bleeding.

The diagnosis of a cervical polyp is quite easy since they can be seen protruding through the cervical opening on a vaginal examination. But a polyp inside the uterus can be neither felt nor seen. Consequently if a doctor suspects that a endometrial polyp is the cause of bleeding, he will advise a D and C. The method of removing polyps depends on where they are situated. Most cervical polyps can be easily seen and are removed in the doctor's office. On the other hand, if it is difficult to see all of the cervical polyp, the doctor will advise a D and C. In this way the base of the polyp can be adequately visualized, and the doctor can then be sure the entire growth has been taken out.

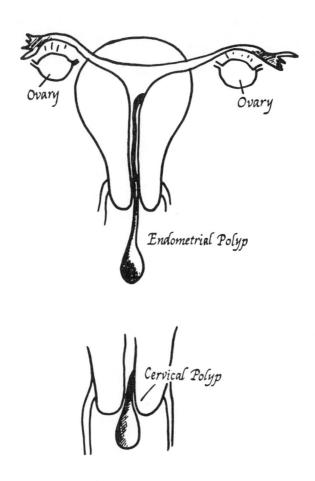

Ovary

Ovary

Endometrial Polyp

Cervical Polyp

Hyperplasia (The Thick Endometrium)

Irregular, frequent, heavy, and prolonged bleeding is sometimes due to an increased thickness of the endometrial lining of the uterus, which doctors refer to as "hyperplasia." It can occur at any age, but is more frequently seen in the young girl who is just starting her periods, and at the menopause. Let us first discuss the problem as it pertains to the teen-age girl.

The majority of girls begin their periods around thirteen years of age. At this time the ovaries produce increased amounts of the female hormone, estrogen, which stimulates the lining of the uterus, causing it to thicken. If ovulation (escape of the egg) occurs around the fourteenth day of the cycle, another hormone, progesterone, is produced and further changes take place in the endometrium, resulting in a period about fourteen days later. Progesterone is the hormone which primarily determines when the period starts. Now the problem is this: Many young girls do not ovulate regularly when the periods first start, which means that only one hormone, estrogen, is present. Consequently, week after week, estrogen continues to thicken the endometrial lining, but the additional changes normally present from the action of progesterone are lacking. This is what causes the trouble and results in the abnormal bleeding, because the endometrium reaches a point where it cannot become any thicker. At that time, heavy and prolonged bleeding may occur. Before this happens, the periods may be a few days or weeks late, and in some instances the period will be late by a few months. Although these changes may cause considerable worry to both the patient and her parents, there is usually no need for concern. Sooner or later ovulation begins, and with the normal production of progesterone the periods become regular and the flow normal. Hyperplasia is therefore like an alarm clock that is continually wound up without being allowed to unwind. When the alarm finally goes off. which we could liken to ovulation, the spring unwinds; and all is well.

Doctors are not certain why regular ovulation is delayed in some girls, but they do know it usually corrects itself in a short time. If it does not, hormones will be used to temporarily regulate the cycle, and this frequently initiates ovulation. In other cases, when the bleeding is excessive, a D and C (dilation of the cervix and scraping of the uterus) is done to remove the thickened endometrium. This, too, is generally followed by ovulation and normal periods. The point to remember is that hyperplasia in a young woman is usually a temporary problem and is in no way a possible forerunner of trouble, as it may be occasionally in the older patient.

Hyperplasia around the menopause is believed to occur by the same mechanical fault: failure of the aging ovary to ovulate. Consequently, the uninterrupted production of estrogen and lack of progesterone causes an excessive growth of the endometrium and abnormal bleeding begins. Usually the bleeding at this age is heavier and may last for several weeks. At other times, bleeding occurs at frequent intervals with the passage of large clots. This too may be a temporary affair, with ovulation occuring spontaneously without treatment and so correcting itself. But in general, hyperplasia is less likely to be reversible at this time of life, either with or without treatment. This, as one would suspect, is because the ovaries are now

Normal Endometrium

Thick Endometrium

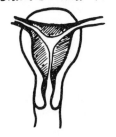

at the end of their productive life, and normally stop ovulating anyway. Therefore hormones which might stimulate ovulation at an earlier age now have little or no effect on the ovary. Similarly, although a D and C may temporarily control the bleeding, by scraping out the thick endometrial lining, it may recur in a few months' time. Why does the bleeding recur? It is because the ovaries still fail to ovulate but continue to produce estrogen in sufficient amounts to stimulate the endometrium, so once again it becomes too thick, and causes heavy, prolonged bleeding. Following the menopause, the ovary continues to produce small amounts of estrogen. But by this time the amount is usually too small to produce hyperplasia. Yet occasionally, enough estrogen will be present to cause a change in the endometrial lining sufficient to lead to light or heavy bleeding.

Abnormal bleeding during the menopause, or years after it, always requires a D and C for an accurate diagnosis. Should the scraping of the uterus show hyperplasia, nothing further may be required. But if the bleeding recurs, doctors are more likely to recommend a hysterectomy at this age, since in a small number of cases the hyperplasia may progress to cancer. A hysterectomy is particularly considered when hyperplasia first makes its appearance following the menopause. The reader should remember, however, that most cases of hyperplasia do not result in cancer, and surgery is primarily done to control the bleeding.

The Menopause

I doubt if there is any other time when women are more confused and worried about changes in the bleeding pattern than at the change of life. It is too bad that this is the case, because like so many things in this life, most of what we worry about never happens. This is certainly true of the menopause, because the majority of women never develop serious bleeding problems. For further information on the subject I would like to refer you to Chapters III and IV, both of which deal with the particular problems that can arise during the menopause.

In the present chapter I intend, therefore, to limit myself to making a few general points on this important subject. As you will find in Chapters III and IV, there can be tremendous variations in the types of normal bleeding at the menopause, but in most cases these slowly lead to a pattern of less bleeding. For some women, this means that the periods are delayed a week or two, or even a few months. These delays and skips usually push the periods further apart until they stop permanently. The point to remember is that doctors prefer to see less bleeding rather than more at this time.

An increase in bleeding is usually the result of a temporary upset in the delicate hormonal mechanism that controls the periods, and only on rare occasions is it due to a malignancy. Also, if you read Chapters II and III, you will see that there are many new and drastic changes in the way an increasing number of doctors are treating women during their change of life.

Why do the periods change and finally stop at this age? The basic reason is that as the ovaries get older they produce smaller and smaller amounts of the female hormones. And sooner or later, one further important thing happens: The ovaries stop ovulating regularly—that is, producing an egg each month. This has further repercussions because when ovulation occurs the female hormone, progesterone, is produced by the ovaries during the last two weeks of the menstrual cycle, and this helps to regulate the periods. When ovulation stops, this hormone is lacking, and only one hormone, estrogen, is manufactured by the ovaries. Sometimes, this lone hormone will be able to regulate the bleeding, but more frequently it cannot, and some change takes place in the bleeding pattern. Finally the periods stop because the ovaries do not produce sufficient hormones to stimulate the inside lining of the uterus to bleed.

How do doctors proceed with patients who gradually or suddenly notice more bleeding than usual? The first step is to do a pelvic examination, although in the majority of instances there will be nothing found to account for the bleeding. This means other tests must be done, because although the doctor can feel the outside of the uterus during a pelvic examination, he must next determine if there is anything wrong *inside* the uterus. This will include the Pap smear test for cancer, which is described in detail in Chapter XV, which may be followed by a D and C (Chapter XII). And the end of this investigation will prove to be good news for nearly all women.

Bleeding after the Menopause

Bleeding at this age may be due to many of the problems discussed in earlier chapters. Polyps, fibroids, a thick lining of the uterus, the aging vagina, chronic cervicitis, and infections may all cause varying amounts of bleeding. And since most doctors are now automatically giving the female hormone, estrogen, to women at the menopause this may very occasionally cause slight bleeding. I've mentioned in other parts of the book that before the menopause tension and worry can alter the periods causing more or less bleeding, or at times completely stopping the periods. However, anxiety on rare occasions can cause bleeding after the menopause. I recall one woman who had three children by the time she was twenty-one years of age; six months later she stopped menstruating for no apparent reason. She was told by her doctor that her ovaries had simply worn out at this unusually early age and that she had started the menopause. During the next seventeen years she was completely free of bleeding until the sudden tragedy of her husband's death—at which time she bled for one day. A D and C was done and no reason was found for the bleeding. So great worry can result in bleeding at any time of a woman's life, although cases such as this are more unusual after the menopause. Patients should also realize that at this age cancer is more common, and therefore, even if the bleeding is associated with some sort of worry, it should never be assumed that this caused the bleeding. It should also be understood that when the bleeding occurs is of no importance. Sometimes spotting or outright bleeding will be present after intercourse, but usually there is no apparent reason to account for it. Pain may or may not be associated with this type of bleeding, but generally it is much more likely to occur without pain. Fortunately the bleeding in most cases is due to one of the benign (noncancerous) problems. But if cancer is present it should be diagnosed as soon as possible. There is only one way to do this: See the doctor at once. More than at anytime in a woman's life this is no time to procrastinate by waiting around another month or two to see if it will recur. What might be 100 percent curable now, may be only 50 percent curable in a few months or, worse still, be beyond cure.

CHAPTER XIV

Common Causes
of Abnormal Bleeding
with Pain

THE DISEASES WE ARE about to discuss are quite common, but it is well to bear in mind that they do not always cause symptoms or require treatment. A small fibroid, for instance, may be deep in the wall of the uterus and remain so throughout the patient's life. Similarly, a small amount of pelvic infection or endometriosis may clear up entirely without causing any trouble. I have already explained that certain problems, such as the tipped uterus, are not associated with any disease in the great majority of cases and require no treatment. This is also true of some ovarian cysts that may occur during a menstrual cycle, only to disappear with the following one. Why, then, are we discussing these problems together? It is because when these diseases *do* produce symptoms, abnormal bleeding and pain are the most common reasons why the patient comes to the doctor. There is one further point to remember: Abnormal bleeding and pain are often seen together —but such bleeding *may* occur without pain, or there may be pain *without* bleeding.

Any of the above problems can occur at any time in a woman's life. But if they do not make their appearance until the menopause, she may make an error of judgment unless she is forewarned. For example, some friend may tell her that the

abnormal bleeding is the result of her age, and there is therefore no reason to worry about it. Do not fall into this trap.
Even doctors are sometimes unable to differentiate between
menopausal bleeding and bleeding which is due to a disease,
unless they do special tests. Your next-door neighbor is neither
a prophet nor a specialist. Don't listen to her. See your doctor.

Fibroids

Most of you know of one or more friends who have
been told they have a fibroid tumor, which is no wonder as
these are the most common benign (noncancerous) growths
occuring in women. They are quite hard, composed of tough,
fibrous and muscular tissue, and occur in various shapes, sizes,
and positions in the uterus. Some are as small as a pea, others
larger than a grapefruit. In some cases, only one will be present,
but there may be many scattered throughout the uterus. As
happens in many of the female diseases, women become quite
confused and worried about fibroids when they foolishly listen
to their friends' advice. One woman, Mrs. X, who was told
she had a fibroid, arrived at my office in a state of a great
anxiety because her neighbor had recently undergone a hysterectomy for the same trouble. Weeping bitterly, she asked me why
her doctor had not recommended surgery, as her friend had
warned her it was the only safe way to treat them. Let me
therefore clear up any confusion that may exist in this regard
by citing two different cases.

Mrs. Jones, who on a checkup examination is found to have
a small fibroid, may be wisely advised to leave it alone if she
does not have any symptoms. This is particularly so if she is
nearing the menopause, as most fibroids do not increase in size
after the change of life is over. Or it may be that her doctor
has been aware of the growth for some time, and since it has
not increased in size has advised against surgery. This happened
to be the case with Mrs. X, and once reassured that all fibroids

do not require hysterectomy, she stopped worrying. After that she also stopped listening to over-the-back-fence medical diagnoses.

Mrs. Smith, on the other hand, consulted the doctor because of heavy, frequent, and prolonged periods. The change from the normal cycle had been quite slow. In fact, looking back she found it difficult to state exactly when it had begun. In addition, her period, which had previously been associated with just an occasional cramp, was now quite painful. The pelvic examination in this case showed a large grapefruit-sized growth, completely distorting the uterus, which required a hysterectomy to correct the problem.

I mention these two different cases to emphasize the fact that a great number of fibroids do not require treatment, but do let your doctor decide, and not a poorly informed friend.

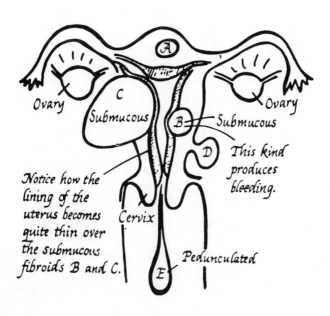

There are many points which the doctor has to consider before making his decision: the age of the patient; the number of children; the location of the fibroids; and last, but not least in importance, how much trouble the fibroid is causing.

However, the *size* of the fibroid may, at times, necessitate surgical treatment, even though the patient is without symptoms. For instance, now and then the doctor will feel a mass in the lower part of the abdomen which on pelvic examination turns out to be a large fibroid. Some patients may be completely unaware of its presence, while others will have noted a heaviness in that region. Yet, in spite of its size, the periods have been normal in all aspects. This, however, is the lull before the storm, and these patients are all advised to have a hysterectomy done. It is recommended for two reasons. First, symptoms such as abnormal bleeding and pain will eventually occur. Second, large fibroids are more likely to develop complications. Cystic degeneration is one of the most common conditions that results from the fibroid outgrowing its blood supply. Stated another way, there is not enough blood to keep all of it healthy, so the central portion, farthest away from the source of blood, starts to degenerate, and hemorrhage may also occur. There is one other interesting complication that may develop, though it is not as common as the one just mentioned. Some fibroids, in the process of degeneration, develop deposits of calcium in the growth. Calcium is a stony, hard substance; so in former years doctors referred to this phenomena as the "womb stone." I'm sure the reader will now realize why it is important to remove large fibroids, even though they are not causing trouble.

There is one type of fibroid that deserves special mention. Doctors refer to it as the "submucous" type, since it starts to grow just under the inside lining of the uterus. Consequently, as it gets larger it distorts the lining, which is believed to result in the abnormal bleeding. There is one further important point. The size of a submucous fibroid is not as important as with fibroids growing elsewhere in the uterus. Small submucous

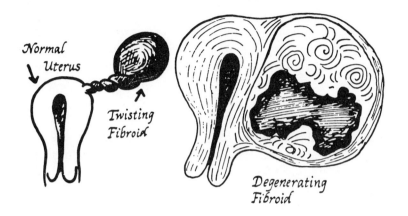

Normal Uterus

Twisting Fibroid

Degenerating Fibroid

fibroids may cause such severe bleeding that a hysterectomy is required since, due to their location, they are hard to remove any other way. There is, however, one type of submucous fibroid that is quite easy to remove. Some submucous fibroids that have been present for years gradually work their way out of the inside lining of the uterus, so that they hang free inside the uterine cavity and are attached to its wall by only a thin pedicle (a stalklike structure). Over a period of months or years, the fibroid may, in addition, fall out of the uterus, and on pelvic examination these are seen in the vagina, but still attached to the inside of the uterus by the pedicle. They can be easily removed by cutting the pedicle close to its attachment to the uterus. If the fibroid is not removed, the pedicle may twist, the blood supply is shut off, and severe pain results. Fibroids can also be attached to the outside of the uterus by pedicles and should be removed.

The majority of fibroids that cause abnormal bleeding such as heavy, prolonged or frequent periods, bleeding between periods, or pelvic pain are treated by a hysterectomy. If, however, a woman hopes to have further pregnancies, and it is technically possible to do so, an operation called a "myomectomy" is done. The fibroids are removed, but the uterus is left in place.

Remember, fibroids are quite common, are in no way related to cancer, and may be present without symptoms. Should symptoms occur, they may start suddenly, with heavy bleeding lasting several weeks, or come on quite slowly with a gradual change in the normal pattern of bleeding. Occasionally, due to their size, they cause pressure on the bladder or rectum, resulting in either frequency of urination or constipation. The diagnosis is easy, since most fibroids are readily felt during a pelvic examination. Some patients may be advised to have a D and C done in cases where the diagnosis is in doubt. During the D and C, the small submucous type of fibroid can then be felt inside the uterus. Don't forget, many fibroids do not require treatment. But if a hysterectomy is required don't feel too sorry for yourself, as the surgery results in a complete cure. Fibroids do not return. Some women with other diseases are not so lucky.

Infection of the Female Organs

Infections may occur in any part of the female organs. You will find, in Chapter XVII, that I discuss trichomonas and fungus infections of the vagina. These were mentioned in this particular chapter because they primarily cause vaginal discharge and itching. Now we will turn our attention to infections of the uterus, tubes, and ovaries which primarily cause abnormal bleeding and pain. Discharge, although it can be present, is in most cases less pronounced.

In the days before antibiotics, severe infections of the female organs were quite common and more frequently due to gonorrhea than is the case today. Furthermore, many acute infections, such as those caused by the streptococcus organism, occurred following a normal pregnancy. The sequence of events was usually the same in all cases. Quite suddenly the patient would complain of severe abdominal pain, high temperature, chills, copious amounts of vaginal discharge, nausea and vomiting, and sometimes pain on voiding. Such patients were acutely ill, and remained so for many days. Many of them developed what doctors refer to as a "pelvic abscess," which is a large collection of pus in the pelvis (lower part of the abdomen). Frequently, these pus areas had to be drained surgically. Furthermore, a large number of these women died, particularly if the infection was associated with childbirth. Other young women who had never been pregnant were left permanently sterile because of damage to the tubes. In these cases, both tubes would be closed by adhesions, and the male sperm would be unable to reach the egg for fertilization to occur. Today, cases such as these are rare. For one thing, doctors now have many different kinds of antibiotics that quickly kill the bacterial infection. Second, the obstetrical care of women has improved tremendously. What, then, is the most frequent type of infection doctors see today? Let me describe a typical case.

Mrs. John Doe at thirty-five had three healthy children, and until a year ago had been in perfect health. Since then she had noted that her periods, which formerly had been associated with a few mild cramps, had now become quite painful. In fact, sometimes the pain in the low abdomen and back would even start a few days before the bleeding began, and occasionally during the period she would have to go to bed. Furthermore, she was frequently left with a dull ache in her abdomen between periods. There had been one other important change. Whereas her periods had been quite regular before, there had now been a gradual change toward more frequent, longer, and heavier periods. On further questioning she admitted some pain on intercourse, which had started during the past year. A pelvic examination revealed that she was suffering from a chronic pelvic infection. How an infection of this type starts is not always known. In some cases, it follows a pregnancy. In others, it may smolder on after a previous acute infection. Sometimes the infection that started it was so mild that it went unnoticed. But whatever the cause, some patients do develop these symptoms. In most cases, such infections could be compared to something like chronic sinusitis—they may annoy you, but they'll never kill you. The majority require little if any treatment. Some clear up on their own with the help of warm water douches. Others require antibiotics. But in general such drugs are less effective in treating chronic infections because the bacteria are protected by scar tissue.

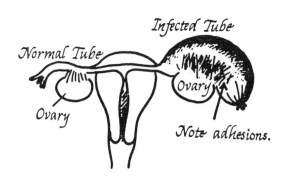

However, if the infection does become extensive, surgery is frequently required. What is done at the operation will depend on the amount of damage present. Sometimes a badly infected ovary and tube is all that is removed. At other times, if the uterus has been pulled back to the spine by adhesions, the tipped uterus will be suspended in its normal position. In other cases, the nerves that carry painful sensations away from the uterus will be cut during an operation called a "presacral neurectomy" (Chapter XII). This will stop painful periods in a large percentage of cases. Such procedures are particularly valuable in the case of women who are anxious to have more children and when the disease has not become too acute. But in those situations where extensive infection exists, and the woman has already completed her family, a hysterectomy is usually done.

Let me emphasize that the symptoms of pelvic infection I have been describing may also be present in many other diseases, some of which may be serious, but which more often prove to be a temporary problem that is easily corrected. So don't jump to any hasty conclusions while reading this or any other chapter. And may I again remind you that this book was written to help you understand your problems *after* you have had them diagnosed by your doctor, not *before* you have seen him.

Pelvic Endometriosis (Internal Bleeding)

An old German proverb states, "what one looks for one finds." This has often proven to be the case in medicine, particularly with such diseases as endometriosis. Originally it was thought to be a rare condition, but as surgeons began to look out for it consciously, they found more and more cases. Now it accounts for about 20 percent of all gynecological surgery.

The typical case of endometriosis has much in common with pelvic infection. Women who formerly had trouble-free periods may notice a slow change. Most will complain that the bleeding is now painful with cramps in the low abdomen and back. Generally these pains will start a few days before the period and may last a day or two after the bleeding has stopped. But regardless of when the pain starts or ends, the important point is that the periods now cause the patient discomfort of a mild or severe type. Another important change usually goes along with the pain: The pattern of bleeding alters. Patients will notice heavier, longer, or more frequent periods. In addition, pain may be experienced for the first time during intercourse. Other women will complain of painful bowel movements at the time of the period. Still others will notice bleeding between periods, or a dirty brownish discharge that lingers for a few days after

the period ends. As the reader will remember, these are practically the same symptoms that are present with a chronic pelvic infection. There is one important exception, although not a
sure rule. The pain of pelvic infection is just as likely to occur
between periods as during them, whereas the pain of endometriosis is actually limited to time of the period. It is this
monthly recurrence of the pain which is quite characteristic of
internal bleeding. But remember, most painful periods are due
to spasm, not endometriosis.

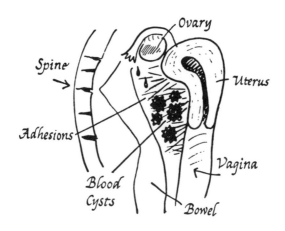

The findings on pelvic examination again bear many similari-
ties to chronic infection. Both the tubes and ovaries may be
tender. The uterus may be pulled back to the spine by adhesions, firmly fixed in this tipped position. But the most characteristic finding of all is small, hard, round lumps at the end of
the vagina which are quite tender. Patients frequently find it
hard to understand what endometriosis is. They have all had a
sore, infected finger, but internal bleeding is another thing. Just
what is it? You will recall from Chapter I that the menstrual
period is the result of bleeding from the endometrial lining of
the uterus. For reasons about which doctors are still not certain,

this lining, which is normally just inside the uterus, somehow appears in places outside the uterus. How it gets there is debatable. Some doctors think that during a period some of the lining, which normally sheds off, works its way back through the tubes, and thereby becomes implanted in the general abdominal cavity. (Much like putting a partial dam across the Niagara.) Others are convinced that small bits of endometrium are carried by narrow channels called the "lymphatics" to these abdominal sites. Still other doctors think it was there all the time and, after remaining dormant for years, finally starts to cause trouble. But why does it?

You will also recall that it is the ovarian hormones that stimulate the endometrial lining of the uterus to grow, and it is this which, after twenty-eight days, results in a period. Stated another way, it is the endometrial lining that produces the period. In fact, without it there can be no period. Why, then, shouldn't these ovarian hormones similarly stimulate the endometrial lining outside the uterus? This is exactly what happens; so, at the time of the period, endometrial glands outside the uterus also bleed. It is this internal bleeding that causes the pain each month, since not only does it irritate the sensitive peritoneum (the inside lining of the abdominal cavity) thereby causing a miniature peritonitis, but it is also, literally, trapped blood, with no way of escaping to the outside. Month after month, with each successive period, the peritoneum becomes scarred, adhesions form, and the uterus frequently becomes pulled back toward the spine and rectum. Furthermore, the trapped blood develops into tiny, hard, blood-filled cysts which can be felt as hard nodules at the end of the vagina. On more rare occasions one of these cysts may gradually enlarge, particularly when it is situated on the ovary, and become as large as a grapefruit and full of clotted blood.

Much can now be done for this common problem. Young married couples, for instance, may be advised not to postpone a family if, during an examination, the woman is found to have early endometriosis. She may still be quite fertile; but five years later it may be more difficult to get pregnant, should the tubes become scarred from the internal bleeding. Doctors have noted that women who marry late, or who put off having children, are more likely to develop endometriosis than those who have children early in life. In other words, early interruption by a pregnancy of the woman's monthly cycles appears to guard against developing the disease. Doctors use this principle in treating patients. They will advise stopping the periods, sometimes for nine months or longer, which can be accomplished in one of two ways: either the patient should become pregnant, or the hormone, progesterone, is given in amounts sufficient to stop the monthly period. The rationale here is that by stopping the periods for nine months no internal bleeding will occur, and the endometriosis present will have a chance to subside. The progesterone also seems to have a specific effect on the areas of endometriosis.

Patients may be advised by their doctor that surgery is the best way to treat this problem. Like that of chronic pelvic infection, there are two types. The conservative operation, in which the female organs are preserved and the areas of endometriosis are destroyed, is performed on women who are young and who desire more children. It is a multiple type of operation, which involves either cutting away or cauterizing the endometriosis wherever it occurs, suspending the uterus in its proper position, and doing a presacral and uterosacral neurectomy. The latter procedure involves cutting the presacral and uterosacral nerves which carry painful sensations from the uterus to the brain, and this frequently relieves the painful periods. If the appendix is still present, most surgeons will remove it, as well, to save the patient the possibility of another operation. A large percentage of patients are permanently cured following the surgery, and many are then able to become pregnant. A smaller number of patients will have a recurrence of the disease, but it is usually mild and is easily treated with hormones. Hysterectomy is usually reserved for those women with extensive endometriosis. If the reader is about to undergo the latter surgery, it is well to remember that this will completely cure the endometriosis, with no chance of a recurrence. Removal of the ovaries at the time of hysterectomy means the ovarian hormones which stimulate the endometriotic areas are no longer present, and any areas of endometriosis that cannot be cut away will shortly disappear. Without the ovarian hormones, the endometriosis cannot survive.

Ovarian Cysts

There are many different types of ovarian cysts, some of which require treatment, and others which are of no importance. Let us first discuss the second, harmless category. And in order to understand this fully we will quickly review how the ovary works during a normal menstrual cycle.

From Chapter I, the reader will recall that immediately following the period a new egg starts developing in the ovary. The egg is enclosed by a small sac, and day by day both egg and sac become larger. Then, halfway between periods, that is on the fourteenth day, the sac normally ruptures, the egg escapes, and if intercourse has occurred pregnancy may follow. Now and then, for reasons of which doctors are not certain, the sac fails to rupture, and gradually increases in size to become an ovarian cyst. Sometimes it is only the size of a walnut. Others become as large as an egg. Doctors refer to them as physiological cysts, that is, cysts that result from the normal workings of the ovary, and not from disease. Fortunately, the majority of these cysts go away on their own. Consequently, if a doctor suspects this type of cyst he will advise another examination in a few weeks. Many will have disappeared by this time. Others that are still the same size, or larger, may require removal, but fortunately these are in the minority. Some women are impatient about waiting and want something done at once. But when it is explained an operation may be avoided by waiting, they are more than willing to do so.

There are many other types of ovarian cysts, which may occur at any age. Doctors refer to them by different names, depending on what is present inside the cyst, and also on the structure of the cyst wall. For instance, some cysts are full of a clear, watery fluid. Others contain a jellylike substance, while still others may contain blood. One of the most interesting of these, and one that is fairly common, is called a dermoid cyst. This cyst contains a number of different types of tissues such as bone, hair, thyroid, brain and other structures. Before the operation, doctors can sometimes diagnose this type of cyst by taking an X ray of the abdomen, and seeing a piece of bone or tooth in the region of the ovary. All of the cysts we have just discussed may be present without symptoms, since the ovary lies in the middle of the pelvic cavity and may therefore reach a large size before

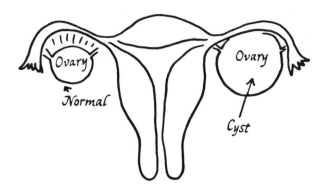

pressing on important structures. Some may cause a heavy sensation in the lower part of the abdomen. Others may be associated with a dull ache or pain at the period time. A few may gradually increase in size to a point where the abdomen begins to swell and the patient's clothes become tight. A few women mistakenly think they are pregnant. Abnormal bleeding may also occur. Sometimes the patient may skip a period, which may then be followed by heavy bleeding. But, generally speaking, benign ovarian cysts are much less likely to cause symptoms than many of the other diseases we have discussed in this section.

A yearly visit to the doctor is the best guarantee that an ovarian cyst will be diagnosed early, and long before symptoms occur. Should one be discovered and persist, surgery may be advised not only to prevent the above symptoms, but also to guard against possible complications. For instance, the cyst can suddenly twist, interfering with its blood supply, and cause acute pain. At other times the cyst may rupture, or bleeding may occur inside the cyst—both conditions causing sudden pain. These complications require immediate surgery to remove the cyst. But, as the reader is well aware, surgeons prefer to remove an acute appendix before it ruptures. The same is true of an ovarian cyst. That is, they would rather remove it before

Rupture of Ovarian Cyst

Twisting of Ovarian Cyst

complications occur. Fortunately most ovarian cysts do not develop complications, but since there is no way of telling which ones will cause trouble, it is better to remove them. The old Arabic proverb of "never troubling trouble until trouble troubles you" certainly does not apply here.

What is done during the operation depends on several factors, primarily the type of cyst present and its size. Some physiological cysts the size of an orange do not involve the entire ovary and can be removed leaving the normal part of the ovary intact. This is particularly important in young women who desire more children. If, however, the entire ovary has been destroyed by the cyst, it must be removed. Most patients only have one ovarian cyst, the other ovary being normal. On infrequent occasions both ovaries will become cystic and may be either so enlarged or adherent to the uterus that a hysterectomy is required.

Before leaving the subject of ovarian cysts there is one common problem that I want to mention. In the early part of this chapter we mentioned that around the fourteenth day of the cycle ovulation occurs, at which time the small sac containing the egg breaks, allowing the egg to escape. Since the sac also contains a clear, watery fluid, this also discharges into the pelvic cavity, which may temporarily irritate the peritoneum (the inside lining of the abdominal cavity) causing a mild peritonitis. Some women are quite aware of this each month, and are even able to tell which ovary has ovulated. It is also a quite convenient method of birth control, insofar as they can avoid intercourse at that time. A few women who have never noticed this phenomenon may suddenly become quite aware of it, with moderate pain which may last from a few hours to a few days. Usually, after a number of months, it goes away as quickly as it came. It is only on rare occasions that ovulation causes enough trouble to warrant more than a few aspirins. If, however, the pain continues to be severe month after month, the doctor may prescribe hormones to stop ovulation for a month or two in the hope that the pain will not recur after stopping treatment. There is just one further problem that may occur on very rare occasions. When the small sac breaks at ovulation a small blood vessel in the sac wall may bleed and, as the blood discharges into the abdominal cavity, severe pain may result. If it is the right ovary that has ovulated, this pain may resemble an attack of appendicitis. In a few cases, bleeding may be so pronounced that an operation is required to stop it, but fortunately this is a rare occurrence.

CHAPTER XV

Cancer

IT WOULD BE FOOLISH to look on cancer as a "good disease," but in some ways certain types of cancer are not that bad when compared to other illnesses. Let's look at it this way. None of us can pick and choose our disease when something eventually goes wrong, for as Shakespeare said, "There's a divinity that shapes our ends, rough-hew them how we will." Nevertheless, most women would immediately place cancer right at the top of the list of the undesirable diseases. They would be correct in thinking this way about certain types of malignancy which are rarely diagnosed early and are consequently less easily cured. Yet they would be totally wrong about cancer of the cervix, which, as long as it is diagnosed early by the Pap test while it is still on the surface of the cervix (Carcinoma-in-situ), is 100 percent curable. Far better to have this type of cancer than a fatal heart attack, the annoyance of diabetes, or many other chronic diseases. Certainly women with frequent migraine headaches or troublesome chronic sinusitis undoubtedly suffer more over the long run than a patient who has this earliest type of cancer at the opening into the uterus and who is permanently relieved of her trouble by the temporary inconvenience of a hysterectomy.

Any of these difficulties can occur at any time in a woman's life. But if none of them appear until her menopause, she may easily make an error in judgment unless she is forewarned. For example, some friend may tell her that any abnormal bleeding is just the result of her age, and there is no need to worry about it. Do not ever let yourself fall into this trap. Even doctors are at times unable to differentiate between menopausal bleeding and bleeding due to a disease, unless special tests are done. Your next-door neighbor is neither a prophet nor a specialist. Don't listen to her. See your doctor.

Fortunately, due to the tremendous and continuing efforts of the Cancer Society and other such organizations, millions of women now have a better understanding of cancer and the importance of both the yearly checkup examination and early diagnosis. And it is the writer's hope that this section of the book will also help to give women a more balanced and optimistic outlook on cancer, for there are enough people around who spend their time spreading gloom. Not too many years ago, doctors had little hope to offer patients who contracted this disease, but happily medicine has progressed a long way since then. In fact, the reader will see that in the case of cervical cancer the Pap smear will detect abnormal changes long before an outright cancer develops. This offers an unparalleled opportunity for cure. Certainly we have now reached the point in cancer diagnosis and treatment when we can start to look up rather than down. Indeed, we should begin to follow the philosophy of F. Langbridge who, in *A Cluster of Quiet Thoughts,* wrote, "Two men look through the same bars, one sees the mud and one sees the stars."

What is cancer? The body is composed of millions of normal cells that help to make up the tissues and the various organs, such as the lungs, heart, and pelvic organs. Under normal conditions, these cells are continually wearing out and being replaced by other normal cells. The important question is what upsets the applecart and makes the body produce cancer cells in a haphazard fashion rather than normal cells Possibly one could liken the process to an intricate computer that for years sorts out all kinds of information and quickly produces the right answers. Then for obscure reasons the machine gets confused and goes off on a tangent, and all the answers become wrong. For years now, scientists all over the world have been working on this problem and sooner or later the various parts of the puzzle will fit into place. Although at the moment there are more questions than answers, some facts are fairly certain. For example, cancer does not appear to be an inherited disease, since nearly all families over the course of several generations will have one or more members who develop it. Furthermore, contrary to what many women think, hormones do not cause cancer. I want to particularly stress this point, because more and more women are being placed on long-term estrogen pills at the menopause to counteract its long-term effects. Old wives' tales, however, die hard, and although there is no scientific foundation to the premise, it nevertheless still lingers on. In fact, recent studies seem to indicate that the exact opposite may be true: namely, that women on long-term hormonal treatment may develop fewer cases of cancer. Consequently, when women are advised to start estrogen pills at the menopause, they should not have any hesitation in going along with their doctor's advice. As I have already said, many doctors now believe the menopause is merely a deficiency disease, and that by supplying the needed hormone, estrogen, the long-term deleterious effects of the menopause can be prevented. (This approach is discussed in full in Chapter III.) Lastly, cancer has never been shown to be infectious; that is, it cannot be passed from one person to another like the common cold. Now, before we proceed further, let's take a bird's eye view of the common and the rare pelvic cancers.

Pelvic Cancer

Cancer of the Cervix is the most common pelvic malignancy and its earliest type, called "Carcinoma-in-situ," occurs most often in the mid-thirties. The term "in-situ" means that the abnormal cellular changes are totally confined to the surface of the cervix, without any penetration into the deeper tissue, and of course it's the best kind to have, since it is completely curable. When women reach their mid-forties, more cases of advanced cancers are seen, although the Pap test is catching more and more of these at the in-situ stage. We still do not know why women develop this type of cancer, and although it is always risky to quote statistics, I'll just briefly mention a few interesting facts about cervical cancer. It has been found, for instance, that for every one Jewish woman who develops cancer of the cervix there are nine non-Jewish women

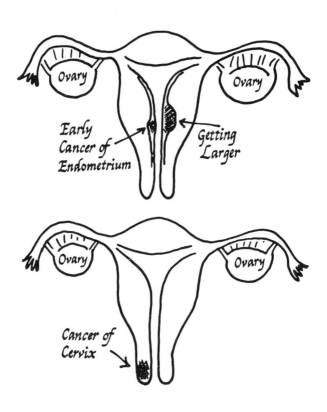

who do so. Why? The theory is that circumcision is automatically performed on all Jewish men, and this in some way prevents the development of cervical malignancy. And, to carry it a step further, this does not appear to be an isolated racial situation, for the Mohammedan people, who also regularly practice circumcision, have a similarly lower incidence of this disease. It is also an established fact that the more children a woman has, the greater the chance she may develop cervical cancer. For example, this type of cancer is extremely rare in nuns. It has therefore been assumed that the tremendous stretching that the cervical opening has to undergo during delivery may injure it and predispose it to cancer. Yet why is it that millions of women have numerous pregnancies without getting this disease? Other doctors believe it is marriage rather than the number of children that sets the stage for cancer, since married women, whether or not they have had children, are twice as likely to have cervical cancer as single women. In fact, one study indicated that early marriage could lead to trouble, since over 50 percent of the women in this group who developed cancer of the cervix had married before the age of twenty. What all this means is hard to say except that in general it is well to realize that statistics can be extremely misleading.

Cancer of the Uterus, the second most common pelvic malignancy, which doctors refer to as "carcinoma of the endometrium" (the endometrium is the inside lining of the uterus), also offers some interesting statistical observations. In this type of cancer, the fact that women have had children is an asset rather than a liability, since women who have never had a child, or have had just one child, are more likely to get uterine cancer than those women who have borne a few children. Doctors are hard put to answer why this should be the case. Then it is also known that three-quarters of the cases start after the menopause, and women who have a delayed menopause are also more susceptible to this kind of cancer. Another interesting observation is that women who suffer from obesity, hypertension and diabetes are more prone to develop it.

Cancer of the Ovary, the third most common pelvic malignancy, can occur at any age, but in general is more common after the menopause. There is no doubt it is the most trying of all the pelvic cancers because of the problem it presents in relation to an early diagnosis. We will talk more about this shortly.

Cancers of the Vulva (Lips of the Vagina), Vagina, and Tubes are rare, and will not be discussed in any detail in this book, because of their infrequency. Suffice to say that a regular medical checkup will reveal any suspicious tumor or ulceration of the vagina and, in the case of cancer of the tube, early diagnosis depends on finding an enlargement of the tube and presents the same problem as ovarian cancer. Possibly the best point to emphasize in talking about these rare cancers is to strongly urge women who notice a lump or sore at the vaginal entrance to quickly have it seen by their doctor. It is amazing how often people will continue for months to use patent medicines of one sort or another, in an endeavor to heal these sores instead of immediately seeking proper help. One would expect that cancer of the vulva would be diagnosed earlier than any other pelvic malignancy, for in this situation women can see and feel the tumor. Yet in the majority of cases it is diagnosed many months after it was first noticed, because the patient thought it was merely an innocent pimple. And, unfortunately, the lost time in diagnosis means that the cancer may have spread to other areas. As the reader can see, we always return to the wisdom and necessity of early diagnosis for, regardless of the type and location of the cancer, it sooner or later spreads if early treatment is not carried out. When this happens, it involves other parts of the body or, as doctors say, "metastasizes" in one or more ways. Initially the tumor enlarges locally, and by expansion may extend to nearby organs.

But eventually cancer cells enter either the blood stream or lymphatic channels to spread to more distant areas.

Diagnosis. When we start talking about the important question of how to diagnose cancer while it is still curable, it largely depends on which of the common malignancies we are discussing, because each one is situated in a distinct location and this is what makes the difference. For instance, cancer of the cervix (opening into the uterus) is closer to the outside of the body than the other two common cancers, because it has the good fortune to lie at the end of the vagina. Consequently, during a pelvic examination, the cervix is easily seen by inserting into the vagina a small instrument called the "speculum," which holds the walls of the vagina apart. It is therefore simple to take a biopsy of the cervix if it should look abnormal. And lastly, the Pap cancer smear is particularly accurate in diagnosing cervical cancer. Cancer of the inside of the uterus, however, lies a little deeper in the pelvic cavity and is slightly more difficult to diagnose, since it cannot be visualized. But fortunately it does connect to the vagina by a small opening that passes through the cervix so that it is easy to obtain samples of tissue from the inside of the uterus by doing a D and C. Cancer of the ovary on the other hand is the most difficult to detect, since it can neither be seen nor reached by instruments, for the ovaries have no connection with the vagina. This means that the only practical way to notice any malignant change is by feeling for any increase in the size of the ovaries during a pelvic examination. Usually this is not too difficult, but in obese women who find it hard to relax it can be a very trying task. In summary, the anatomical location of the cancer makes the diagnosis either simple or difficult.

Before I go on to talk about the symptoms of cancer I think it is wise to repeat what I mentioned in Chapter X. *Minor problems not only occur more frequently than cancer, but many of these benign conditions have the very same symptoms as a pelvic malignancy. It is impossible for it to be otherwise, be-*

cause there are not enough symptoms to go round. So when women notice pain, abnormal bleeding, or discharge they should not fall into the trap of thinking the trouble is due to cancer, when 99 percent of the time it is due to benign disease. And, lastly, it is important to remember that symptoms are only part of the story, since the final diagnosis depends on what the doctor finds both from the tests and his examination.

I don't want to say too much about the symptoms of cancer, because I wish to get the message across that it is better to have regular checkup examinations than to wait until symptoms appear. The point is that early symptoms do not always mean early cancer, since some cancers can be present a long time before they make their presence felt. This is actually what one would expect, for all cancers start out being quite small, and it is only when the cancer increases in size, or develops ulceration, that abnormal bleeding or bloody discharge occurs. Similarly, cancers cause pain only when they have either increased in size and produced pressure on a normal organ or nerve, or have spread to other parts of the body. It is therefore just as logical to arrange for a yearly visit to the doctor so he has a chance to diagnose cancer *before* any symptoms occur, as it is to have a mechanic check on your car before the wheel falls off. Yet for various reasons many women fail to follow this advice. Some believe that because their parents are still alive at eighty that they, too, will last that long. So why see a doctor? Longevity does run in some families, and it has been said somewhat facetiously that "you can't be too particular who your parents are." But there are exceptions to every rule, and all doctors have seen patients dying of cancer at an early age when their parents are still living. Other women put off seeing their doctor because they feel fine and besides, they don't like the idea of pelvic examinations. Still others who have symptoms may foolishly compare them with those of someone else when actually no logical comparison is possible. Irrational thinking is certainly not limited to attitudes to cancer, for there are still millions of people who think it is necessary to have a bowel movement every day in order to enjoy good health. But the big difference is that taking unnecessary laxatives is not going to cost them their life, whereas, should an early cancer be present, senseless procrastination in seeing the doctor may easily do so.

Symptoms of Cancer

What are the symptoms of cancer? Again it depends on the type of cancer, so I'll briefly mention each one separately.

Cancer of the Cervix is most likely to cause bleeding between periods. This may occur for no apparent reason, or following a long car ride, intercourse, or douching. This is because the cervix is at the end of the vagina and anything that irritates the cancer can make it bleed. Sometimes the bleeding is better described as spotting, since it is not enough to require wearing a pad. And because the largest number of cervical malignancies occur around the menopause, many women use poor judgment at this time, and write off this bleeding as being due to their change of life. This of course may be the case, or it may result from benign polyps, fibroids, or other minor problems; but this is for the doctor to decide, not the patient. And while we are talking about the menopause and the type of bleeding one should expect at this time, I would like to refer you to Chapter III, which deals with menstrual problems, and to Chapter XIII and XIV, which deal with all types of abnormal bleeding and their causes. It is very important that you understand what type of bleeding is normal and what is abnormal. Otherwise you are playing a very dangerous guessing game. For example, if your periods start to get heavier, prolonged, or more frequent during the menopause, this can be a danger signal. Increased bleeding is *usually* due to temporary hormonal changes, caused by the aging ovaries gradually producing less and less hormones or by other benign conditions. However, now and then, it is due to an early malignancy. A thin, watery discharge is another symptom, and it may become quite brownish, depending on the amount of blood that may mix with it. It has been said that he who treats himself has a fool for a patient, which is certainly true at this time (or for that matter, any other time) in a woman's life.

Cancer of the Uterus can cause all the symptoms we have just mentioned, but some form of abnormal bleeding is by far the most common result. Some patients may notice either irregular, heavy bleeding, prolonged periods, frequent periods or slight spotting between periods, but in all cases there is a change toward more bleeding, not less. Again it should be stressed that this type of bleeding frequently occurs at the menopause, and that 99 percent of the time it is not due to a malignancy. Yet it is only by doing a D and C, and by removing tissue from inside the uterus that this type of malignancy can be ruled out. There is one further type of bleeding that deserves special mention: that is any bleeding that occurs six months or more after the periods have, to all intents and purposes, stopped. Doctors call this postmenopausal bleeding, and it is particularly significant because 75 percent of the uterine cancers start after the change of life. This bleeding may vary from a slight spotting to a large, sudden gush of blood. And although the bleeding may be intermittent, it can also be an almost daily occurrence. Postmenopausal bleeding can also occur from other benign conditions, but since it frequently results from cancer, no time should be lost in consulting a doctor. One of the good things about uterine cancer is that whether it occurs before or after the menopause, it frequently causes some form of abnormal bleeding while the tumor is still quite small and easily curable. Consequently, reporting early symptoms can indeed be lifesaving. Cancer of the uterus can also cause a brownish or blood-tinged discharge and, as in the case of the other cancers, pain is usually a late symptom.

Cancer of the Ovary sooner or later causes pain, but rarely abnormal bleeding. In the initial stages patients complain of a bearing-down feeling, a sense of fullness, or an aching sensation in the lower part of the abdomen which sooner or later develops into outright pain. But remember there is hardly a woman living who does not have a sense of fullness in the stomach at one time or another, so this vague symptom is often hard to evaluate. And although a gradual enlargement of the abdomen can result from ovarian cysts it is also good to bear in mind that most women who notice their clothes getting tighter are just eating too much. As mentioned earlier, the ovaries have no connection with the outside of the body, and consequently cannot cause vaginal discharge; and it is only on rare occasions that abnormal bleeding occurs. Furthermore, since they are situated deep in the pelvic cavity, surrounded by loops of bowel and empty space, they can reach a fairly large size before causing any pressure symptoms.

The Diagnosis of pelvic cancer consequently rests on yearly checkups and the reporting of any of the above symptoms, should they occur. In the event symptoms such as abnormal bleeding are present, doctors frequently advise a D and C, so that the inside lining of the uterus can be studied microscopically to see if cancer is present. But for the woman without symptoms the annual pelvic examination combined with a Pap test is the best method for detecting cancer in its earliest stages. Henry David Thoreau once wrote "if a man seems out of step with his companions perhaps it is because he hears a different drummer." He implied that not all people think alike, and those who don't always follow the crowd may be even better than those who do. To be sure, more than one road may lead to Rome in some things in life, and it makes little difference which one you take. But in the diagnosis of cancer there are absolutely no choices. The only good way is to have a yearly checkup examination and a Pap smear. In this case all people had better hear the same drummer.

Since the Pap smear is now so widely used, let me explain what it is and the rationale for having it done. Actually the idea is quite simple and logical and, as with so many things, it is amazing that no one thought about it earlier. For instance, while you are actually reading this chapter, the cells on the outside of your skin are continually falling off and, in turn, being replaced by younger cells. This is also happening to the tissues and organs inside your body, such as the lungs, stomach, and pelvic organs. Cells from the vagina, cervix, and uterus are constantly being discarded into the normal vaginal discharge, and thousands of these cells can be seen when a drop of discharge is placed under the microscope. At this point, you may justifiably be wondering what normal cells have to do with cancer cells. Actually, they have nothing to do with cancer cells except for one important point. It is this: normal cells are constantly thrown off into the normal vaginal discharge; therefore, isn't it logical to assume that if a cancer is just starting to grow, it will also discard some of its cells? This is exactly what happens, and doctors are able to see cancer cells mixed with normal cells in the "Papanicolaou smear," commonly known as the "Pap test."

The Pap Test has also brought to light one other extremely interesting fact. Doctors have always wondered how long it takes to develop cancer. Is it a slow process or does it happen quite suddenly? It appears that cancer is like most other things which are not white one day and black the next. Our cars don't suddenly collapse on the highway, but fall apart piece by piece. And our hair usually takes many years to turn gray. The body's cells act in the same way. Therefore, they are not normal one day and cancerous the next, but go through a definite series of changes on their way to becoming malignant cells. These changes in normal cells can be picked up by microscopic examination of a Pap smear, sometimes many years before cancer occurs, which obviously offers the patient a 100 percent chance for cure.

With the Pap test becoming such a routine practice, it follows that an occasional patient will be told the smear was not normal. And it is only natural that when this happens a woman will quickly jump to the conclusion that she has cancer. But as we have just pointed out, such is rarely the case. There are two main reasons for this. First, most abnormal smears merely indicate that the cells have undergone some change from the normal, but they are still far away from being outright cancer cells. Looking at it another way, the cellular changes are neither white nor black, but lie somewhere in the large gray area; so that there is plenty of time to do further tests and, if necesary, to carry out treatment. Second, vaginal infections or inflammations of the cervix may temporarily produce changes in the normal cells that can at times look very similar to the changes seen in early cancer cells. Once the infection is cured, the cells return to normal. All this means is that the Pap smear is an extremely sensitive test, which more often finds the early changes in cells rather than definite malignant cells. Depending on just how severe these changes are, doctors may advise a biopsy of the cervix and possibly a D and C, to determine more specifically what part of the cervix or uterus these cells are originating from.

The Pap smear is undoubtedly the most significant advance in early cancer diagnosis to the present time. Women who submit to this painless test every year, which takes about one minute to do, can be assured that they will never die of cervical cancer. I say this because, even if the smear failed to pick up an early change one year, it would surely do so the next; and since these cellular changes take many years before they become 100 percent cancer, there is ample time to catch them. Unfortunately what I have just said about cervical cancer is not true for cancer of the uterus, since the Pap smear is accurate in only 70 percent of these cases. This is because the cancer is inside the uterus, so not as many cells fall down into the vagina as in the case of cervical cancer.

The Treatment of Pelvic Cancer either involves surgery, radiation, or a combination of both. The early in-situ cancers of the cervix are best treated by a hysterectomy, and most surgeons will also remove the tubes and ovaries. In some cases, when the malignancy occurs in young women who desire further children, doctors will remove only the diseased portion of the cervix, and will then continue to give these patients regular and frequent Pap smears during the years they are completing their family. But when cervical cancer is no longer a surface growth and has slightly invaded the deeper tissues of the cervix, the standard treatment is radium, which may or may not be followed by a radical hysterectomy, in which not only the uterus is removed, but also the various lymph nodes in the pelvis. Cancer of the uterus in the early stages is again more likely to be treated by surgery because, fortunately, uterine cancer tends to remain localized longer than cervical cancer. But many surgeons will initially advise radium treatment, and then follow this with a hysterectomy a few weeks later. For ovarian cancer, the initial treatment is to remove the cancerous ovary along with the uterus and the other ovary. Very often radiation in the form of deep X-ray treatment will then be given. No doubt other ways to treat this disease will be found in the future, for a great deal of work is now being done on various chemicals to treat the several types of malignancy. And in some cases the results have been very encouraging. But I hope this chapter has impressed on the reader that at the moment the only sure way to cure cancer is by early diagnosis and treatment before it has spread to other parts of the pelvis. So I think it is worthwhile repeating once more that you should not procrastinate if there is a suspicious symptom. Remember that putting things off until tomorrow is a very human trait. In fact some highly intelligent people have made fatal mistakes by pushing their luck too far in postponing important decisions. For instance, long after he knew he was in desperate trouble, Napoleon still refused to accept the reality of the situation and retreat from Russia. An earlier decision might have salvaged most of his army. Don't make the same mistake. See your doctor early.

Cancer of the Breast

Despite the fact that most breast lumps are benign, cancer of the breast is nevertheless the most common malignancy in women, and therefore deserves special attention in attempting to insure its early diagnosis and treatment. It is unfortunate that, like all cancers, doctors still have no idea of its cause. It is equally unfortunate that any disease for which the cause is unknown invariably over the years gets surrounded with all sorts of curious stories regarding its origin. In the case of breast cancer, an injury to the breast has been the favorite old wives' tale to explain its onset. Doctors totally discount this, and believe the blow merely focused the patient's attention on a lump that was already present. I am sure there is not a woman reading this book who on one or more occasions has had her breast struck one way or another and has not developed breast cancer. Yet pet theories like this die hard, and no doubt this one will continue to cause unnecessary worry.

There are some facts, however, that doctors have noticed over the years in studying breast cancer. For example, unmarried women or married women, who either have no children or a small family, are statistically a little more likely to develop breast cancer than those women who have an average-sized family. It has also been found that women who do not nurse their children are more likely to develop this disease than women who do breast-feed their babies. But statistics in medicine, where there are so many variables to consider, can be extremely misleading; and what one doctor believes can be proven by statistics, another doctor is able to prove to the contrary.

Breast cancer rarely occurs before thirty years of age; and at whatever age it starts, it is almost always present without any pain. However, once the lump is found either by the patient or her doctor, a burning, aching, stabbing or throbbing pain frequently starts, because of the fear that it may be a malignancy. It is a well-known fact that focusing one's attention on any part of the body can bring on pain. If the lump is an early one, no other signs of cancer are present; but later on, the skin over the cancer may become depressed or pulled down by the growth and may eventually look pitted and thick like orange peel. Discharge which may be either clear or bloody can occur, yet it is well to know that most women with nipple discharge do not have a cancer. There is one further sign to look for, nipple retraction. Many women have a depressed or retracted nipple, which may have made breast-feeding either difficult or impossible, and if it has been that way for years it is of no importance. If, on the other hand, a normal nipple starts to be pulled in or off to one side then it is vitally important to have it checked by the doctor.

When the lump is discovered by the doctor, there is never any delay in treatment. The problem arises only when the patient finds a lump. I have known many intelligent women who procrastinate week after week before they seek advice. In fact, on more than one occasion it has even been women who have been doing volunteer cancer work and obviously should know better. They usually delay because of combined feelings of fear, hope that it isn't cancer, and the desire to put off that frightful moment of hearing the verdict if it *is* a malignancy. Yet nearly all admit once a diagnosis has been made, that the *fear* of cancer was much worse than its diagnosis. A quick trip to the doctor not only makes an early diagnosis possible, but also results in complete reassurance for the majority of women, insofar as most breast lumps are benign.

The method of treating any suspicious lump is to remove

the mass quickly and examine it microscopically by a procedure called a frozen section, while the patient is asleep. This immediately tells whether the lump is benign or malignant. As previously mentioned, the great majority prove to be either cysts full of clear fluid, or solid, benign tumors, called "fibroadenomas." But if the report shows a cancer, further surgery is required, and a radical mastectomy is done. This involves removing the entire breast, and also the glands in the arm pit, in the event the cancer has spread to that area. In recent years some doctors have also advised removal of the ovaries in women still in their reproductive years, since they believe in certain cases this improves the chance of cure. In other instances, chemical drugs or hormones may be used with good results.

It is because of the continuing efforts of family doctors, specialists, and the Cancer Society that each year more and more women who develop cancer have it diagnosed early because of regular checkups and the Pap test. But there are still large numbers who for one reason or another are not so fortunate. When this happens, and the cancer has spread to other areas, the outcome is frequently bad. But neither the patient nor the family should give up hope, for present-day surgical techniques and improved methods of radiation can cure large numbers of patients, even with fairly advanced cancers. Furthermore, some patients seem to be able to live with a tumor without it progressing any further, and there are instances where tumors have been known to disappear. Just why this occurs in the rare case is unknown, but in some way patients develop an immunity and a resistance to the malignancy. Unfortunately these situations do not occur too often, but nevertheless authentic cases have been reported in medical journals by eminent doctors. And with so many scientists working on this problem, sooner or later a breakthrough will be made, and who can tell how soon this may be? There is little doubt that medicine has progressed further in the last few decades than in all the centuries before, and there is surely no reason to suspect it will slow down. Tomorrow or the next day may mean an entirely different story for patients who have cancer. We all eventually meet our Waterloo in one way or another; but faced with a serious problem that occurs before old age, it is always a good idea to play for time. I sometimes tell patients the ancient story of the flying horse, which concerns a long-ago king who sentenced a man to death. The man begged a reprieve, and finally obtained one by assuring the king that he would teach his Majesty's horse to fly within a year. The reprieve was granted on the condition that the horse must be able to fly by the time the year was up. Otherwise, the man would once again face execution. Afterwards, when people started criticizing and asking him what possible good such an absurd promise could do him, the man shrugged his shoulders. "Within a year the king may die," he said, "or I may die. Or the horse may die. And in a year—who knows? Maybe the horse will learn to fly!"

CHAPTER XVI

Lumps at the Outside of the Vagina (Vulva)

LUMPS AT THE OUTSIDE of the vagina may be of many types, and fortunately nearly all are benign (noncancerous). There are many reasons why doctors see so many different types of problems in this area. Situated here are a combination of structures, such as skin, various types of glands, hair, and numerous blood vessels that are not all present in other regions of the body. In addition, these structures are subjected to the irritation of childbirth, intercourse, and sometimes increased amounts of vaginal discharge over a long period of time. No wonder something abnormal occasionally develops in this area. Let us now discuss some of the more commonly encountered problems.

Bartholin Cyst

Situated at the vaginal opening are two small glands, one on each side, which in normal circumstances are small, soft, and cannot be felt. They frequently become infected by different types of organisms and may then become quite swollen, sometimes reaching the size of an egg or an orange. This causes fever and severe pain in the area, and the patient may have difficulty walking. Admission to hospital is then necessary in order to drain the abscess and administer penicillin or other types of antibiotics. In a few days the infection and swelling are usually controlled, and sometimes nothing further is required. Not infrequently, an acute infection so injures the gland that it is followed by a chronic infection which may flare up time and time again. During this chronic stage, the gland can usually be felt as a small, hard marblesize lump at each side of the vagina. Either removing this mass or cutting a hole in it will result in a complete cure.

Sebaceous Cyst

Sebaceous cysts are quite common, being formed from sebaceous glands which are situated in the skin. Usually they are quite small, about the size of a pea and, under normal circumstances, painless. Small, and sometimes even large, cysts that are present just inside the lips of the vagina may go unnoticed by the patient for years until the patient has a routine pelvic examination. Should they become infected, however, they quickly make their presence known, and will become swollen and painful. Most doctors will therefore advise excision of the cyst long before this complication occurs.

Boils

Boils do occur now and then around the vaginal entrance and can be extremely annoying and painful, in fact the throbbing can be so intense that physicians in the past have often referred to it as the "devil's pain."

In order for a boil to form, a hair somewhere on the skin has to become infected by a bacterial germ known as the "staphylococcus." This germ then works its way down the shaft of the hair, penetrates the skin surface, and the boil gradually but surely starts to appear. The question that is sometimes hard to answer is why some women are more prone to develop boils than others. In some instances the reason is fairly obvious among women with poor bathing habits. But the fact remains that most patients who develop boils in this area do wash themselves well, and the cause for the infection must be found elsewhere. Some women have had a chronic discharge which, for either months or years, has constantly irritated the skin, making it more susceptible to the staphylococcus germ. Other women may be quite obese, so that during hot weather the constant rubbing and perspiration produces irritation in the area. Patients who have diabetes are more prone to develop them, but certainly the majority of women with this problem do not have diabetes. Still others may get them for no apparent reason.

The diagnosis is frequently apparent when the patient walks into the office with great difficulty with her legs apart. Examination will show an extremely tender swollen area that may still be fairly hard if the boil has been present for a short time, or an abscess that is ready to be opened and drained if the boil has been present for a number of days. Not infrequently the glands in the groin area are swollen and tender.

What treatment the doctor advises depends on when he first sees the patient. For instance, in its extremely early stages, the prompt use of hot baths and antibiotics may stop the boil from going any further, and it may fade away. But after a certain point, this will not happen, and a combination of frequent hot baths, antibiotics, and bed-rest are needed to help the boil form quickly, so that the pus can be drained. Sometimes the boil will break on its own during a hot tub bath, but if this does not happen a small incision may be necessary. Women should remember one thing above all others: Never, never squeeze a boil in the hope it will break, for this may break down the protective wall nature has formed around the boil, and if this occurs blood poisoning may be the result. Furthermore, patients should never open a boil themselves with any sharp instrument as, if this is done too early, blood poisoning may also result. In the treatment of a boil at this stage the exact timing of when to open it is very important.

Women who get one boil after another present a difficult problem, but one that can be frequently helped by the use of a staphylococcal vaccine. By gradually injecting larger and stronger amounts of the vaccine, patients frequently develop an increase in resistance to the staphylococcal germ, and in many instances boils become a thing of the past.

Warts of the Vulva

Soft, raised, cauliflowerlike warts around the vaginal opening are occasionally seen and are caused by a virus infection. Women who suffer from copious amounts of vaginal discharge for a long time, or who are lax in their personal hygiene, are more prone to develop them. It is thought that the irritating action of the discharge lowers the skin resistance and the virus can then more readily penetrate the tissue causing the formation of the warts. Generally a number are present, scattered about the vaginal opening; and some may occur inside the vagina. During pregnancy they may grow to a large size and may cause trouble with the actual delivery if they are not treated. In a woman who is not pregnant, they may or may not cause symptoms, depending on their number, size, and situation. Some women will complain of pain and an irritation around the vaginal opening. Others may notice bleeding, and if the opening of the bladder is involved, there may be pain on urination. Regardless of whether a woman is or is not pregnant, it is important to treat them as quickly as possible to prevent their spread. Small warts are usually treated by placing an ointment called "podophyllin" over them, allowing it to remain in contact with the wart for about six hours, following which it is washed off with soap and water. Before the ointment is applied, the skin surrounding the warts is first covered by a jelly such as petrolatum, to protect it from the irritating action of the podophyllin, since it is an extremely powerful irritant. Why will an ointment of this kind cause the wart to dissolve and finally disappear? It is thought that the irritating action of the podophyllin causes injury of the blood vesels which supply the wart. This results in decreasing the blood supply to the wart, and it gradually shrinks and dies. Depending on the size of the wart, one or more applications of podophyllin may be necessary. Another way to treat these warts is by the use of an electric needle that doctors call electro-dessication. This can be done in the office, and usually after a number of treatments the warts gradually fade away. Large masses that have been present for a long time and that do not completely respond to treatment may require excision by surgery.

Varicose Veins

Varicose veins, involving the lips of the vagina, are quite common and may be associated with varicose veins of the leg. Usually they are seen for the first time during a pregnancy and, following delivery, usually subside only to recur with a subsequent pregnancy. The varicosities can reach a large size without becoming too troublesome. Some women will notice a heavy dragging sensation in the area, particularly at the end of the day. A few may experience pain, if one of the veins either forms a thrombosis (small blood clot) or ruptures. In the latter case, blood may collect under the skin, and result in swelling of the vaginal lips. Neither of these complications is serious. In fact it is quite amazing how women with large varicose veins can deliver a child in a normal way without any of the veins breaking. If, following delivery, the veins continue to be troublesome, they can be either injected or removed by surgery, but most women require no treatment.

Injuries to the Vulva

Childbirth is the most common cause for an injury to this region, when the vaginal opening may be torn. This used to be extremely common when most deliveries took place in the home. Under these conditions, tears of the vagina were either not repaired, or were repaired under such poor conditions that infection was common, and tender scar tissue would sometimes form. Now the reverse is true. Nearly all women are delivered in a hospital and, as the baby is being born, the doctor usually makes a small cut in the vaginal opening to avoid a ragged tear. Doctors refer to this cut as an "episiotomy," and following delivery it is neatly repaired. There are of course other ways the vulva can be injured. Some young girls can't seem to resist walking along the top of a picket fence and should they fall, serious injury can of course occur. Many injuries are, however, less serious, resulting only in a bruised, swollen area on the lips of the vulva. Should bleeding occur, a blood clot may form which occasionally may reach a fairly large size. Most cases of this kind will usually heal gradually on their own, if heat is applied to the area. More recently, pills have been developed which, when taken by mouth, help to reduce the swelling and size of the blood clot in more extensive injuries. Injuries that cause tears require surgical repair.

Prolapse of the Urinary Tube

The "urethra" is the name given to the tube that carries urine from the bladder to the outside. It is lined with a membrane called the "mucosa," which, in old age, may on rare occasions become weakened and fall slightly to the outside forming a small lump. Should this occur most women will be completely unaware of it, while a few will either notice a lump or complain of some burning on voiding. Usually no treatment is required, but infrequently the mass will increase in size or cause symptoms enough to require its removal.

Prolapse of the Bladder and of the Uterus

These conditions, particularly the prolapsed bladder (cystocele), are quite commonly seen in a doctor's office. Many patients are often quite unaware of their existence, though they may have been present for years. But when they do produce trouble, they cause an annoying symptom which doctors call "stress incontinence." This means when a patient coughs or sneezes a small or large amount of urine is lost. At other times it may be lost sitting in a chair or walking down the street, and may be quite troublesome when it necessitates wearing a pad constantly. Although patients may have been aware of the annoyance for some time, many first become worried when they either see or feel a lump protruding from the vagina. But these problems do not occur suddenly; rather it is a gradual progression occurring over a period of years. Yet when the mass is first noted at the vaginal entrance many women immediately jump to the wrong conclusion that it is a tumor.

What causes the female organs to fall down? The most important reason is childbirth, for during delivery of the infant the vagina is stretched to many times its normal size. In addition, the ligaments and other structures supporting the bladder and uterus are stretched and sometimes injured. Large babies, prolonged labors, difficult deliveries, and repeated pregnancies in rapid succession, all help to cause a weakness in the supports of these organs. Women who are born with strong tissues are, of course, less likely to develop trouble than those born with weak tissues. This is shown by the fact that the occasional woman with a dozen children may still have adequate support, whereas another woman with only one pregnancy may have poor support of the organs. When one considers the tremendous stretching of the vagina during delivery it is amazing that this problem is not more common than it is. Yet in most cases, a few weeks after delivery the pelvic tissues are back to normal

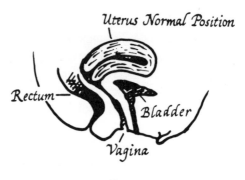

Uterus Normal Position

Rectum — Bladder

Vagina

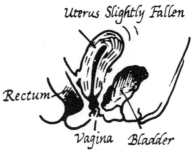

Uterus Slightly Fallen

Rectum

Vagina   Bladder

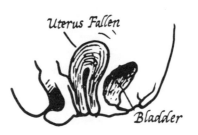

Uterus Fallen

Bladder

size. Those women who do develop trouble are more likely to have a prolapsed bladder. A smaller number will have both the fallen bladder and the fallen uterus.

As mentioned earlier, the common and most bothersome symptom is loss of urine, usually on coughing and sneezing. In addition, many patients will complain of a heavy or bearing-down feeling in the vagina or lower part of the stomach, particularly on standing. Usually it is more pronounced at the end of the day or after a long walk. Other women will have the feeling of never being able to completely empty the bladder. In order to do so it is necessary to insert a finger into the vagina and push up the bladder. A few patients who have

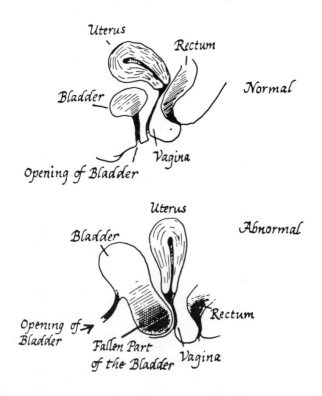

suffered from this condition for a number of years may develop
an infection of the bladder due to stagnation of urine from
incomplete emptying. This causes increased frequency of urination during the day and night, and there may be pain or
smarting on passing the urine. Patients who have a complete
loss of the supports may end up with the uterus falling completely out of the vagina. This in addition to other complaints
mentioned above may also cause backache.

What is done for these problems depends on many factors.
Everything in life is relative, and so it is here. The majority of
women have only a slight falling down of the bladder and,
if it is not causing trouble, no treatment is needed. One might
again use that old saw about "why trouble trouble till trouble
troubles you?" Yet some women, without symptoms, whose
bladder has fallen more, may be advised to have an operation
as a prevention against future trouble. For one thing, a bladder
that has fallen down considerably usually does not empty com-
pletely- on voiding, and as mentioned earlier may cause a
bladder infection if left this way for a number of years. We
all know that a stagnant pond is much more likely to become
polluted than a flowing river. Second, the doctor may feel that
the bladder is easier to repair at this stage than it will be in a
few years' time. Furthermore, the sooner it is repaired the
better the results. Most women with this trouble are past the
child-bearing years, but if they want more children an operation should be temporarily postponed. Another pregnancy would
probably undo the results of surgery, unless a caesarean is done.

The operation to repair the prolapsed bladder (cystocele
repair), is performed entirely within the vagina. And since
absorbable catgut sutures are used throughout the procedure,
there are no sutures to remove following surgery. The operation consists of stitching the bladder back into its normal
position, so that the front wall of the vagina, which supports
the bladder, no longer sags down into the vaginal passage.

But just as the front wall can be weakened by childbirth,
so can the back wall, which supports the rectum. Consequently,

rectocele repair is usually done at the same time, because this will provide additional support to the vagina.

Some patients inquire whether the doctor can guarantee a cure by surgery. This, of course, is not possible. For example, if a patient has a fibroid uterus, the doctor can assure the patient it will be 100 percent removed by a hysterectomy and will never return. But a mechanical problem such as this is a different story. Here the surgeon is attempting to narrow the small opening, which allows urine to escape from the bladder. Fortunately the operation is successful in most cases, and patients once again have complete control of the urine. But a few patients, although helped by the operation, still continue to lose small amounts of urine, and further treatment is required. Sometimes exercises will help to control the loss. Women are advised to tighten the rectum twenty-five to fifty times a day which exercises not only the muscles of the rectum, but also those of the bladder opening. Doing these exercises conscientiously for a number of weeks may control the incontinence. If it does not, and the urinary loss continues to be a difficulty, another operation will be advised. Some doctors will again operate th ough the vagina. Others will resort to an abdominal operation. A more extensive operation of this type will usually correct the problem.

Let us now turn our attention to the patient who has both a prolapsed bladder and a prolapsed uterus. Here, too, there are various degrees of the fallen uterus. Those that are slightly fallen do not usually cause symptoms, and no treatment is required. But as the uterus, over a period of years, gradually works its way down the vagina, it also pulls the bladder along with it. Consequently, a badly fallen uterus is always associated with a fallen bladder. This means there are actually two lumps protruding from the vagina, although the patient may be aware of only one. Most patients who have this trouble are most commonly treated by a vaginal hysterectomy; that is, the uterus is first removed through the vagina without making an abdominal incision. Once the uterus is out, the bladder and rectum are then repaired to give the necessary support to the vaginal canal. There are cases, however, in which the vaginal hysterectomy is not considered the best procedure. The uterus, for instance, may have only a minor degree of prolapse (falling down), and other diseases may be present which would make it difficult to operate entirely by way of the vagina. The surgeon will therefore repair the bladder and rectum first by a vaginal operation. An abdominal incision is later made to remove the uterus.

Elderly patients who do not wish an operation can be fitted with various rings that help to hold the organs in place. During the last few years, pessaries made of soft plastic materials have become available that are much more satisfactory. But often even these cause irritation, discharge, and occasional vaginal sores. However, I have finally concluded that tampons provide the most effective support, and they also have the further advantage of not causing any vaginal irritation. Patients can easily insert one or two tampons themselves by gently wetting the ends with water, and then inserting both at once. But the great majority of elderly patients are advised to have surgery to correct this problem.

Benign Tumors

The lips of the vagina are composed mostly of fibrous and fatty tissue, particularly the latter. It is the fibrous tissue that helps to hold the various tissues of the body together, acting like a cement or glue. The bulk of the body, on the other hand, is composed of fat, often too much of it in the case of many people. For reasons that doctors do not yet know, these two types of tissue can develop a benign (noncancerous) tumor, and in rare circumstances one of these may develop in the lip of the vagina. At the start, the growth may be no larger than a marble, and it remains this size for years. A few, however, continue to grow and gradually work their way out of the vaginal lip. Stated another way, as the growth gets larger it also gets heavier, and the force of gravity when the patient stands gradually pulls it away from the surrounding tissues of the labia. This takes place over the course of many years after which the growth—now about the size of an egg—will be hanging from the labial lip by a thin strand of tissue, sometimes no larger than the size of a pencil. I have, in fact, been consulted by a number of women for other problems, and find that in addition to their primary difficulty they also have a large tumor of this sort. Some women have been aware of this lump for twenty years or more, and interestingly refuse to have it removed. Of course most women, due to the annoyance of having it hang between their legs, will readily agree to its removal, which requires only a minor surgical operation.

CHAPTER XVII

Vaginal Discharge and Itching

DOCTORS HAVE COME a long way since the horse-and buggy days in curing vaginal discharge and itching. In earlier years a physician had very little in his black bag to offer a patient with these complaints. In fact, it has been said face-tiously that the only thing a doctor could do then was to prescribe a tonic that would at least give the patient sufficient energy to scratch.

Vaginal discharge and itching are two of the most common reasons why women consult their doctors. Either one or both of these symptoms may be present, but discharge is more frequently the problem. Usually they are not the result of serious disease, but they do cause a great deal of annoyance and worry. Of course, just as women vary in their tolerance of pain, so they differ in their tolerance of a discharge. Some patients complain bitterly about even a small amount of discharge, whereas others either never notice it, or never bother to mention it. It is important to bear one point in mind. All women have a small amount of vaginal discharge. It is only when it is enough to constantly stain the underclothing or if there is a sudden increase or if it is associated with itching, that there is usually a cause. Certainly, a discharge that is blood-tinged should be looked into immediately. Even a bloody discharge does not mean serious disease, and in most cases is the result of an easily correctible condition. But only by examination can a definite diagnosis be made. Waiting to see if it will clear up may mean the loss of valuable time should a serious problem be present. Two of the most common causes of vaginal discharge and itching are trichomonas and fungus infection. Let us discuss the more common problem of trichomonas infection first.

Trichomonas Infection

Hardly a day goes by that a doctor does not see a patient with this common problem. It is seen in all ages, young and old, but it is much more common in the childbearing age group. This infection is due to a very small protozoan organism called "trichomonas vaginalis." "Protozoa" literally means first animal, because this organism consists of a single cell, and therefore represents the simplest form of animal life. Of course, it cannot be seen by the naked eye, but when magnified four hundred times under the microscope it is about the size of a pea. Most of them are pear-shaped, with a long, thin projection at one end which beats back and forth in a whiplike fashion, causing the trichomonas organism to move about. There appear to be many different varieties of trichomonas, and doctors are learning more and more about these organisms each year. Some of them are round and do not appear to move, whereas the others described above are extremely active. Just how women pick up this infection is not known, but in all probability infected bathtubs, swimming pools, or towels may be a major source of this infection.

What are the symptoms of trichomonas infection? Again, like many diseases, women may be completely unaware of its presence. Most, however, do have symptoms, the most common of which is a persistent whitish or yellowish discharge. Some patients have noticed it for just a few days, others for years.

A majority of women seem to be troubled by it more after a period, but it usually never clears up completely. After it has been present for some time, there may be irritation and itching at the vaginal entrance. Others complain of painful intercourse. Certainly a large number of patients become depressed and worried in the more persistent cases, and frequently worry that they have a serious disease. This is not true. Trichomonas infection can be extremely annoying and persistent, but it is not a serious disease.

The diagnosis of trichomonas infection is quite simple in most cases. On a pelvic examination the diagnosis is suspected by the finding of a frothy vaginal discharge, and frequently the wall of the vagina is quite reddened and sore-looking. A definite diagnosis, however, depends on finding the trichomonas organism in the vaginal discharge. To discover this the doctor puts a very small amount of the discharge on a thin glass slide, mixes it with a small drop of water, and then examines it under the microscope. In the average trichomonas infection, large numbers of these organisms can be easily seen under the microscope. In mild cases, however, a number of such examinations may be necessary on different days in order to find the trichomonas. A great many women who suffer from this complaint are so embarrassed by the discharge that on their first trip to the doctor they take a douche on the day of their appointment. This is, of course, commendable, but it does make it more difficult for the doctor to find these organisms. It also makes it more difficult for him to determine how much discharge is actually present. Frequently, the doctor will have to ask the patient to return to his office in a few days' time for a repeat examination, with a request to the patient not to douche during that intervening period. So if you are planning a visit to your doctor for this condition remember not to douche prior to the examination.

What can doctors do to treat this infection? The old time-honored treatment was the use of douches, using one teaspoon of white vinegar to a quart of lukewarm water; the rationale being that the trichomonas organisms seem to occur more frequently when the normal acidity of the vagina is changed. Although douches tend to decrease the symptoms they rarely result in permanent cures. This is now accomplished by various types of pills (suppositories) which are inserted into the vagina at night. Not all patients respond the same to these pills, consequently it is not infrequent that more than one type of pill has to be used. It is important that patients realize this, because failure to respond to a single type of medicine does not mean that the infection is a serious one. Furthermore, it does not mean that it cannot be cured. But there is another important point. To obtain a permanent cure sometimes the treatment must be continued over a period of weeks, sometimes months. Just as important, it must be continued *during* the period. Patients, after a few days' treatment, usually find a marked decrease of their symptoms and, thinking themselves cured, stop the treatment only to find that the problem shortly recurs. More recently, various drugs that can be taken by mouth are being tried. This is a new approach, as up to this time the treatment has been entirely local, that is the insertion of pills or jellies locally into the vagina. Many doctors feel that it is for this reason that the treatment is not always saitsfactory, since the trichomonas organisms may be in places such as the vaginal glands and cervix and the bladder, which are not accessible to local treatment. In other words, the pills just can't get to the organisms. There is one other problem. More and more it is being realized that a high percentage of men harbor this infection in the prostate gland. This means that as soon as the wife is cured she is immediately reinfected by her husband during intercourse. Doctors have referred to this problem as a ping-pong infection. Now these new oral drugs treat not only the wife, but also the husband more effectively. Also, they usually clear the infection up within ten days.

As the reader might suspect, the speed with which a cure is obtained depends on many factors. How quickly is it diagnosed and treated? Patients who put off treatment for years are certainly less likely to respond as quickly as those who see their doctor immediately. Another important point is that trichomonas organisms do not all respond to drugs in the same way. Some trichomonas are easily killed by drugs; other trichomonas organisms are more resistant to them. Fortunately, most cases are cured within a few weeks and do not recur. Others, however, require a longer period of time for treatment, but it is unusual to find a case now that sooner or later does not respond to one of the many drugs available for treatment. The patient is considered cured, however, only when repeated smears of the vaginal discharge fail to show the trichomonas present.

Fungus Infection

Fungus infections are very common, but are seen less frequently than the trichomonas infection discussed in the first part of this chapter. What are fungus infections? Certainly the type that most of you have heard about are the yeasts, molds, and mildews. Just like the trichomonas organisms, fungi too have a very simple structure and are present all around us. Fortunately, most fungi have a very useful purpose, such as the raising of bread. Just as important, they cause the decay of dead plants and animals, and by so doing break down the complex constituents of the body into simpler components and return these to the soil where they can be used again for the growth of plants and animals. Without this process, these chemicals in a dead body or plant would be permanently locked up, and would not be available for further use. What a terrible waste of these materials if it were not for the lowly fungus! Unfortunately, fungi also cause disease both in plants and animals. In fact, in some cases, they have helped to change the course of history. The loss of the Irish potato crop many years ago caused such a famine in Ireland that it resulted in mass migration of the Irish to the United States. Possibly the city of Boston today would be without its Irishmen if it had not been for fungus infection. Some fungi also cause disease in the human body and, as the reader will see, the one called "monilia" is the most common. Let us talk about this particular fungus in some detail. I am sure that a number of my readers have seen newborn infants suffering from a common fungus infection of the mouth called "thrush." It is this same infection that frequently locates itself in the vagina. Pregnant women are more prone to develop it, due to the increased amounts of sugar in the vagina during a pregnancy. As you would suspect, diabetic patients are also more likely to be troubled by it, due to increased amounts of sugar in the vaginal wall. But let me reassure you that it is only the rare patient with fungus infection who also has diabetes.

Other people who are more likely to get it are those who have been on antibiotics, particularly if this has been for a long time. What happens is that the antibiotics not only kill off the germ that they are intended to get rid of, but also normal bacteria in the vagina. This upsets the delicate balance of nature, and a fungus can more easily start to grow. This same principle is always at work in nature. For example, if hunters kill too many wolves the deer multiply too quickly. Of course, this occurs in only a very small percentage of patients receiving antibiotics. The great majority of patients who get a monilia infection do not have any of these problems. How do they catch it? In most cases doctors cannot track down the original source. Some patients no doubt infect their fingers and then carry the fungus to the vaginal area on their hands.

While many patients suffer from a trichomonas infection without knowing it, this is rarely the case with a fungus infection. Nearly all patients suddenly complain of an intense itching in and around the opening of the vagina. This comes on quite suddenly and, in spite of repeated douches or anything else the patient may try, it continues on unabated. Due to the intense itching, patients frequently aggravate their problem by scratching the area so that a vicious cycle is started. Usually the outside of the vagina becomes sore, so that voiding is usually associated with a burning sensation. Some patients also complain of frequency of urination. Nearly all notice a discharge which may be watery, but in most patients it is thick and looks very much like cottage cheese. As you would imagine, intercourse becomes either impossible or extremely painful. Sometimes patients will endure these symptoms for days before they seek advice. But with such diseases most patients usually beat a hasty path to the doctor's office. The diagnosis in most patients is easy. Examination of the vagina shows the characteristics cottage-cheese-like discharge, which is usually quite adherent to the vaginal walls. Nevertheless, the only sure way to make a diagnosis is again by microscopic examination. This is done by placing a small piece of the discharge on a glass slide, mixing it with a little water, and then examining it under the microscope. What the doctor sees are numerous branching interwoven stems or rods along which are small buds.

Fortunately, most of the fungus infections are simple to treat, and the chances of obtaining immediate relief and permanent cure are excellent. Usually the doctor will prescribe one of the newer pills or ointments to be inserted into the vagina. In addition, he will give an ointment to be applied around the vaginal opening. In other cases, he may also prescribe pills to be taken by mouth for a number of days. Douches may or may not be recommended. Should the doctor advise it, he may also suggest a douche containing a couple of tablespoonsful of baking soda to a quart of lukewarm water. A time-honored treatment for fungus infection has been painting the vagina with a 1 percent solution of gentian violet. This will give almost immediate relief of the itching, but due to the fact that it is purple in color and stains the clothing and that some patients become sensitive to it, it is now not used as frequently as before. Regardless of the type of treatment used, nearly all patients respond quickly to the drugs. There is, however, a small group of patients who either fail to respond immediately or, following what is thought to be a cure, develop a recurrence. There are many reasons for this.

First, the fungus may be a resistant one, that is, one that is difficult to kill. Second, the patient may be reinfecting herself, possibly from a contaminated bathtub or an infected douche nozzle (see Chapter XVIII), which should always be sterilized by boiling for ten minutes after each douching. If it happens to be an organism that is difficult to kill, changing the patient to another drug will often rectify the situation. If, on the other hand, the patient is being reinfected from another source, such as household pets, this problem must be corrected.

Bacterial Vaginitis

This is the third common type of infection causing discharge and itching. Nearly everyone has had a bacterial infection of some sort during their lifetime, such as a boil, sore throat, or infected finger. The vagina can become similarly involved with many kinds of different bacteria. Like the other infections we have discussed this too is not serious, but now and then it may be a hard problem to quickly cure. Various antibiotics, sulfas, or a jelly to insure the normal acidity of the vagina, are just some of the medicines used to treat this problem.

Chronic Cervicitis

This is generally considered to be the most common problem in gynecology. The reader will recall that the cervix is the neck or opening into the uterus, which can be seen at the end of the vagina during a pelvic examination.

What is chronic cervicitis, and why is it so common? Doctors use this term when referring to a rawness at the opening of the cervix and in nearly all cases it results from pregnancy. The cervical opening is normally smaller than a piece of spaghetti and during the process of labor and delivery it has to undergo tremendous stretching. The amazing thing is that after delivery it gradually returns to its normal size but, as would be expected, it is left frequently with a small amount of injury.

The majority of women with chronic cervicitis are neither aware of its presence nor have any symptoms. But others, usually following a pregnancy, will notice increased amounts of vaginal discharge. Usually the discharge is colorless and fairly thick, but since the raw area on the cervix bleeds easily, the discharge may sometimes be blood-tinged. These small episodes of bleeding are more likely to occur following intercourse or douching. And should the discharge become extremely heavy it may cause irritation at the vaginal entrance.

The diagnosis of chronic cervicitis is simple. Pelvic examination shows a beefy-red area around the cervical opening. Sometimes it will completely encircle the opening. At other times, only a part of the cervix will be involved. Just touching it lightly with an instrument is usually enough to make it bleed, which explains why intercourse or douching may cause slight bleeding. In the past it was impossible to distinguish between chronic cervicitis and extremely early cancer, as they both looked alike to the naked eye. This meant that doctors had to take a biopsy (cut out small pieces of tissue) from the cervix, and look at it under the microscope. Since only a fraction of 1 percent of the cases turned out to be cancer, this involved a lot of unnecessary work for the doctor and inconvenience for the patient. Now all this is past history, for the painless Pap test quickly distinguishes between cervicitis and cancer. (How the Pap smear works is discussed in detail in Chapter XV.)

The treatment of chronic cervicitis by cauterization is similarly simple and effective. This can be quickly performed in the doctor's office and is a painless procedure, since the cervix does not contain any nerves. Most doctors will then advise the patient to take douches starting a few days after the cauterization and continue them for a number of weeks. They may also tell the patient to avoid intercourse for a few days. How long it takes the cervix to heal depends on the extent of the cervicitis, but generally six to eight weeks is the average time. While the healing is taking place there may be a temporary increase in the amount of discharge and occasional spotting or bleeding. The period may also come a little early or late, and now and then there is increased bleeding for a month or two.

Foreign Bodies

This is a very rare cause of discharge, but now and then doctors find objects of various sorts in the vagina. Usually the patients are unaware of their presence. I recall one lady who consulted me because of a persistent discharge for many years. Pelvic examination revealed a pessary which had been placed in the vagina some five years previously by a doctor because of a tipped uterus. Despite the fact that her doctor had told her to return for monthly examinations she had failed to do so. She had also forgotten the pessary ring was still in the vagina. Failure to remove it regularly for cleansing purposes had resulted in a severe irritation and infection of the vagina. Once it was removed the discharge cleared up promptly. But there are many objects besides pessaries that are found in the vagina. Some women who use vaginal tampons occasionally forget to remove one. And young children will sometimes push safety pins or small toys into the vagina.

On another occasion, a graduate nurse came to my office. She was suffering from a persistent discharge of several weeks duration. Pelvic examination revealed a tampon which she had neglected to remove several weeks earlier after being out on the town one evening and indulging in too many martinis. But on very rare occasions doctors encounter remarkably strange objects. One gynecologist during a pelvic examination was surprised to feel two sharp prongs suddenly strike his fingers as he felt along the front wall of the vagina. This patient, who was mentally ill, had inserted a small pair of tweezers into her bladder, and from that location they had gradually worked their way through the bladder wall and partially into the vagina.

Regardless of what is left in the vagina, it always produces the same result: discharge and infection. The longer the foreign body is left, the greater the trouble. Sometimes discharge will be associated with bleeding. Sometimes bleeding will occur without much, if any, discharge. Pain may or may not be present. But sooner or later one or the other always occurs. Fortunately once the object is removed the symptoms quickly clear up. Usually douches are advised, and antibiotics may also be given, depending on the degree of infection.

Senile Vaginitis (The Aging Vagina)

One of the most neglected problems in gynecology is the condition that doctors refer to as senile vaginitis, which, if untreated, causes a great deal of unnecessary annoyance. Aging, of course, affects every organ in the body, but in some it goes along unnoticed and without causing any perceptible trouble. The skin wrinkles, and the hair turns gray, but these things do not produce pain or other symptoms.

The vagina is quite different, for it requires adequate amounts of the female hormone, estrogen, to remain healthy. During a woman's reproductive years this hormone is produced by the ovaries and by circulating in the blood it keeps the lining of the vagina thick and healthy. But later in life, when women go through the menopause, or what is commonly referred to as the "change of life," the aging ovaries produce less and less female hormones.

This gradual decrease in the amount of estrogen is responsible for the hot and cold spells, headaches, nervous tension, the cold hands and feet, insomnia, and crying spells that many women experience at this time. But lack of adequate estrogen also produces a thinning of the vaginal lining, and this is what causes trouble. A thin lining of the vagina is less able to withstand infection and becomes easily irritated by intercourse. Consequently it is quite common for women to complain of vaginal itching and irritation, increasing vaginal discharge, pain or bleeding, which may or may not be related to intercourse.

During the menopause one or all of these vaginal symptoms may gradually occur. In fact, it is often difficult for many women to be certain how long their symptoms have been present, in view of the insidious nature of onset. Yet in other instances they may start rather quickly when the weakened vagina suddenly becomes infected from a bacterial, fungus, or trichomonas infection.

The vagina may also age within a few weeks following a hysterectomy, when both ovaries have been removed. Sudden surgical removal of the ovaries produces an abrupt drop in the female hormone, since it is primarily manufactured by the ovaries. Unless the patient has been given estrogen pills the vaginal lining becomes thin, and discharge, irritation, and bleeding may occur.

It is amazing how frequently the sore vagina goes unnoticed, sometimes for years. One elderly nurse, whom I had considered a wise old owl, once consulted me because of vaginal irritation that had annoyed her for ten years. She had not bothered to see anyone about it and had been treating herself ineffectively with weekly douches. On examination she had a marked degree of senile vaginitis. This was completely cured in just one week's time by the daily use of estrogen cream, followed by daily estrogen tablets.

It is impossible to calculate how many women are daily suffering from the annoyances of this condition, but without a doubt there are a great many—primarily because women are living much longer with each passing year. Just a mere sixty-five years ago the average age of death for women was forty-eight— now it is seventy-three years of age. Stated another way, most women died before they had time to develop this problem. Now, for the first time, women are living beyond their reproductive years and are literally running out of the female hormone, estrogen.

The diagnosis of senile vaginitis does not require any fancy tests, since a direct visual examination of the vagina is usually all that is required. This reveals a vaginal lining that is thin, sore, with small reddened areas of bleeding, so irritated that it looks as if it had been scraped by a razor blade. In more advanced cases, areas of ulceration are present. In most cases there are also varying degrees of redness and irritation on the outside of the vagina, in part due to lack of hormone and in part due to chronic irritation from the discharge.

Doctors can also make the diagnosis by doing a "Pap smear," the test which, although more frequently used to detect cancer, also shows specific cellular changes characteristic of senile vaginitis. And if the physician suspects that infections have been superimposed on the underlying senile vaginitis, other tests to detect them will be carried out.

Ninety-nine percent of the time the diagnosis is obvious, and so is the treatment. Unfortunately, when some women are told a hormone cream is needed to cure them it causes unnecessary worry. Many have been told that hormones cause cancer and are therefore sometimes reluctant to use the treatment. This is just another of the old wives' tales that abound in medicine and cause needless concern. Not too long ago there was no good treatment for senile vaginitis. Doctors could only advise their patients to use cleansing douches, which would temporarily decrease their symptoms, but in no way cure them. In short, they had to endure this constant daily irritation as long as they lived, and it no doubt caused as much suffering as some of the more serious diseases.

Today it is an entirely different story, for it has become just as important to relieve patients of chronic annoyances as to save them from lethal diseases. Now that most of the infectious diseases have been controlled, scientists in recent years have more and more directed their attention to the cure of the degenerative diseases of aging.

Senile vaginitis is one of those important aging problems that can be cured by the use of the female hormone, estrogen. When the patient is first seen, the symptoms can be quickly relieved by inserting an estrogen cream into the vagina every night for about a week. Then, to stop the condition from recurring, doctors will advise the continued use of the hormone in a number of ways. Some doctors will recommend using the cream once every week or two. Other doctors, including the writer, are now fully convinced that this example of a localized lack of hormone in the vagina is only part of a general process that goes on in many parts of the body after the menopause. They therefore advise the daily use of an estrogen pill, which prevents the aging of the vagina and also helps to slow down the aging of the heart, blood vessels, bones, and other parts of the body. Two kinds of hormone pills are available, the synthetic or the natural hormones. Since the synthetic ones so frequently cause troublesome nausea, most doctors prefer the natural estrogens. To understand more about this the reader is advised to read Chapter III, which deals with the subject in detail.

Like any drug, estrogen cream must be used correctly to get good results. For instance, on one occasion I was treating an elderly lady for senile vaginitis. She failed to improve, even though I had given her a number of prescriptions for an estrogen cream. While I was pondering why she should be so resistant to treatment it was necessary to admit her to hospital for another problem. She was such a model patient that she even brought her own estrogen cream to the hospital. But then the puzzle started to unfold. The first morning in the hospital a student nurse kindly offered to insert the cream for her. But being an independent woman she gracefully declined and insisted on doing it herself. Luckily the student nurse watched her, and to her amazement the patient inserted it into the rectum. Later that day we had a little chat about anatomy, and a few days later her vagina was back to normal.

One final point. There is a certain pitfall that women too easily fall into. Estrogens are so rapidly effective that many women fail to follow their doctor's advice and think they will not need to continue using them once their condition has been cured. But this is not so. Let me explain further. When a patient has a vaginal infection, drugs will usually kill whatever organism is causing it. And if all the germs have been effectively killed the infection does not recur. But with senile vaginitis the trouble is not an excess of something that has to be gotten rid of—rather it is a lack of the important hormone, estrogen, that must be supplied as long as that person lives. A small price to pay for relief.

Exterior Vaginal Itching of Unknown Cause

Just why women suffer from this condition is still an unanswered question. Since many of these patients are tense and emotional it has been thought that psychological factors may be the cause. Psychiatrists have postulated that it is a desire to avoid intercourse that causes the itching. Others feel that it may be related to other marital problems, guilt complexes, or fear of cancer or venereal disease. Other doctors feel that the nerves are more sensitive than normal, and consequently they are more easily stimulated. Regardless of the cause, the itching results in much annoyance and suffering. Some patients complain that it is present all the time. Others notice it more at night. Most have tried numerous ointments without success. Nearly all have caused more harm by scratching. The more the patient scratches, the more the skin becomes irritated, and the more likely it is to become infected. Thus a vicious cycle is started: the more the patient scratches, the more it irritates the skin and the more it itches, causing more scratching.

Although doctors are still unable to explain the cause of this condition adequately, fortunately they are learning more and more about how to treat it. Now most patients can be cured. One of the most successful approaches is to inject the nerves around the outside of the vagina, using a long-acting anesthetic in a solution of oil. It is believed that this causes a scarring of the ends of the nerves, so that they do not function as well as normally. Consequently, although the irritating factor causing the itching may still be there, the nerves are less likely to react to it. Certainly the majority of women, once they undergo this treatment, are either cured completely or helped to a large extent. Relief may occur either immediately, or over a period of two or three months. Some women who find that the itching is about 50 percent improved will frequently be relieved of the remaining itching by a second injection or even a third injection. Following this procedure there is a reasonable amount of swelling of the lips of the vagina for a few days which gradually subsides.

There is one further way to attack this problem. Doctors are now able to cut the nerves around the vagina by a surgical operation. Interrupting the nerves in this way usually gives good results, but it is not done until all other ways have failed.

CHAPTER XVIII

Personal Hygiene

AN ASTUTE BUSINESSMAN once remarked that if he had two men on his board who thought alike, one was unnecessary. Differences of opinion can be refreshing and useful in evaluating certain problems. But in matters such as female hygiene it may be more of a liability than an asset, for it can cause a good deal of confusion for women.

Douching

Douching is one aspect of female hygiene regarding which there has been considerable comment and diversity of opinion. Many women have an inherent reluctance to insert anything into the vagina, whether it be a tampon or water. This stems from a lack of knowledge of the female anatomy, and a general worry that whatever is placed in the vagina might get lost. To add to the problem, medical opinion seems almost split down the middle on the merits of douching. One school of thought says it is best to leave the cleansing of the vagina to nature. They argue that a normal vagina cleans itself, and that douching destroys the beneficial bacteria that help to keep the vagina healthy. Furthermore, they say, why wash out the vagina when the rectum and nose do not require this ritual? The other school says nature frequently does a very inadequate job, that douches no more affect the vaginal bacteria than brushing the teeth affects those in the mouth, and that the rectum and the vagina are rather poor comparisons.

The writer shares this latter view, and considers douching just another refinement of an increasingly sophisticated society. It would be just as foolish to throw away the douche kit as to discard the toothbrush. Nature certainly does a poor job of looking after the teeth without adequate dental hygiene, otherwise doctors would not see a large number of girls in their twenties wearing complete dentures.

What is the best and the most convenient method of douching? The majority of older women will recall the type of douche bag that looked like a hot-water bottle and was hung on the wall after filling it with warm water. The water then flowed down a long tube and a nozzle was inserted into the vagina. It was a rather cumbersome, unwieldy piece of apparatus; particularly in these days of increasing travel. Today, the douche kit consists of a large bulb syringe that can be filled with water and a teaspoonful of white vinegar, and then gently squirted into the vagina. Most doctors usually recommend vinegar because the vagina is normally acid; however, in certain conditions, such as fungus infections, a teaspoonful of baking soda will be advised. And when vaginal infections are being treated doctors will also suggest boiling the nozzle for about ten minutes before douching to destroy any germs that may be present.

But one company has come out with even a more novel and practical method of douching. And like so many simple things it's amazing that no one thought of it sooner. It consists of a small plastic handle with a sponge-like piece at one end that can be used to gently swab out the vagina after dipping it in a cleaning solution. Why is it more effective than the usual method of douching? Let's look at it this way. Everyone would agree it's plain common sense that the toothbrush does a better job of cleaning the teeth than merely rinsing the mouth out with water. Since this douche apparatus resembles a large soft toothbrush it also gets rid of vaginal debris better than merely squirting water into the vagina. Furthermore, it is a compact, convenient design which is much easier to store, and also handy to take away on holidays. So far it is not too well known, but I'm sure more intelligent women will use this method in the future. How frequently women should douche depends primarily on personal preference. Those who have more than the average amount of discharge may feel cleaner by douching every few days. Others may elect to do it every week or two. How this is done also depends on individual taste. Those women who are still using the douche bag may find it more desirable to hang this next to the bathtub, allowing the solution to run gently into the vagina while they are lying down in the tub. Others, who have switched to the large bulb syringe, or are using the spongelike apparatus mentioned earlier, may find it more desirable to stand over the toilet.

I have already mentioned in an earlier chapter that many women instinctively douche before having a pelvic examination. This is commendable, but there are also several reasons why it is a mistake. For instance, if the visit is prompted by troublesome discharge it is better to let the doctor see how much is present. Furthermore, doctors usually do a microscopic examination of the discharge to determine if various types of infection are causing the problem. A douche prior to the visit often makes this test less accurate. In addition, doctors prefer to do the yearly Pap smear *before* douching.

Sanitary Protection

How to prepare adequately for the menstrual period has also been a point of controversy, further confused by much misinformation. This is an important consideration when one realizes that month after month the inconveniences of the menstrual period add up to about a twelfth of a woman's life, or a total of six years of this physiological menstrual discomfort. To handle this problem the time-honored method has been the use of the external pad, and this is still quite popular with a large number of women. But it does have certain disadvantages for it is bulky, requires the wearing of a sanitary belt, and is awkward to change. Furthermore, the cumulative effects of motion, warmth, and dampness are not conducive to antiseptic safety, since the pad represents a self-made bridge between the rectum and the vagina. It also favors the development of unpleasant odors, which in many cases make deodorants necessary.

In view of these disadvantages, more women are now using internal vaginal tampons. This is not a new idea, as in the Greek and Roman civilizations absorbent cotton placed in the vagina was used by athletic or theatrical performers and by women in the upper classes of society. But this method of protection never caught the public fancy because there was a good deal of illogical prejudice and hearsay about its use. Now, however, there has been a swing back to tampons as many women find that by using them they can continue their daily activities with a minimum of inconvenience. This is in part because, unlike the external pad, once the tampon is in place women can forget about its presence until it has to be removed. It also seems much more sensible to place tampons in the vagina where the blood is, rather than wait until it flows to the outside. But the old wives' tales still continue to frighten some women away from this method. One story is that tampons obstruct the menstrual flow. This is nonsense. In actual fact tampons act more like a wick in drawing blood away from the cervix. Another tale is that the tampons can get lost, but again this is fiction and not fact. As the reader will have learned from Chapter I, the vagina is practically closed at its far end except for a small opening into the uterus. A mother will often ask whether her daughter can and should use a tampon. The majority of virgins can insert them without any trouble since not only is the hymen usually quite soft and pliable, but also the vaginal opening itself is usually large enough to insert a tampon. And in these days of tight-fitting clothes and mini skirts most young girls prefer tampons to the cumbersome external pad. Girls who use tampons are also more free to participate in vigorous athletic events, including swimming, than they would be if they used other forms of menstrual protection. In addition, married women who are using the intrauterine device for contraception are perfectly free to use tampons.

Vaginal Deodorants

Just one other point about an important feminine matter. Some women in spite of special care are troubled by an unpleasant vaginal odor, and nothing distresses a woman more than the fear it might be detected by others. Fortunately, vaginal deodorants are available and they represent a major breakthrough in feminine hygiene. These effective yet gentle female deodorant sprays are recommended to eliminate odor from the external vaginal area, even during the menstrual period. By using these deodorant sprays daily, women can be assured that their private problems remain private.

To Sum Up

THE ARCHITECT DOES his best to design a building that present and future generations will admire. Similarly, the producer of a musical show fervently prays the audience will go home humming his best tunes. Authors are no exception, since we all hope to create an acceptable product. And what most writers desire to get across is some message, some philosophy of life, which will add to people's appreciation and understanding of the world around them.

Since I am primarily a doctor, my intention in writing this book has been both practical and philosophical. I have hoped by giving women a better understanding of how their bodies work I can also prevent them from needless worry over some of the problems which can beset them at all ages. Life is short, and to waste one's prime years worrying about insignificant difficulties is both tragic and unnecessary.

Mark Twain once said, "There is no point in worrying, because half our troubles never happen." Armed with the information in this book the reader now knows that the odds are even better in gynecology, for 99 percent of the symptoms women fear are due to cancer are, in reality, caused by benign conditions. And not only can you now laugh at the scaremongers, you can also be a great help in reassuring others who have fallen prey to alarmist gossip.

In earlier chapters, I particularly chastised women for talking too much. I am not naive enough to believe that this book will succeed in forever silencing them. But hopefully they will now at least know what they are talking about. Because today we are more interested in facts than in fancy. For many years the public was kept largely in the dark regarding medical matters, but we now realize how wrong this was. Modern women are becoming increasingly well informed as to what is going on in medicine. They are therefore less and less willing to put up with minor complaints that can easily be cured. For example, the majority of educated women now realize the value of a yearly medical checkup and also automatically expect that a Pap smear will be done at this time. As a result, doctors are finding that they do not have to work nearly so hard at selling new ideas to their patients.

I hope that this book has also shown that we really have entered a new era in medicine. For the first time, doctors are now focusing more of their attention on the degenerative diseases of aging and, as the reader has seen, are solving many of its problems. Thousands of elderly women have already gained relief from the constant annoyance of vaginal irritation, which was previously caused by a deficiency of the female hormone, estrogen. Those of you who have leafed through these pages are now also cognizant of the new attitude toward the menopause as a stage of aging which needs medical treatment like any other disease. And the dramatic change in the medical approach to this problem means that untold numbers of women are now taking a daily estrogen pill. When you take all these benefits into consideration, you have to admit things are a lot better now than they were in the "good old days." In fact, rather than just adding years to your life, doctors have also found a way of adding life to your years!

And this is just the beginning, for it has been said that in the last decade medicine has advanced further than in the two thousand preceding years. There is little doubt that this is the case, and that in the next few decades we will see even greater achievements, as medicine succeeds in conquering many more of the problems which have bedeviled us. Organ transplantation will become commonplace, the population explosion will slowly but surely be solved, and computers will add a new dimension to resolving some of the riddles of health versus disease. And, at a not-too-distant date, the greatest disease of all will be mastered—when we finally find the means to postpone death indefinitely. Even today, although there are still many riddles left unanswered, life for all of us—and for women in particular—is far better than in the past. And remember, things do not have to be perfect to be good!

Index

Aorta, 192–93

Abdominal pain. *See:* Painful periods; Pelvic pain.

Abnormal bleeding, 36, 40–44, 168; as cancer symptom, 262, 268, 270–71; and chronic cervicitis, 236; D and C for, 199–200; as disease symptom, 162, 187–88, 205, 217; dysfunctional, 42–43; and endometriosis, 208, 253–57; and female organ infections, 250–53; and fibroids, 246–50; and hyperplasia, 239–41; during menopause, 241–43; painful, 245–60; painless, 236–44; and polyps, 237–38; postmenopausal, 41–42, 243–44, 270. *See also:* Blood clots; Bloody discharge; Spotting.

Abortion, 85, 97, 104; criminal, 109–13, 201; legal (*see* Legalized abortion); self-imposed, 112; spontaneous (*see* Miscarriage); therapeutic, 92, 109–10, 123, 138, 142–43

Abortion Act of Great Britain, 119–20

Adoption, 159–60

Afterbirth. *See* Placenta.

Aging: menopause as disease of (*see* Menopause, as disease); reasons for, 12–13, 25; scientists' attacks on, 11–12; surgery and, 14–15. *See also* Osteoporosis.

Aging vagina (senile vaginitis), xii, 26–27, 173, 243, 302–06

Alaska, legalized abortion in, 109, 128

Albumin in urine, 230

Alcohol: and intercourse, 56; and venereal disease, 183, 186

American Baptist Convention, 121

American College of Obstetricians and Gynecologists, 21, 122

American Medical Association (AMA): and birth control pill, 66–68; and legalized abortion, 121–22

American Public Health Association, 121

Amniotic fluid, 109

Amphetamines, 66

319

Breast tenderness: and birth control pill, 79; in cystic disease, 181; and pregnancy, 45, 97, 103; premenstrual, 32, 180

Breasts: changes in, 100, 180; cystic disease of, 180–81; development of, 38; differences in, 180; sagging, 26

Breech delivery, 228

Bronchitis, 74

Buddhists: and abortion, 115; and contraceptives, 86–87

Caesarean section, 109, 227–32; and prolapsed bladder, 288; reasons for, 228–31; safety of, 227–28

Calcium deposits, 248

Calcium loss. See Osteoporosis.

Canada, legalized abortion in, 137–43; abortion committees in, 142; Bourne case in, 139–40; doctors' attitudes toward, 138–39; and French Canada, 138, 140; and N.Y. State abortion law, 132–33; obstacles to, 141–43; compared to U.S., 140

Cancer, 261–78; and birth control pill, 72–75; bleeding changes and, 43, 242; of breast (see Breast cancer); of cervix (see Cervical cancer); definition of, 262–63; diagnosis of, 267–69, 271–72; (see also Pap smear); D and C to determine, 24, 200; disappearance of, 277; and DNA, 13; endometrial (see Uterine cancer); of Fallopian tubes, 260; fear of, xi, 44, 313; and fibroid tumors, 250; and hormone pills, xiv, 20; and hyperplasia, 241; and hysterectomy, 216, 219–20; incidence of, 162; of lung, 74; after menopause, 244; of ovaries (see Ovarian cancer); and pelvic pain, 167; spread of, 266–67; symptoms of, 262, 267–71; treatment for, 274–75, 277–78; of uterus (see Uterine can-

cer); of vagina, 260; of vulva, 260

Cancer Society, 66, 163, 262, 277

Carcinoma of the endometrium. See Uterine cancer.

Carcinoma-in-situ, 73, 261, 263–64. See also Cervical cancer.

Castration, 93

Catheter following surgery, 198–99, 222

Catholic Church, and legalized abortion, 121, 126, 138

Cervix, 3; cancer of (see Cervical cancer); in miscarriage, 106–09; infections of, 186, 273, 295; and IUD, 88; polyps of, 237; rawness of (see Chronic cervicitis); removal of, 214; "ripe," 235; stretching of, 35

Cervical cancer, 214, 263–65; diagnosis of (see Pap smear); hysterectomy and, 216; symptoms of, 269–70; treatment for, 274

"Chancre," 191–92

"Change of Life." See Menopause.

Childbirth: infections and, 251; prolapsed bladder and uterus resulting from, 285–86; and vulva injuries, 284. See also: Caesarean section; Labor.

Chronic cervicitis, 157, 236–37, 299–301; and vaginal discharge, 169, 299–301

Chronic cystic mastitis, 180

Circumcision (and cervical cancer), 264–65

"Climax" (orgasm), 55–58

Clitoris, 3, 55

Clomiphene citrate, 80, 153–55

Codeine, 35, 88

Cold spells in menopause, 22, 24

Conception, 145–46

Condoms, 63, 83–84, 91–92

Constipation, 250

Contraceptive creams, 90; for women in 40's, 30; during menopause, 84. See also Jellies (contraceptive).

Legalized abortion, 67; AMA and, 121–22; in Canada (*see* Canada); and Catholic Church, 121, 126, 138; in Great Britain, 109, 119–20; history of, 127–28; in Japan, 109, 114–19; methods of achieving, 133–34; and Planned Parenthood Association, 121, 142; in U.S. (*see* United States)

Life expectancy: changes in, 11–14; of women, 21, 175

Loop, the. *See* Intrauterine device (IUD).

Low back pain. *See* Backache.

Low-dosage pills, 81–82. *See also* Birth control pills.

"Low pain threshold," 165–66

Low-salt diet, 230

Lumps. *See* Breast lumps; Urethra, lumps at; Vulva, lumps at.

Lumbo-sacral strain, 176–77, 204

Lung cancer, 74

Malignant tumors. *See* Cancer.

"Mask of pregnancy," 79

Mastectomy, radical, 277

Masters, Dr. William, 56–57

Membranes (Bag of water): in miscarriage, 108–09; and prolapsed cord, 231

Menopause, 8–9, 22–24, 37, 48, 74, 84, 216; and birth control pills, 29, 83–84; bleeding during (*see* Bleeding, during menopause); bleeding following (*see* Abnormal bleeding, postmenopausal); complaints and symptoms of, 21–25, 302 (*see also* Aging vagina); as disease (of aging), xii, 20, 314; fears regarding, xii, 22–23; and hyperplasia, 219, 240–41; and intercourse, 14, 23; treatment for (*see* Estrogen replacement therapy).

Menstrual cycle, 8, 45; breast

changes during, 180; hyperplasia and, 239–40; ovarian cysts and, 257; variations in, 41–42

Menstrual period, 5–6, 8, 31–50; in adolescent girls, 46–47; age of onset, 16, 38–39, 46, 239; anxiety and, 49; backache and, 174–75; and birth control pill, 80, 82; changes in pattern of, 23–24, 44, 162–63; and cervicitis, 301; D and C effects on, 202; failure to have, xiv, 6–8, 44–50, 97, 100; hyperplasia and, 218–19; during menopause, 241–43; myths regarding, 44; obesity and, 48–49; pain during (*see* Painful periods); following pregnancy, 83; sanitary protection during, 310–12; symptoms preceding, 205; and tubal pregnancy, 102

Mice, breast cancer in, 74

Miscarriage (spontaneous abortion): D and C following, 200; reasons for, 104–05, 151, 158–59; symptoms of, 103; treatment to prevent, 107–09; types of, 105–06

Misconceptions (about gynecology). *See* Old wives' tales.

"Missed abortion," 105–06

Missed period. *See* Menstrual period, failure to have.

Monilia albicans, 170, 297

Morning nausea. *See* Nausea, as pregnancy symptom.

Multiple births, 153–54

Mumps and male sterility, 148

Muscle spasm, 165, 177

Myomectomy, 24, 159

National Health Service (British), 120

Nausea, 32, 103, 186, 223, 251; and birth control pill, 78–79; as pregnancy symptom, 45, 97, 100; and synthetic estrogen, 28, 305